7000588212

BRISTOL'S GREEN ROOTS

BRISTOL'S GREEN ROOTS

The growth of the environmental movement in the city of Bristol

Emmelie Brownlee

Supported by the Heritage Lottery Fund

LOTTERY FUNDED

Published by the Schumacher Institute for Sustainable Systems

First published in 2011
by The Schumacher Centre Ltd
31-34 High Street, Bristol, BS1 2AW
www.schumacherinstitute.org.uk
© The Schumacher Centre Ltd, 2011

Photographs used in this book are acknowledged where the source is known, and are the copyright of the organisations and individuals who supplied them.

Front cover photos, left to right: Windmill Hill City Farm (© Windmill Hill City Farm Archive), Avon Gorge (© Brownlee) and Bristol to Bath Railway Path (© Sustrans)

The Schumacher Centre has made every effort to ensure the accuracy of the information in this book at the time of going to press. However, they cannot accept any responsibility for any loss, injury or inconvenience resulting from the use of information contained therein. The Schumacher Centre has made every effort to contact copyright holders of photographs.

The opinions, perspectives and thoughts expressed in interviews are those of the people interviewed and The Schumacher Centre does not accept any responsibility for them.

Text printed on Regency Satin FSC paper and covers on Claro Silk FSC board by Latimer Trend, Plymouth, UK

A catalogue record for this publication is available from the British Library.

ISBN 978 0 85784 028 8

Contents

Acknowledgements   7

Foreword   9

Introduction   11

The darker side of Bristol   19

The start of the environmental movement   21

The growth of the environmental movement   25

Bristol's environmental movement: 1960 – 2011   39

Bristol's green heritage   81

    Energy   82

    Food   97

    Transport   115

    Recycling and resource management   131

    Wildlife, biodiversity and green space   147

    Construction, property and urban planning 164

Thinking about the city: top-down and bottom-up actions   185

2011 and onwards: the future of Bristol   217

Is Bristol on its way to becoming a sustainable city?   221

What are your hopes for the future of Bristol?   227

References   236

Bibliography   245

About the author   248

Acknowledgements

The Schumacher Institute would like to thank all of those who have contributed to this project including our interviewees; the organisations, initiatives, community groups and individuals who donated archive material and photos; the individuals who attended our community workshop and those who have suggested interviewees. Particular thanks to:

Helen Ball, Ben Barker, Tim Barker, Mark Barough, Hugh Barton, Peter Basset, Thomas Beale, Celia Beeson, Vicky Beckwith, Karen Bell, Jonathon Bewley, Mike Birkin, Jeff Bishop, Paul Blakemore, Eric Booth, James Bruges, Darryl Bullock, Diane Bunyan, Douglas Burnett, Joy Carey, Susan Carter, Georgia Catt, Sara Chapple, Ed Cook, Stephanie Coombs, Ryan Corkery, Mike Crabbe, Andy Cunningham, Savita Custead, Juliet Dearbugh, Nigel Dudley, Mark Durk, Iris Ealing, Elizabeth Ellis, Rob Enticott, Bekki Farrar, Bill Flinn, Martin Fodor, Matt Fortnum, Jenny Foster, Nick Francis, Abby Frary, Mike Frost, Sandra Fryer, Irene Galant, Penny Gane, Lucy Gatward, Suzanne Gaved, Mike Ginger, Chris Gittens, Tess Green, John Grimshaw, Darren Hall, Keith Hallett, Alison Harris, Phil Haughton, Patrick Holden, Helen Holland, Simon Hooton, Gary Hopkins, Trevor Houghton, Gus Hoyt, Paul Humphries, Phil Insall, Jeremy Isles, Jill Kempshall Andy King, Andy King (BCC), Robert Lambourne, Rik Lander, Tim Lawrence, Mark Leach, Johanna Le-Poidevin, Peter Lipman, James Lucas, Martin McDonnell, Miguel Mendonça, Steve Micklewright, Andy Moore, Stephen Moore, Ben Moss, Jackson Moulding, Wilf Mound, Mo Mulligan, Ciaran Mundy, Dan Naryanan, Simone Osborn, Jim O'Shaughnessy, Rocky Pearce, Lucy Pedler, John Pontin, Brian Price, Sarah Pugh, John Purkiss, Angela Raffle, Paul Rainger, Chris Richards, Amy Robinson, Simon Roberts, Alastair Sawday, Steve Sayers, David Saunders, Miles Sibley, Ray Smith, Kristin Sponsler, Paul Stepan, Jane Stephenson, Richard St George, Jane Stevenson, Emily Stokes, Chris Sunderland, Sennen Timcke, Sam Valentine, Glenn Vowles, Richard Walker, Sue Walker, Kate Watson, Leslie Watson, Dan Weisselberg, Tim Weisselberg, Carolyn Whitwell, Claire Wilks, Matt Wood, Mike Zeidler.

We would also like to thank the young people of Digital Fish at Knowle West Media Centre: Ashon Barwich, Alice Butler, Emily Butler, Lydia Butler, Chanel Carter, Jordan Davey, Connor Segsedy, Kayleigh Segsedy,

Chloe Shiner, Michael Summers, James Wall, for their input and Sandra Manson for facilitating the workshops.

Thank you to the volunteers of the project: Julia Ankebrand, Trish Appleton-Fox, Basia Cieszewska, Charlie Clemoes, Sian Easton, Adrian Estment, Jolyon Firth, Helen Gunn, Amaya Iriondo-Coysh, Billy Launder, Graeme Morpeth.

I would like to thank the project advisor, Ian Roderick, for his support and help (including writing several of the case studies) and my work colleagues Alice-Marie Archer, Lucy Fleetwood, Olivero Mannu.

Thank you to Jane Stephenson for writing our foreword, Barbara Szente of Expressive Print for designing the cover and Green Books for handling the production of this book.

On a personal note I would like to thank Liz and Pete Brownlee, Jake Larcombe and Helen Taylor for their support, help and advice during the course of this project.

Foreword

When I first arrived in Bristol early in 1983, just back from 18 months travelling in South America, I was looking for something to 'get my teeth stuck into' that 'made a difference'. I had witnessed a society in which nothing was wasted and returned home to what appeared to me, even then, a consumer-driven economy with little or no regard for safeguarding the earth's resource base or for what happened to products once they were thrown away.

The early 1980s in the UK were epitomised by high unemployment particularly among young people – this too struck me as a tragic waste of human talent. Bristol at that time was a hive of radical, and to some no doubt, subversive activity. Friends of the Earth had 'usurped' the council's waste paper collection vehicle and started their own collections, City Farms were springing up on derelict land, the Bristol Energy Centre were converting a couple of terrace houses as 'energy efficient' demonstrations, at the weekend buses left to support the Greenham Common protest, the 'Stop Hinkley C' campaign was warming up, the 'Greenleaf' bookshop opened . . . the list goes on.

What struck me then was that alongside the campaigners and community activists this 'movement' included a number of local businesses and entrepreneurs. In my field this included Clarfield Waste Paper and Harris & Co (textile merchants), without whom the pioneering recycling work undertaken by Avon FoE could not have taken place. Nor could the wide range of environmental projects have been developed without the 'workforce' and funding provided by the Government's various unemployment programmes: thousands of young people must have passed through the various practical projects delivering loft insulation, recycling services, and conservation work.

So what does this all mean for us now in 2011? There are plenty of similarities: economic uncertainty, public expenditure cuts, high unemployment, questions over Government defence policies and practices, the arguments about nuclear power . . . the list goes on. There has clearly been some progress, but what is equally apparent is that there is still a long way to go. It is, I think, useful to look back, not in a self-congratulatory way, but to ensure that the lessons learned and the expertise developed during that period is built on. Most of the organisations that led the environmental movement in the 1980s now operate at a national level, with expertise and experiences that are relevant to the city today.

We are getting better at providing meaningful mechanisms for organisations and groups to work together, and this must remain key to making the city-region work better. The other major lesson would have to be that despite the fact that in the intervening 30 years the council and the leading business organisations have embraced the sustainability agenda to some extent – the truly cutting-edge work then, and I suspect the same is true today, has not been led by local authorities or big corporations. For this we continue to rely on NGOs, community activists and SMEs.

I'm glad to say that there are a healthy number of new initiatives and a myriad of ways that local people can get involved in making Bristol a more sustainable city – you only have to look at the Transition movement, Co-exist, Shift Bristol (practical training courses on sustainable living), the Happy City Project and the Bristol Food Project as examples to see that the environmental/sustainability movement is alive and kicking. Sometimes that kicking will be uncomfortable for those in powerful positions. What the authorities need to remember is that sometimes it requires a leap of faith to support work during its development stage and to fight against the tendency to try to control things. My own organisation and others were lucky that at the crucial time there were some who were prepared to make that leap.

Jane Stephenson
Chief Executive, Resource Futures

Introduction

An ounce of practice is generally worth more than a ton of theory
E. F. Schumacher

Bristol has an enviable reputation for 'alternative living'. The city has a diverse scene in music, art and performance and is populated by many thriving independent bars, clubs and shops. There are regular talks, events and workshops which encourage the city's population to come together and discuss new ideas, books and pressing topics. Festivals promote vegan, vegetarian, local and organic food. There are protests and demonstrations. In Bristol, 'alternative' is almost the mainstream.

Enhancing this reputation are Bristol's 'green credentials', which can be traced as far back as the late 1960s. The city is home to some of the UK's biggest environmental organisations as well as a thriving low-carbon technology sector. Local businesses, organisations, communities, individuals and the council all contribute to developing Bristol as a more pleasant place to live for everyone; a city which minimises its environmental impact as well as developing quality of life and social and economic equality.

In 2008, Bristol was the only UK city to be nominated for the European Green Capital award and topped the Forum for the Future's Sustainable Cities Index. The Schumacher Institute felt that these achievements deserved to be recognised, and so we started a project to explore Bristol's development as a 'green' city.

Bristol's Green Roots has documented some of the pioneering examples of 'sustainability' in the city: the environmental action and the organisations, initiatives and community groups that want to improve Bristol's social and environmental justice or fairness. We wanted to do this before the information, the documents and the narratives are lost.

The project has looked at the period 1960 – 2011, and explored how the city gained its 'green' reputation, the impetus and social context behind the development of some of the city's sustainability organisations, initiatives and community groups, and the reasons people get involved.

It is a valid concern that Bristol is green in name but not always in action. Environmentalism is only one part of Bristol's identity. Like all urban areas of the world, the city has behaviour, planning decisions and

Figure 1. Bristol's harbourside

industries which are hard to reconcile with the environmental movement and go against what those in the environmental movement are calling for.

The long and rich history of environmental action within the city, however, is still important and we want the project to celebrate and improve upon what has gone before as well as encourage more of these activities and initiatives.

It is useful to discuss what we mean by some of the terms used in this book. 'Sustainability' and 'sustainable development' have been used with an increasing frequency in recent years. Essentially, they refer to the desired outcome of the environmental movement; human activity leaving minimal impact on the planet.

Something is deemed as sustainable when it is "capable of being maintained at a certain rate or level".[1] As present levels of consumption are not capable of being maintained on our finite planet, we are damaging not only the environment but our ability to live on this planet. For the human population to act sustainably in all areas of life is the ultimate achievement for those in the environmental movement.

In 1987, the Brundtland Commission defined sustainable development as development which "meets the needs of the present without compromising the ability of future generations to meet their own needs."[2] Sustainability is not just about the environmental issues that we face – it is also about creating a fair and equal society so that people "are not subject to conditions that systemically undermine their capacity to meet their needs."[3]

Defining 'needs' is complex, but it seems obvious that everybody should have equal access to shelter, clean water, food, and energy as well as healthcare, education, jobs and welfare, and that this access is completely regardless of sex, age, race, social class, mental and physical health or sexual orientation.

Global behaviour has led to inequity for both present and future generations – needs go unmet locally, nationally and globally. Women, men and children across the UK, Europe and the world are consistently prevented and denied access, because of social, political, economic and cultural factors, to the same resources and quality of life as others.

An awareness that both social and environmental factors are at play in 'sustainability' is important, as you cannot have a sustainable society without fairness and justice. The concept of convergence, which we will discuss further later, promotes the meeting of the developed countries and developing countries somewhere 'in the middle', so 'everyone has a fair share of the resources that the Earth can easily provide... where everyone has a fair and equal share of, and access to, human-created resources such as knowledge.'[4]

Figure 2. View over Bristol toward Clifton Suspension Bridge

This 'meeting in the middle' is an important notion, as Bristol has a long way to go before it can be deemed socially just and equal. The city has a big 'economic gap', with some of the least deprived areas in the country side-by-side with areas with multiple indicators of deprivation, and these areas can often be more exposed to environmental issues such as air pollution, fly-tipping and lack of green space.*

Many of the sustainability organisations in Bristol, therefore, realise that 'environmental issues are inseparable from social justice' and are concerned with highlighting the connections between social and environmental issues in order to improve the city's environmental impact as well as the quality of life for its residents.[5]

In carrying out our research we have spoken to over 100 people and tried to get different perspectives from different parts of the city; from the communities to the council to the organisations and businesses. The interesting thing about the environmental organisations in Bristol (and

---

* 'People on low income are also more likely to endure the worst environments in terms of poor quality housing, busy roads, dirty streets, dereliction and inadequate local amenities' Burningham and Thrush (2001). http://www.jrf.org.uk/sites/files/jrf/1842631462.pdf p.1

would imagine elsewhere) is that many of them started as personal ̱eys by groups of individuals who just wanted to make a difference. ̱ project has sought out these stories and narratives as they are inspirational, illuminating and relatable.

We have tried our best to give a balanced view, but the purpose of this project is to document the action on sustainability in the city. This means that the people we have been interviewing are heavily involved and have both personal and professional dedication to the cause. It can be difficult to gather unbiased material, as environmental and social issues are topics that create impassioned and personal responses.

As with any historical research, there are issues with memory, selective remembering and personal involvement and so we have tried to talk to as many different people as possible, from all sectors of the city, to try to make the stories as multi-voiced as possible. It is unavoidable, however, that people will remember things differently.

We will begin by highlighting Bristol's well-known but less than ethical past. In the mid-18th century Bristol had the biggest slave trade in the world, and founded much of its wealth on the trafficking of humans and the industries associated with it; sugar, tobacco, chocolate and alcohol.[6]

We will then set in context the history of Bristol's environmental movement by giving a brief overview of global environmentalism, from early conservation to the 'watershed' moment for the modern environment movement: the publication of Rachel Carson's *Silent Spring* in 1962.

Carson's pivotal text discussed her concerns about the impact that synthetic pesticides could have upon the natural world and human health, placing environmental discussions firmly in the public domain. From 1960 onwards, set against a backdrop of social, political and cultural change, a wave of anti-establishment thinking and cultural, social, economic and political critiques paved the way for the emergence of the modern environmental movement.

The growth of scientific understanding and global communications made clear the impact that humans could have upon the planet. The next four decades saw the development of environmental concerns from a fringe movement to a mainstream discussion. We will look briefly at this growth and the rise of issues such as resource depletion, climate change, convergence, sustainable development and environmental justice.

We will then move on to a discussion of Bristol's early modern environmental movement, which can be traced back to the work of local amenity groups in the late 1960s who tried to preserve the city's communities, landmarks, buildings and green space from a series of planning

> *I think Bristol's a very positive place for green activity . . .*
>
> *I think that people who wanted to get engaged in green activities were drawn to the city, back in the 70s and 80s, because of its location in the west country, because it seems an energetic sort of place, things get done here, and after a while that starts to create a nucleus and other things are drawn in.*
>
> **Mike Birkin, South West Campaigner,**
> **Bristol Friends of the Earth**

proposals. It was these campaigns that helped prevent the development of the Outer Circuit road which would have completely changed the land-scape of Bristol. Those involved set a precedent for community involvement in urban planning.

The majority of environmental action in Bristol, however, started in the early 70s, perhaps visibly marked by the launch of Bristol Friends of the Earth in 1971. Bristol Friends of the Earth and Avon Friends of the Earth provided a platform for some of Bristol's most pivotal and influential environmental organisations to begin; they were a "seed-bed for new ideas and new projects".[7]

The organisations, initiatives, and community groups will be discussed through a series of 'themes': energy, food, transport, recycling and resource use, biodiversity and green space, property, construction and urban planning.

The study of sustainable development considers a wide variety of issues, but the interconnections between these themes are important. Energy influences transport and food, construction influences protection of green space, recycling and resource use influence energy use, and so on.

The chapter called 'Thinking about the city' will look at the role of the different sectors in the city – community, council, business and NGOs – and the role of cross-sectoral action in Bristol's environmental movement, something which has been cited over and over again as essential to the development of Bristol as a sustainable city.

It is important not to forget that local authority involvement and application of UK and EU legislation, such as the Local Agenda 21 strategies, have contributed positively to Bristol's journey of environmental action. We will also look at the issues that can arise due to differing perspectives between the public, private and voluntary sectors.

The publication is about our more recent history as well; we wanted to discuss some of the initiatives and community groups responding to today's concerns to show the growth of the environmental movement. The recent boom in sustainability initiatives dealing with local resilience and a variety of issues ranging from food to energy to transport is testament to the hard work done by the organisations that began 40 years ago.

In 2006, The Transition Movement began and local Transition groups emerged across the UK. These were 'community-led responses to climate change and shrinking supplies of cheap energy' and looked to build our resilience against these issues while improving well-being and happiness.

The growing talk about 'preparing for change' and protecting ourselves from climate change, peak oil and resource depletion can be seen as a negative narrative but, as the Transition Movement shows, this preparation brings about opportunities to develop our communities and cities for the better through developing local resilience and self-sufficiency.

In the final section we have included some of the transcripts from two of the questions we asked everybody during the filmed interviews: Do you think that Bristol is on its way to becoming a sustainable city? What do you hope for the future of Bristol?

The responses to these explore and discuss what the future of Bristol could hold, what a sustainable city might look like, what has been done well, what continue to be Bristol's biggest problems and what is obstructing individual and city efforts to become more sustainable.

The aim of the project is not self-congratulation but rather to look at an important part of our shared history and identity and to be proud of how far we have come, while recognising how far we have to go. A connection with, and knowledge of, the past can stimulate informed decisions and enable us to understand what can work and what does not.

Most importantly, we cannot afford to be complacent, as Bristol is in danger of falling behind its UK counterparts. We are already behind most EU cities in terms of provision for sustainable living such as transport, housing, energy, recycling and legislation.

In a filmed interview for this project George Ferguson CBE, whose involvement with Bristol's environmental movement dates back to the 60s, said that "it's too easy to think that because we talk about Bristol being a 'green city' [and] because we talk about our ambitions to be a 'green capital' that therefore we are somewhere near it." [8] We should not let a head start make us overconfident.

The environmental movement is often accused of being all talk and no action, and change is slow to happen, which can be demoralising and disillusioning. This is why we hope that the collection of case studies and stories presented here will be both uplifting and inspirational and demonstrate that things can be achieved through partnership and dedication.

When faced every day by a series of messy and complex issues, it can become disheartening and difficult to recognise when any real progress has been made. It is important to recognise simultaneously what has been done well as well as what needs to improve. During one of the project's community workshops it was discussed how important it is not to overemphasise Bristol's 'greenness', but it was equally strongly suggested that we should not ignore this element of our city's history.

By exploring Bristol's achievements and mistakes, as well as seeing them in a historical context, we hope to show that positive and successful change can be made. The stories and case studies that we have collated are, quite simply, examples of how people can make a difference, how powerful collaboration can be and how sustainable development can positively develop a city, both socially and environmentally.

The darker side of Bristol

There is not a brick in the city but what is cemented with the blood of a slave – **Anonymous**

It is ironic that a city which prides itself on its engagement with concerns of social and environmental sustainability founded its wealth through the slave trade. By the late eighteenth century, it was not just the biggest slave port in the UK or Europe, but in the world. The city, however, had been involved in the trafficking of humans as early as the twelfth century. At this time the people being sold were local people including kidnapped men, women and children.

Over the next few centuries, as international trade and the popularity of overseas goods such as sugar, tobacco and cacao (to be made into chocolate) grew, there was an increase in demand for enslaved people as these required a large workforce.

Ships would leave Bristol for Africa with local goods such as textiles and glass which would be exchanged for enslaved Africans. The African people would then be taken to the Caribbean to be sold and to work on plantations and in the homes of the plantation owners. The luxury goods would be part of the exchange or bought with the money and were then taken back to Bristol; this journey was called the 'Triangular Trade'. Between the years 1698 and 1807, a known 2,108 ships left Bristol for Africa.[9]

Bristol, therefore, was able to import many luxury goods such as rum, tobacco, cacao and sugar, and become an extremely wealthy city. Victoria Coules states that slavery was "driven by the western greed for profit [and] it is estimated that between 9 and 11 million Africans were transported to a new continent . . . all to satisfy the Europeans' taste for luxuries."[10]

Slavery began a long-lasting practice of using overseas labour and resources to satisfy the growing needs and desires of those in the west. The legacy of the slave trade is unavoidable, and today racial discrimination is still a serious issue. There are studies exploring the continuing effects of slavery on Bristol's black population today.[11]

During its involvement with the slave trade Bristol developed culturally, socially and economically as a city. As a port, it became a point of entry for the 'new', whether that be foodstuffs, new cultural influences or intoxicants. These advancements, however, relied heavily on the exploitation of people, and this began to be seen as unethical.

In 1788 Bristol became the first city outside London to set up an Abolitionist movement.[12] This was the one of the first political movements in which women became a driving force through campaigning and boycotting slave trade products such as sugar.

Despite, however, the overwhelming concern and call for action, there was also a great deal of social apathy. There was a fear of what the abolition of slavery would do to the economy of Bristol, as the economy was almost entirely dependent on the triangular trade. Businesses, traders and those with economic vested interest were primarily responsible for this backlash. As Britain soared to the top of the world's economy, any social movement which threatened this position was considered dangerous.

Can we draw parallels with the present day? Despite an awareness that the slave trade and its associated industries were exploitative, there were still those who did not want to abolish slavery; a concern about the environmental movement is that living sustainably will damage our economic system, as 'infinite and unregulated growth' would no longer be the aim.

In 2008, Andrew Simms spoke at The Schumacher Lectures in Bristol drawing this parallel. He suggested that the abolition movement shows us that we can shift an economy towards a fairer and more just model.[13]

The discussion of the slave trade was to illustrate the long history that every society has of exploiting the planet and people for our own gain. This is especially easy when this exploitation does not happen in front of our eyes, but rather in other countries where we do not see the environmental or social impacts.

But as those in the abolitionist movement fought for those they never knew, we have seen over the last fifty years a rise in people fighting to prevent environmental damage they may never see and for people they will never meet.

The start of the environmental movement

To determine a specific date that the environmental movement began is difficult. The term 'environmental movement' is itself a flexible term which means different things to different people. You could say that the environmental movement began the moment a society gained an appreciation for the natural world that surrounded it.

For the purposes of this book we are looking at the modern incarnation of the environmental movement, which is concerned with how technological, scientific and social advancements have changed the way we treat the planet and how our behaviour threatens both our and future generations' ability to live upon this planet. This is usually understood to have had its roots in the early 1960s and developed throughout the next five decades.

While the 1960s, and particularly the 1970s, saw a boom in environmental activism, there were people concerned about human activities, and their impact on human health and the natural world, in the nineteenth century. As the Industrial Revolution gained momentum, it quickly became very apparent that humans were capable of having a negative impact upon the environment.

The improvement in social and physical infrastructure, economic stability and quality of life that the Industrial Revolution developed was of great benefit to Bristol and the UK, but it began the systematic and unrelenting exploitation of the earth's resources to fuel the new obsession with progress and advancement, both scientific and economical.

Air, water and soil pollution and the diseases associated with these became rife, especially in urban areas. Environmental health, therefore, became a major issue, especially in economically deprived areas.

Concerns about resource depletion also began to surface as coal, timber and other natural resources began to be consumed at alarming rates. The systems to exploit natural resources, such as mining, transport of resources and large industry needed those resources themselves. This developed a self-perpetuating loop.

The environmental movement in the 1800s and first half of the 1900s was therefore primarily concerned about environmental health matters as well as conservation and protection of wildlife, water quality, soil and forests.

The conservation movement split into two distinct strands in the late nineteenth and early twentieth century. Protectionists, such as John Muir, saw that there was an inherent value in nature and wildlife, and suggested that a connection to the natural world was beneficial to humanity for a sense of well-being and harmony.

Muir's famous dictum that "when we try to pick out anything by itself, we find it hitched to everything else in the Universe" demonstrates his understanding of the systemic nature of the world and how the smallest action can impact the world in ways that are not always realised.[14]

Conservationists, like Gifford Pinchot, wanted to manage natural resources to maximise exploitation. This utilitarian attitude towards nature and its resources had the aim of ensuring that the Earth's resources were preserved for their long-term exploitation to maximise economic gain. He and Muir were contemporaries, and while both had similar aims in trying to preserve forestry, they disagreed at a philosophical level.

This disagreement is worth noting. Even today it is a mistake to think of the environmental movement as a unified campaign. At times, seemingly environmentally friendly decisions can have environmentally damaging consequences, as we will see later with the debates surrounding the Severn Barrage. Although this would generate sustainable energy, wildlife protection groups are concerned about the impact upon the species that live in the Estuary.

This said, you would be hard-pressed to find an environmental organisation that would advocate maximising economic gain from wildlife and natural resources. There is, however, undoubtedly an element of self-protectionism to environmental responsibility.

There is both a realisation that we cannot carry on our current levels of consumption for our own safety as well as a concern that the way we are treating the natural environment, and the wildlife that we share the planet with, is wrong on moral grounds.

The reasons that environmentally damaging behaviours have developed are far too complex to go into here, but it is important to see that technological and scientific advancements have both required us and enabled us to damage and exploit the planet for its natural resources. To develop we have needed the resources of the planet, but that development has meant that we can then use even more of the resources.

It is our ways of thinking, rather than the advancements themselves, that determine our behaviour. Fritz Schumacher suggested that we do

not experience ourselves "as a part of nature, but as an outside force des-
tined to dominate and conquer it." [15]

This way of thinking has defined how we develop as a civilisation,
nationally and globally.

John McNeil suggests that "one reason the environment changed so
much in the twentieth century is because prevailing ideas and politics –
from an ecological perspective – changed so little." [16] The dominance of
capitalism, and consumerism, has meant that the way we treat the natural world has changed little. As people become increasingly concerned
about the implications of this behaviour for both humanity and the
planet, the environmental movement has grown.

There is, however, a backlash to this. The cultural and social preva-
lence of capitalism and consumerism has meant that people distrust
those who try to implement environmental protectionist measures on
business. Unlimited economic growth is desired, and those who try to
stop it are trying to restrict freedom.

The environmental movement, therefore, continues to fight against
big corporations and governments, as well as dominant modes of thinking, to try and shift to a more sustainable way of living which is better for
us and the planet.

We have looked at how Bristol has responded to environmental
issues and concerns, and how the organisations, initiatives, individuals
and communities have tried to show that environmental thinking is
about going forward, not backward.

The growth of the environmental movement

We stand now where two roads diverge. . . The road we have long been travelling is deceptively easy, a smooth superhighway on which we progress with great speed, but at its end lies disaster. The other fork of the road — the one less travelled by — offers our last, our only chance to reach a destination that assures the preservation of the earth.[17]

Rachel Carson

In 1962, Rachel Carson's *Silent Spring* was published. This polemical text looked at the environmental consequences of the overuse of pesticides, specifically DDT, on human health and wildlife. While Carson's work was not the first instance of environmental thinking, her book placed environmental concern within public consciousness.

The title referred to Carson's fear that one day spring would no longer be marked by the song of birds, which was a powerful evocation of a future without nature. Her passion and dedication to exploring our ability to have such an impact on the world marked a new chapter in the environmental movement.

The book's reception was controversial. Some saw it as a threat to the economy, as without pesticides agriculture would suffer and therefore environmental protectionism would be damaging to economic growth.

Carson was not calling for a total ban on pesticides, rather their controlled and responsible use, but her work was seen as a threat to the freedom of corporations and seemed to call for state intervention, which led to fierce criticism. Concerns about limiting corporate freedom still pose one of the greatest challenges to those in the environmental movement.

Furthermore, as Carson identified DDT (which was used in the controlling of mosquito populations) as one of the most harmful pesticides, she was accused of attacking the prevention of malaria. While the reception of the text was contentious, Carson had encouraged a mainstream awareness of the reality of human interference with nature which would only grow over the next fifty years.

The 1960s were a decade characterised by social, political and cultural rethinking, protest and radicalism. Those involved in the alternative 'counter-culture' of the 1960s were concerned with, among other things, race relations, women's rights, sexual morals, and traditional modes of authority. People were becoming disillusioned with the status quo and sought alternative ways of living, which saw the rise of 'hippies' who travelled and lived in non-standard community and family structures, including communes or 'on-the-road'.

These protests by women and men about issues of discrimination developed a section of society which openly questioned authority and refused to accept exclusion and oppression. While environmental concerns were not a dominant aspect of the protests, it was this culture of questioning and examination which paved the way for the beginning of the modern environmental movement. Many of the values of this era, such as self-sufficiency, non-standard community living, moving away from consumerism, acceptance of difference and political activism for social justice, can be seen in today's environmental movement.

In 1970, the 'Don't make a Wave Committee' developed in order to protest against a second nuclear weapons test at Amchitka Island in the Aleutians.[18] The group was officially founded in 1970, and went on to become Greenpeace who are now present in over 40 countries. Their main way of campaigning – direct action – became a vital tool to the global environmental movement.

Direct action is a form of protest where people, quite simply, take direct action to voice their concerns. This can range from sit-ins, occupations to road blocking. They are often non-violent, but can be judged as 'civil disobedience'. For example, when a piece of land is in dispute over development, protesters will trespass in order to stage a sit-in to prevent that development.

The level of civil disobedience can differ, however. A practice known as 'monkey wrenching' is sometimes used, which usually involves the disabling of machinery or damage to property to prevent environmentally damaging behaviour. Direct action is sometimes used as the last port of call when all other forms of protest have been unsuccessful or ignored.

The Don't Make a Wave Committee, as their first campaign, chartered a boat and "set sail to Amchitka to 'bear witness'", which is a Quaker tradition of silent protest.[19] A member of this expedition, Bob Hunter, later wrote about the issues with collaborative decision-making that arose during the voyage. The voyage remains a pivotal moment in the environmental movement, however. As Bob Hunter puts it, "whatever history decides about the big picture, the legacy of the voyage itself is not just a bunch of guys in a fishing boat, but the Greenpeace the entire world has come to love and hate."[20]

In 1969 and 1970 another environmental protest group was being founded: Friends of the Earth (FoE). This group was also keen to take assertive actions to highlight and prevent environmental damage. David Brower, one of the founder members, hoped to change the environmental movement for the better as he became increasingly "frustrated at the conservative orthodoxy of mainstream nature conservation".[21] Brower felt that those in the environmental movement were not doing enough to prevent the damage that humanity was causing upon the planet, noting that "polite conservationists leave no mark save the scars upon the Earth that could have been prevented had they stood their ground." [22]

Like Greenpeace, FoE has gone from strength to strength and has 76 national member groups, 5,000 local activist groups on every continent and over 2 million members and supporters worldwide.[23] While both were founded in America, the UK closely followed, with a UK Friends of the Earth and Greenpeace UK in 1971.

Brower founded FoE with the motto "think globally, act locally", which is still a dictum that many environmentalists abide by today [24] The structure of both Greenpeace and FoE (a global organisation with national and then local groups) encourages this way of thinking.

The development of both Greenpeace and Friends of the Earth demonstrates the growing concerns about the environment and human activity. The shift towards grass roots action and public protest made it clear that people understood that if they wanted change, they needed to be willing to take clear and, sometimes, radical action.

In 1970 a U.S. Senator, Gaylord Nelson, put in motion the development of 'Earth Day'. Nelson, concerned by the 1969 Santa Barbara oil spill and inspired by the student anti-war protests, realised that there was a great source of untapped energy in people protesting for their beliefs. He put together a team to develop the concept of the protest, and on the 22nd of April 1970 22 million Americans, united through a shared aim, campaigned for better treatment of the environment.

Environmental concern was not limited to protest. In 1968, a varied group of people, including academics, economists, scientists and civil servants, met in Rome to "discuss the dilemma of prevailing short-term thinking in international affairs and, in particular, the concerns regarding unlimited resource consumption in an increasingly interdependent world." [25]

This group was known as the Club of Rome, and their first report, 'Limits to Growth', published in 1972, became an integral text within the burgeoning environmental movement. Their concerns over resource depletion, the economy and population growth were discussed as the report "demonstrated the contradiction of unlimited and unrestrained growth in material consumption in a world of clearly finite resources."[26]

Their report demonstrated how environmental issues were complex, interconnected, and dependent on the way humanity had developed social, cultural, political and economic structures. Yet there was no long-term thinking about what this would do to the planet.

An economy based on the consumption of finite resources was not sustainable and would be compounded by a growing population. The work done by the Club of Rome shows the shift towards a new chapter in the environmental movement – the rise of 'sustainable thinking'.

In the year after *Limits to Growth* was published the Western world was catapulted into an unprecedented oil crisis. The Organisation of Petroleum Exporting Countries (OPEC) placed an embargo on exporting oil in response to international political tension. This led to oil prices skyrocketing. The crisis demonstrated that the developed world's ability to access cheap and easy fuel depended not only on physical availability but also on international political stability. It also showed the realities of living without cheap oil and how energy availability played a pivotal role in economic security, transport and leisure.

The benefit of this crisis was that it exposed the vulnerability of the developed world and the possible issues of resource depletion. It became clear that a world without easy access to oil, or other resources, would be difficult and likely to generate conflict. E. F. Schumacher reportedly stated that "the party's over".[27] Those, like the Club of Rome, who were concerned with resource depletion, had evidence for their fears of unlimited consumption and the future consequences of this paradigm. We will see that this oil crisis had a direct effect on Bristol's environmental movement, specifically in the development of Sustrans.

Climate change

The 1980s saw the growth of public interest in the environmental movement at a local, national and global level with the growth of environmental groups such as Friends of the Earth and Greenpeace. Towards the end of the 1980s global warming, or climate change, became a discourse that was to dominate public opinion about environmental issues for the next thirty years.

The nineteenth century had the discovery of greenhouse gases and the regulation of the biosphere and by the end of the century scientists were discussing the implications of an increase of carbon dioxide and other gases in the atmosphere.

In 1938 Guy S. Callender suggested that the warming trend revealed in the nineteenth century had been caused by a 10% increase in atmospheric carbon dioxide from the burning of fossil fuels.[28] There was little concern as it was generally thought that carbon capture by the ocean would self-regulate the CO_2 levels in the atmosphere.

In the late 1950s, two oceanographers, Hans Suess and Roger Revelle, questioned this assumption and employed David Keeling to measure the levels of carbon dioxide in the atmosphere. Within 18 months, Keeling's work had shown that carbon dioxide levels were continuing to rise at both the sites where he was performing tests. Revelle, Suess and Keeling, however, had to fight continually to keep this monitoring process going throughout the 60s and 70s as there was still no widespread concern within the scientific community or the public domain.

In the mid-70s Wallace Broeker wrote a paper called 'Climate Change: Are we on the brink of a pronounced global warming?' Broeker, and others, had conducted a series of studies examining 'ice cores' from glacial sheets. This work showed that the Earth's climate was capable of rapid, short-term shifts between climates. Broeker suggested that the rise in carbon dioxide levels might lead to "abrupt changes in the Earth's climate".[29]

This began the exploration into the natural environment, the atmosphere, the ocean, the land, the forests and how they interacted with one another in a series of systems that created feedback loops, had emergent properties and could be unpredictable. The notion of 'tipping points' and rapid change created a fear that we were not acting quickly enough to prevent the causes of global warming. Scientific opinion remained divided, and climate change was not a dominant discourse in the public domain. Mike Hulme, in his book *Why we disagree about Climate Change*, identifies the year 1988 as the year that this changed.

In the January of 1988 it was announced that 1987 had been the warmest year within the 130-year global temperature series published by the University of East Anglia. In May, an intergovernmental conference on climate change was held in Toronto which concluded that industrialised nations should reduce their carbon emissions by 20% by 2005.

This year also marked the founding of the Intergovernmental Panel on Climate Change by the UN.

National leaders including Margaret Thatcher, George Bush Sr. and Mikhail Gorbachev entered the debate, and mainstream media noted the importance of this topic as *Time* magazine ran an edition calling the Earth 'endangered'. While this 'awakening' was primarily in the Western world, it still marked a major change for the environmental movement.

The 1990s and 2000s therefore saw the involvement of international governmental figures and the proliferation of environmental organisations and community groups, as people became concerned about what 'climate change' meant for them. It was an issue, however, that often other environmental issues took a backseat to the public discourse of climate change. Throughout the twentieth century, human actions and behaviour were responsible for a range of environmental damage through air and water pollution, damage to agricultural land and contamination: oil spills, nuclear testing, overuse of pesticides, resource depletion, holes in the ozone layer and the acidification of the oceans.

The viability, resilience and sustainability of our society relies on the alleviation and prevention of many more environmental issues, including pollution, resource depletion, energy and food security, water use, loss of biodiversity and deforestation.

Global warming is possibly the most controversial environmental issue. We can see the depletion of resources; we can see the loss of biodiversity; we can see deforestation and desertification. We cannot see carbon dioxide in the atmosphere and it is hard to conceptualise and communicate the various effects climate change may have, all in some indeterminate future.

The actions taken by many of the environmental initiatives, organisations and community groups in Bristol place the reduction of carbon emissions alongside other environmental and social work, as climate change is recognised as only one issue in among many others.

Sustainability

We do not inherit the world from our ancestors; we borrow it from our children.
Native American Proverb

The late 60s and early 70s had seen a proliferation of work surrounding issues such as overpopulation, resource depletion and the economy. These included Paul Erlich's *The Population Bomb,* Club of Rome's *Limits to Growth*, E. F. Schumacher's *Small is Beautiful*, The Ecologist's *Blueprint for Survival* and Barbara Ward and Rene Dubos's *Only One World*.

These texts inspired an understanding of how issues such as population growth, environmental damage and resource depletion interacted, and we can see these texts, among other work, as the beginnings of what later became known as sustainable development or sustainability.

As discussions of climate change dominated media representation and overshadowed the public discussion of other environmental issues, sustainable thinking promoted a holistic understanding of environmental damage and placed climate change as only one part of a much wider problem.

The Brundtland Commission's original definition of sustainable development was perhaps too general, and perhaps has been taken to mean too many different things, but the notion of sustainable thinking is still useful to us as the word simply means to enable things to last.

Sustainability can be seen as "enlightened self-interest".[30] We have become aware that is not just about the common mantra of 'saving the planet'; it is also about 'saving' ourselves, and enabling planetary resources to last is an important part of this. Schumacher's statement that "infinite growth in a finite environment is an obvious impossibility" simply refuses to allow his reader to think otherwise.[31]

E. F. Schumacher's work on sustainable economics inspired the Schumacher Institute to explore sustainable thinking and to recognise that understanding the interconnections, interdependencies and complexity of social, cultural, political, economic and environmental systems is vital to developing a sustainable society.

Small is Beautiful argued that our economic system was not sustainable, and discussed notions of appropriate scale, use of technology and the prioritisation of economic growth over human well-being. Schumacher's work explored not just how we exploit the environment but why. The inability to see ourselves as part of nature has made us feel separate and immune to the natural world, able to exploit it without consequence.

Schumacher also said:

"It is clear that the 'rich' are in the process of stripping the world of its once-for-all endowment of relatively cheap and simple fuels. It is their continuing economic growth which produces ever more exorbitant demands, with the result that the world's cheap and simple fuels could easily become dear and scarce long before the poor countries have acquired the wealth, education, industrial sophistication, and power of capital accumulation needed for the application of alternative fuels on any significant scale."[32]

This again shows the interconnections between social and environmental issues. The way developed countries have acted has left developing countries in a position where they are going to feel the brunt of environmental degradation having had very little, or no, part in it. This is why we feel that social and environmental justice and convergence are such important aspects to creating truly sustainable societies.

Convergence

The Schumacher Institute is leading a European-funded research project to explore convergence. This idea links the need to live within planetary boundaries with the ethical desire to do that as fairly as possible. Everyone on the planet should share in the resources available so we can have as high a quality of life as possible. Our research is to understand better what this simple, yet powerful, concept means and how we might find ways to achieve it. How can we organise the world so that everyone has fair access to the services needed to live well –in a way the preserves the earth's capacity to provide those services.

In November 2001, the Economic and Social Research Council and Friends of the Earth published a paper on environmental justice under the umbrella of the Global Environmental Change Programme. This paper stated that environmental justice's "two basic premises are first, that everyone should have the right and be able to live in a healthy environment, with access to enough environmental resources for a healthy life, and second, that it is predominantly the poorest and least powerful people who are missing these conditions." [33]

It would be a failing not to talk about how Bristol cannot be sustainable without the rest of the UK, Europe and the world doing the same. No matter how environmentally friendly Bristol is, it will make little difference if the rest of the world carries on regardless of these issues. Even though there is a strong emphasis on local self-sufficiency within the environmental movement, it is unrealistic that in an age of globalisation we will not remain part of a world network, heavily dependent on people we never see or know about.

This is why the maxim 'Act Local, Think Global' is important as a framework for thinking. Local action should be a way of not just helping your own country but also helping other countries, especially developing ones. A simple example of this would be buying an organic, fair trade chocolate bar from your local independent shop. You are supporting your local retailer and those who grew the chocolate abroad.

We are aware that so far our discussions have been West-centric, which is because we are discussing the modern environmental movement and its role in a specific location – Bristol. It would be wrong not to mention that the actions in the developed world are negatively affecting those in the developing world, both environmentally and socially.

Environmental and social injustice happens on a global scale as developing countries are exploited for their natural resources and often have less temperate climates, which means they are the first to be hit by climate change. The IPCC stated in their report 'Climate Change 2007: Impacts, Adaptation and Vulnerability' that "there is high confidence that developing countries will be more vulnerable to climate change than developed countries." [34] This vulnerability is compounded by poorer physical and economic infrastructure, leaving developing countries unguarded against extreme weather or resource disputes. Without the necessary economic stability, these countries will find it difficult to protect themselves and bounce back from environmental degradation, climate change or resource scarcity.

Convergence has its origins in the work of the Global Commons Institute, led by Aubrey Meyer, whose Contraction & Convergence™ proposal lies at the heart of the Kyoto Protocol to reduce carbon emissions.

This notion of convergence is not just useful in a global context. Many of the organisations, initiatives and community groups that we will look at in Bristol are concerned with ensuring that people across the city – and the UK – are not subject to social and environmental injustices which affect their quality of life.

Nature

In 1973, Arne Naess, drawing on the work of Aldo Leopold and Rachel Carson, discussed his concept of 'deep ecology'. Conservation of the natural environment, including wildlife, is one of the most recognised forms of environmental protection, and Naess's work advocated a move away from utilitarian treatment of nature towards the principle of 'biospherical egalitarianism or equality' and stated that 'humans have no right to reduce this richness and diversity [of life forms] except to satisfy vital needs.' [35]

An article in *Resurgence* magazine in 1985 stated that "ecological consciousness and deep ecology are in sharp contrast with the dominant worldview of technocratic-industrial societies which regards humans as isolated and fundamentally separate from the rest of Nature, as superior to, and in charge of, the rest of creation." [36]

This echoes Schumacher's assertion that we see ourselves as separate from nature, which has allowed us to exploit natural resources for our own gain. Deep Ecology tries to encourage an understanding that we are part of the natural world and dependent on its self-regulating systems, and that a connection with nature can give a sense of well-being.

As much of the discourse surrounding climate change and environmental degradation, including resource depletion, is to do with the effects they will have upon humans, certain organisations and individuals have been keen to highlight the effects it will have on non-human animals and plant life as well.

Further discussion of wildlife and nature conservation will take concerns for humans, non-human animals and nature into consideration. As we are indeed part of interconnected and interrelated systems, all three are often linked. For instance, when we destroy rainforest and woodland we destroy the habitat of thousands of species as well as trees that have survived for hundreds of years. We also however lose huge areas of 'carbon dioxide sinks' which clean our air and regulate the atmosphere.

It is often the bigger, more 'iconic' animals that we see calls to protect, such as tigers, pandas and other endangered species. The growing recent awareness of the decline in the bee population, however, has encouraged an understanding of the interdependence of the diversity of life on this planet. A recent United Nations Environment Programme report stated that "declines in managed bee colonies date back to the mid-1960s in Europe but have accelerated since 1998, especially in Belgium, France, Germany, Italy, the Netherlands, Spain and the United Kingdom." This is an issue because "of the 100 crop species that provide 90 per cent of the world's food, over 70 are pollinated by bees." [37]

There are many theories as to why bee populations are declining, including pesticide and insecticide use, air pollution, mite infestations, declining levels of flowering plants and even electromagnetic fields. What is clear, however, is that their decline will adversely affect our human ability to feed ourselves. This is worrying now, without even taking into account that our global population is expanding and expected to hit 9 billion people in 2042. [38]

Calls to preserve biodiversity have only grown as environment problems, including deforestation, desertification and climate change, become more apparent. 2010 was the International Year of Biodiversity, and we will see that there are organisations in Bristol, and the rest of the UK, which deal with issues of local, national and global nature conservation and enjoyment.

Issues within the environmental movement

Being 'sustainable' or 'environmental' means different things to different people and as we will see later, these different opinions and values can lead to tension. Our earlier discussion of Muir and Pinchot's fundamental philosophical disagreement is just one example of this.

To this day there are divisions evident in the different sectors and organisations involved in the environmental movement. People have different standards of what constitutes environmental dedication, use different language, different methods and have different priorities.

From the person who recycles to the person who lives off-grid, we differ in our interpretation of what the most pressing issues are. The ability to be environmentally friendly is also an issue. Lifestyle choices, like not flying, being vegetarian, buying organic and local food, can be alienating to people outside the environmental movement, for personal, cultural or financial reasons.

Guilt, purposefully or not, is often invoked through the discourses in which the environmental movement speaks, and people have become tired of hearing 'Doomsday' narratives and often simply react against what they feel they are 'being told to do'. Furthermore, environmental behaviour and protection can be at odds with social justice. Implementing taxes and charges on environmentally damaging behaviour can be successful, especially in relation to big corporations, but when these taxes are implemented at a household level, they impact lower-income households much more than the more affluent ones. (Eames 2006) [39]

We believe, however, that consideration of environment justice and sustainable thinking can improve social equality. There are, as we will discuss later, issues of involvement and representation from every area of the population within the environmental movement which requires attention to ensure that the environmental movement speaks for everyone, not just a select few.

Prepare for change: the case for resilience

One noticeable aspect of the environmental movement in Bristol and elsewhere is the shift in the last decade towards a 'prepare for change' mentality.

Peak oil (the point at which global oil supplies reach a peak and then enter a decline) has become a much more discussed term in the last four or five years. Once this has happened oil prices will continue to rise and, unlike the oil crisis of the 1970s, will never fall. This will not only affect our access to energy but also the price of our food, our transport, the warmth of our homes, leisure activities, national security and our economy.

A synonym for sustainability has become 'resilience', and groups such as the Transition Movement have started to look at ways of preparing for events they see as inevitable, such as the effects of climate change and peak oil. Rather than adopting a 'doom and gloom' outlook, Bristol's Transition movements are about celebrating this change, looking to the positives of a low-carbon society which makes more time for family, friends and loved ones, cities where communities work together and share skills, thereby creating a society which is centred around people, not things.

The effects of environmental change, resource depletion and energy instability will, however, widen the socio-economic gap, which makes discussion of environmental and social justice even more important.

By developing resilience through localisation, low-carbon 'behaviour' change will naturally follow. Transition calls for all sectors of the city to think about how they might prepare for change, to strengthen our infrastructure (economic, physical and social) where vulnerable, and to find opportunities among problems.

Governmental legislation and local authorities

While community and grass roots action can achieve many things, it can, at times, only go so far. Government legislation and local authority policies can protect the environment by making city-wide decisions which encourage sustainable behaviour, including recycling schemes, curbing carbon emissions or providing funding for fitting sustainable energy technologies in homes (retrofitting).

There will not be much mention of centralised government, as our stories are about Bristol, but governmental legislation and implementation of environmental measures can have a great effect in reducing carbon emissions and environmentally damaging behaviour, especially for businesses.

Legislation allows local authorities to have a degree of control over environmental issues in the local area, such as on air or water pollution by companies. The Clean Air Act of 1968, which was followed by the

Control of Pollution Act in 1974, began to restrict the levels of environmental damage by corporations as well as encourage them to think about their impacts.

Calls for tougher environmental legislation have become more regular as concerns about the environment have grown. This is often where campaign groups and the government, local authorities and big corporations come into dispute, as campaign groups demand change which corporations or the government are not willing to give.

Demands for stricter controls on polluting practices and carbon emissions are labelled 'prohibiting' to economic growth, and governments are fearful of imposing stricter controls in fear of becoming unpopular with their electorate as well as with corporations that hold a lot of power.

These tensions are visible within Bristol, but there are also good examples of ways in which the people of the city, businesses and the council have worked together – sometimes having to compromise – to share skills, funding and support to achieve a common aim.

Bristol's environmental movement: 1960-2011

Bristol's reputation as a 'green city' is controversial, and we do not want to suggest that it is anywhere near being a 'sustainable city'. We have a high proportion of sustainably minded individuals and environmental organisations and the city's environmental awareness has spread into all sectors of the city, including the council and businesses. As we will see, there has been a great deal of innovative and creative sustainable thinking within the city.

Often, however, there has been too much thinking and not enough application. Bristol has examples of poor urban planning which creates chock-a-block traffic, a transport system with room for improvement, areas of the city which have been divided by roads, and a high level of socio-economic disparity.

This is before we even consider the other attributes that Bristol shares with every other UK city: an insatiable appetite for and reliance on fossil fuels, a dependence on supermarkets, roads dominated by the car, a diminishing wildlife population, green space under threat and a growing gap between the rich and more deprived areas of the city.

There were many aims of this project. We wanted to document examples of early environmental action as well as some of the more recent pioneering stories. We also wanted to share this information with the public and look to the future. One thing we were not seeking to do however was to 'prove' that Bristol was or is the UK's greenest city. It is not.

We do, however, have a lot to feel proud about even though we still have far to go. The stories that we will begin to detail now are but a few of the many, many examples of sustainable action in Bristol but will hopefully give a sense of the successes, achievements and problems in the city.

1960s Bristol

The early twentieth century changed the face of Bristol. During World War I and II the city sustained serious damage through bomb attacks. Post-1945, Bristol was faced with the long task of rebuilding the city. The

1950s were seen as a period of opportunity for the city to reclaim some of the glory and beauty of the architecture which had been lost. The emphasis was on modernisation, which encouraged Bristol to try and create a city designed for the motor car which was "necessary to. . . the advance of civilisation".[40]

The Fight for Bristol: Planning and the Growth of Public Protest describes the struggle against many of the planning decisions which the city's residents felt would damage Bristol. These decisions arose because "at the end of the war there was an all-pervading mood for a clean sweep of everything tawdry, dirty and inefficient."

In 1952, a 'Development Plan' was published which detailed how the city was going to be renewed through housing estates developed into communities which could function without the private car, which was still not a prevalent form of transport. Each of these communities would have local amenities, like a school, church and shops and would create new jobs.

These plans did not take off as quickly as planned, and Bristol in the 1960s still bore the marks of a city heavily damaged by the war. It was therefore understandable why the town planners and local authorities wanted to regenerate and modernise the city. A plan for a new road to improve car mobility throughout the city was proposed in the Bristol Development Plan in 1966.

The plans for the Outer Circuit Road, as it was known, were less than desirable for many of Bristol's residents. While the environmental campaigning boomed in Bristol in the 70s, the public protest against the road laid the foundations for the city's determination to protect Bristol's geographical landscape, community coherence and green spaces. It seemed as if roads and cars were being valued over communities and people. This encouraged Bristol's residents to try to stop these plans. Fight for Bristol states that the Outer Circuit Road threat "was vastly greater to the east and south of the city. In these areas, property was cheap, the topography was generally less difficult and the residents were thought to be less vociferous."

The campaign against the road united the whole city, across social and geographical barriers, and was supported by local media, Bristol Friends of the Earth and some local MPs.

This campaign continued through the early years of the 70s until the plans were put on hold, and eventually scrapped, due to the combination of the protests and, ultimately, economic recession. Easton, however, still remains split in two by the first section that was built and in Totterdown 550 houses were demolished and 2,000 people evicted from their homes.

> *"It was an urban motorway that was going to bridge over the area where the SS Great Britain is, then go over the city docks with this great urban motorway bridge...*
>
> *... tear up the side of Brandon Hill, dive into the hillside and underneath Clifton...*
>
> *... reappear behind the Victoria Rooms with a great spaghetti junction, go up Tyndall's Park...*
>
> *... tearing through houses...*
>
> *... dive down through Cotham into St Paul's and then join up with the M32 as it now is where the motorway comes into Bristol...*
>
> *... and then it was going to go beyond, right round to Totterdown".*
>
> **George Ferguson, a local architect and an individual who protested against the plans, remembers what the road would have done to Bristol**

The reasons behind the campaign were not entirely environmental. Local residents objected to the notion of splitting communities in two, destroying houses and degrading local amenities. Air pollution, car domination and the destruction of green space, in Victoria Park and Brandon Hill, were also major concerns.

Bristol and Avon Friends of the Earth

As Bristol entered the 1970s the environmental movement was growing, and Bristol found itself in the midst of it with one of the first UK Friends of the Earth groups outside of London.

Over the next ten years, Bristol's environmental movement grew and several key organisations were developed that dealt with issues such as sustainable transport, recycling, local food and sustainable energy.

The actions of Bristol and Avon Friends of the Earth contributed heavily in these early days, as did the help of the Youth Opportunities Scheme and Community Programmes which gave new small organisations and initiatives the workforce they needed.

The Youth Opportunities Programme was essential to our success. We used dozens of young people who were given six-month placements, they were paid a minimum wage and they were supervised by other very long-term unemployed people . . .

. . . YOPs was crucial, it did a lot of really good work in Bristol and there was an explosion of Community enterprise under the YOPS banner . . .

. . . which is interesting because that sort of thing could happen again, I think. But those were halcyon days in a way for the people of my generation because we watched an enormous amount of good work being done by YOPs.

**Alastair Sawday,
founder member of Avon Friends of the Earth**

In 1971, Bristol Friends of the Earth officially launched with their first big campaign: a protest against non-returnable bottles from Schweppes. In a nationally co-ordinated protest, they collected and left 500 non-returnable bottles on the doorstep at Schweppes Offices in Brislington.

The protest was organised by several local people, including Dr. Stephanie Tyler, a local biologist, and a young Bristol University student named Brian Price. Brian had worked at the national FoE office and quickly ended up helping to run the Bristol FoE group out of the Student's Union.

As the group grew they moved to Brunel House and began a project, with some funding, to look at levels of pollution with local schoolchildren. This was the first proper FoE office outside of London.

The group's work was not limited to any one environmental issue and they worked on local and national campaigns including recycling and resource use, mining, nuclear power, whaling and pollution. In 1972 they campaigned against the proposals for the Outer Circuit Road. Along with other amenity and environmental groups in Bristol they held a candlelit vigil on College Green to raise awareness.

In the same year the group drew attention to Bristol's lack of adequate public transport by running a free bus for the day from Knowle West through to the centre. The bus was driven by members of Bristol FoE and aimed to demonstrate that "if public transport was free, or at least a lot cheaper, then more people would use it and there would be less pollution and resource wastage from cars." [41]

The group also protested nationally against lead in petrol, concentrating on the effects it had on children's development and how it contaminated food through soil pollution.[42]

The 70s also saw protests against nuclear power, with anti-nuclear rallies at Windscale, cycling campaigns, and in 1976 Bristol FoE called for more research into the Severn Barrage plans.

In 1976 Bristol FoE began a small-scale recycling service when the council cut back their service. This proved to be a key moment in Bristol's environmental movement as it formed a core group responsible for the development of the city's recycling. They had to work on a shoestring budget, and the waste paper collected was initially stored in Brian's flat until his landlord pointed out it was a fire hazard. The paper was taken to a local waste paper merchant, Nick Francis, who guaranteed Bristol FoE a decent price for the paper. Bristol FoE then used the proceeds from this scheme to insulate houses of older people.

In 1976, Alastair Sawday moved to Bristol and joined Bristol Friends of the Earth. He and others developed the waste paper scheme after Bristol City Council stopped collecting it altogether in 1980 when St Anne's Board Mills, the local waste paper mill, closed down. They acquired trucks from the council and started a much bigger recycling collection and Nick Francis continued to provide them with a guaranteed market for the paper they collected.

They used the Youth Opportunities Scheme to employ people to work for them; this both benefited them, as they had a workforce which they did not have to pay, as well as contributed to a programme which provided previously unemployed people with a steady wage.

The initiatives that grew from the recycling programme developed quickly and so Alastair set up Avon Friends of the Earth which became responsible for the recycling programme, known as Resourcesaver, and ACORN (Avon Conservation of Resources Network).

In 1978 Bristol FoE promoted their work and ideas through a local environmental publication called 'Spaceship Earth' which looked at both local and national environmental concerns and took "a critical look at the impact that human activity has had".

Resourcesaver worked throughout the 1980s to collect Bristol's waste materials through a kerbside scheme. They had little funding but worked tirelessly to improve the city's recycling facilities. At one point they were using a horse and cart to collect waste paper from around the city!

In 1979 and 1980 the UK had been hit by a strike by rubbish collectors. As refuse piled up in the streets for days, the concepts of 'waste' and

> *I would go round with [the volunteers] collecting newspaper,*
> *bundled newspaper in a van, trundled it down to Avonmouth where we*
> *sold it to Clarfield Waste Paper run by Nick Francis who was a very*
> *keen to support us.*
>
> *At the time we were getting £25 a tonne, which was a lot . . . within three*
> *or four years, we had about a hundred people working for us mostly on*
> *the recycling programme. By that time we were recycling glass as well*
> *and textiles.*
>
> **Alastair Sawday,**
> **founder member of Avon Friends of the Earth**

the consequential impact of no services to dispose of it, were thrust into the public consciousness. This helped the recycling schemes encourage people to think more about their waste.

Avon FoE started a quarterly magazine, the *Western Environmental Bulletin*, in 1981. In the first edition, Brian Price stated that "ten years ago, the word 'environment' was on everybody's lips. Newspapers, magazines and television programmes were full of stories about pollution, over-population and resource depletion . . . more than a few have expired as public attention has shifted to other issues." [43]

This was exactly 30 years ago. Oddly, in 1981 there was an economic and social situation similar to that faced by the UK today: there were serious problems with unemployment and with the economic system. Brian's words still ring true when he asserts that in spite of these issues "we must never lose sight of the fact that all the money in the world can never buy us a new planet should we be so foolish as to ruin this one."

Bristol FoE continued campaigning throughout the 80s about local and national issues which concerned them. One local issue was the air pollution in Avonmouth which was identified as a massive problem for that area, due to the combination of the different types of industry working there.

In 1984, a paper was published entitled 'Health Inequalities in Bristol' (Townsend, P., Simpson, D., Tibbs, N., University of Bristol, 1984) which looked at indicators of material deprivation to show the big differences in premature mortality between the more affluent and deprived areas of the city. In an edition of the *New Scientist* in 1986, Townsend discussed the Avonmouth health issues and suggested that it was "startlingly new

Figure 3. Avon FoE Horse and Cart Recycling (photo © Ray Smith)

evidence of the effect of environmental pollution on health". The area "house[d] a petrochemical complex and [was] the site of one of the world's largest smelting works . . . Avonmouth ranks 18 out of the 28 wards for deprivation but has the worst health record." [44]

Townsend went on to suggest that while "levels of zinc, lead and cadmium are well below internationally agreed safety limits . . . levels of cadmium were 60 times greater than in other areas of the city [which is] why Avonmouth sticks out like a sore thumb amid the generally high correlation between health and deprivation."

While Avonmouth was not what was termed a particularly 'deprived' area, the level of industry, and the cumulative effect of this pollution, was a serious concern and an interesting example of environmental health problems in the city.

We see clearly that Bristol FoE was involved with issues of environmental justice early on in their work through identifying the effects that environmental problems could have on health. They have continued to work on the various local and national environmental issues and later we will look more at their role and activities in Bristol.

Avon FoE's initiatives

Avon and Bristol FoE worked alongside one another but attempted to effect change in different ways. While Bristol FoE continued campaigning, Avon FoE became more involved in social enterprises and business.

Avon FoE was based in King Street, then Old Market, and in 1983 they moved to the Cameron Balloon Building. They were concerned with developing a market for materials they were collecting so that recycling would become viable and cost-effective. The Youth Unemployment Programme, later the Community Programme, was integral to Avon FoE's ability to run these enterprises. As we will see, the scheme supported many tiny grass roots initiatives that provided the means for new businesses to employ a workforce without having to pay them.

Avon FoE, keen to encourage community enterprise and aided by this scheme, provided a platform which spawned several other initiatives and businesses, all of which were concerned with providing a market for recycled materials. Children's Scrapstore was one of these initiatives. In 1982 Simon Hooton had recently moved to Bristol and he saw an advert for a job advertised through Avon Friends of the Earth to set up a 'play resource centre'.

This became the Children's Scrapstore, and it employed its staff under the Youth Opportunities Scheme. When it began it was a team of four young people who were put in charge of converting an unused garage in Bedminster into a space suitable for a scrap store. They had to put in a toilet, office heating and all the plumbing but managed to open within six weeks. They gained a lot of media attention through their work with children. Simon suggests that the premise of the organisation was win-win: they collected waste materials, which companies therefore did not have to pay for to have disposed, and children's groups got cheap materials.[45] Their slogan was 'Make waste things play things!'

Within two years they had member groups stretching from West Wales to Cornwall – right across the whole of the south-west. They had even donated to a school in Ethiopia. They realised that they should help other groups to set up across the UK to cater for their local needs.

When Avon FoE moved in the Cameron Balloon building, Children's Scrapstore joined them and gained more space. As Children's Scrapstore progressed and grew they decided that their main aim was to encourage creative children's play rather than recycling, although it did remain a central concern. This meant that their agenda separated somewhat from Avon FoE.

In the mid-1980s they set up a loan scheme for big items, such as badge-making machines and laminators, so that groups did not have to buy these. They also developed three social enterprises for the purposes of funding. They started an office stationery business, converted a building in West Wales into a holiday centre and retreat, and developed an enterprise called 'Greenplay', which promoted sustainable ideas through play. Children's Scrapstore is still going strong today, and remains firmly about creative ways to reuse waste.

In 1982, the SOFA Project also developed within the Avon FoE family. It began as a project to recycle big items like sofas, chairs, washing machines, cookers and other household items that people no longer wanted. This prevented these items from being sent to landfill. The scheme then refurbished these items and sold them to people who were on restricted incomes. The scheme began as an Avon FoE initiative and, in a common pattern we can see emerging, started with just a few members of staff and a truck.

As they grew, so did their collections. The project had difficulties along the way, as the goods they collect needed to be of good quality and to be safe in order for them to be able to sell them on.

In the mid-1990s, due to new regulations, they could no longer sell on foam-filled furniture which had been made before 1988. This meant they had to turn away a lot of donations, which hit them hard as it coincided with a recession. People were buying fewer pieces of new furniture and therefore there were fewer donations of older pieces. In the early 2000s, however, they found funding which enabled them to build a new base and encouraged a phase of growth.

The funding also allowed them to set up a workshop where damaged items could be repaired and sold on, and this created jobs, training and experience for people who had been unemployed or were excluded from the jobs market.

Figure 4. Sofa Project (photo © Recycling Consortium / Resource Futures)

This project demonstrates the importance of rethinking our methods of purchase and examining the ways in which recycling can offer a way to provide goods that are inaccessible to people due to cost. The SOFA Project continues to work in Bristol today.

The Recycling Consortium and Resource Futures

The beginnings of Resource Futures, a waste consultancy organisation that works with government organisations, local authorities, waste management companies and communities, can also be traced all the way back to these early schemes.

Resourcesaver, Avon FoE's kerbside scheme, had steadily grown throughout the 80s and started to collected textiles, glass and cans as well as paper.

The loss of the Community Programme in the late 80s however meant it was hard to support the full scale of their recycling operations, and a small group decided to continue the recycling collections on a more com-mercial footing with finance coming from sale of materials and recycling credits paid for by Avon County Council. At the same time they began actively campaigning for the collections to be supported directly by Bristol City Council.

The council found the money to make a series of one-off grant pay-ments, and included recycling within the waste collection contract. Resourcesaver/Avon FoE continued to manage the recycling collections under a sub-contract with SITA, the council's waste management company, until 2003.

As Avon FoE campaigned for funding from the council they were also working hard to secure suitable premises for their own and others' envi-ronmental projects. In 1985 Resourcesaver moved into Avon Environment Centre in Brislington along with Children's Scrapstore and The SOFA Project. This building, however, was knocked down to build the spine road between the M4 and the M32. All of the organisations had to move out in the early 1990s.

This loss of shared space was a blow to the organisations, and as a result Resourcesaver, Avon FoE, Children's Scrapstore and the Sofa

Figure 5. Resourcesaver (photo © Community Recycling Network Archive)

Project decided to form a consortium of recycling initiatives and look for another building in order to develop a purpose-built recycling centre. At this stage the Bristol Recycling Consortium was formed to develop this idea further. After a year or so of looking for suitable sites either for redevelopment or new build, the council offered them B-Bond, which was one of the warehouses in the Cumberland Basin. The building was large enough but did not have the accessibility or outside space needed for the deliveries and operations of the recycling organisations.

The operational aspects of the recycling schemes, therefore, went elsewhere – Resourcesaver to Eastville, SOFA to Old Market and Children's Scrapstore to Welsh Back – all premises owned by the council which had fallen into disuse. The fact that the groups had worked together had proved successful in terms of increasing their lobbying potential, and they decided to continue with the Consortium in order to develop new initiatives that would benefit each of the members.

The Consortium became one of the key organisations in the development of B-Bond, which became the Create Centre. They were joined by the Urban Centre for Appropriate Technology, which we will discuss later, and both organisations worked with the council to develop the warehouse into a mixed-use development which had community and office space.

The Consortium began to get involved with Bristol's community recycling action and encouraging grass roots action. As they grew they developed work in other locations and their work became nationally recognised. They changed their name to The Recycling Consortium (TRC) to reflect this national outlook.

TRC became well-known for its work with communities. Jane Stephenson, now the Chief Executive of Resource Futures, notes that the groups which had set up TRC "had really started from small groups of local activists who were committed to making a difference and had set up projects which over time grew and became substantial enterprises in their own right, in many cases becoming exemplars of environmental action across the UK."

As a result of this, TRC had a theory that new innovations primarily started through community action, and they thought that different communities would devise different ideas and plans to reduce waste, suited to their own locality. In order to test this theory they secured funding to work with different communities across Bristol: Westbury Park, Hartcliffe, Patchway, Easton and Hawkbury Upton.

Through consultation with each community, TRC met the local 'movers and shakers' and discovered what waste issues interested and concerned the local people. Support and was then offered to help them develop different community waste reduction, reuse and recycling initiatives to meet their particular needs.

This work continued throughout the 90s. TRC also identified partnership as a key factor to success and so tried to involve all the local schools and businesses in their areas of work. This community engagement work attracted a lot of national attention. Further funding was secured to produce a 'Community Waste Action Toolkit' and to develop new initiatives with other local authorities including Oxfordshire – where the local project continues to this day.

During the 1990s funding was available to organisations like TRC through the landfill tax credit scheme, and through this funding TRC expanded its local work to include education work with schools and community composting. They also developed new initiatives to engage local people in the 3Rs (recycling, reducing and reusing) including door-to-door canvassing, which at the time had not been done within the waste industry.

This included working closely with Bristol City Council managing 'The Rubbish Revolution', a publicity and promotion campaign to improve recycling rates alongside the change to a weekly recycling collection service. This work continued to attract national attention, and during the late 1990s and early 2000s TRC did work across the UK.

The withdrawal of the landfill tax credit scheme for waste work in the early 2000s posed new funding issues. From 2004 onwards TRC began to develop their commercial and consultancy work and worked in partnership with other similar organisations.

In 2006 TRC merged with Save Waste and Prosper (SWAP) in Leeds

---

Resourcesaver was very instrumental in getting the Bristol City Council to accept that supporting the kerbside collection was an important part of its programme of improving its waste management facilities . . . the Director of Health and Environmental Services at the time, Robert Lambourne, was very instrumental in helping us to make sure that recycling services were maintained and were written into future waste contracts, and Councillor Diane Bunyan was [also] very supportive.

Jane Stephenson, Chief Executive of Resource Futures (involved with Avon FoE and Resourcesaver since the early 1980s)

and Network Recycling in Bristol to form Resource Futures. They are still going strong today, and continue to work across sectors aiming to improve resource efficiency and alleviate and prevent environmental issues which stem from over-consumption.

In 2011, Resource Futures supported 30 local action groups working on a wide range of sustainability initiatives, and they have recently secured work to support May Gurney in the development of new recycling services in Bristol during 2012.

Sustrans

Sustrans is another example of how the actions of a few people can, with the right dedication and support, develop an organisation which truly effects change.

In the 1970s Bristol, like the rest of the UK, was in the throes of an oil crisis. The unprecedented move by the oil-producing countries in the Middle East left the developed world in shock, as people were unaccustomed to shortages of what seemed like a never-ending supply of cheap fuel.

In July 1977 Bristol Friends of the Earth decided to organise a rally in response to the oil embargo. The oil crisis also coincided with a wider concern about resource consumption stimulated by the work of E.F. Schumacher, the Club of Rome and others. At the rally, Bristol Friends of the Earth were encouraging local authorities to create more provision for cyclists in the city as they were sidelined by the dominance of the car. Furthermore, the bicycle provided cheap, reliable transport which was not dependent on fuel.

John Grimshaw MBE, a local civil engineer, was known as a cycling enthusiast and so was asked to be a speaker at this rally. He says that he thought that "the most sensible thing [was] to say during the course of the speech; 'let's set up a campaign group.' "[46] A group of about 30 interested people met in the Nova Scotia pub. As there was so little provision for cyclists in the city it was decided that a campaign group was definitely needed. The group was initially called Cyclebag.

They began with a demonstration outside the council house, and then groups visited cycling-friendly UK and EU towns. Although they focused on advocacy and lobbying, Cyclebag's work was original. Early in its development, it carried out practical work. Researching the practicalities of cycling provision became important and James Bruges, a local architect and urban planner, conducted their first study in 1978, which looked at building cycle paths along disused railways.

Figure 6. Cyclebag Rally 1977 led by George Ferguson
(photo © Sustrans/David Sproxton)

Figure 7. In 2007 the founding fathers of Sustrans revisit the Nova Scotia as Sustrans celebrates its 30th birthday (the inaugural meeting of 'Cyclebag' was at the same pub, The Nova Scotia, Ashton, Bristol on the 7/7/1977. Left to right: John Grimshaw, Alastair Sawday, George Ferguson and David Sproxton (photo © J Bewley/Sustrans).

Virginia Chainless developed this notion further by conducting a study about the possibility of a cycle route between Bristol and Bath. Clarks, the shoe company, gave Cyclebag £10,000 to build a key 8km section between Bath and Bitton, and over the course of three months in 1979 a cycle route was built solely by Community Programme volunteers. It was hugely popular, and it became clear that if good quality cycle paths were built then people would use them.

In 1981 the Minister of Transport at the time was invited to visit the path to see its popularity. In 1982, the Bitton to Mangotsfield section of the path was opened and in 1984 the final stage of the route, up to Bristol, was completed. Most of the labour was provided by the Community Programme volunteers.

In 1981, after the visit from the Minister, John Grimshaw and Bill Clark, Cyclebag's Secretary at the time, were commissioned by the government to conduct a study of all disused railways in England and Wales.

The results were published in 1982 and they included 33 appendices which showed the possibilities for every county in England and Wales.

Although the government did not embark upon much action from this report, Cyclebag had a blueprint for cycle routes for every county in England and Wales with the official government stamp on it.

Through the success of the Bath to Bristol Railway path, Cyclebag built up a good relationship with the Railways Commission. Cyclebag felt that every town deserved and needed a good route where people could cycle safely and easily. They began to lease more disused railways to make cycle paths.

As their operations became bigger, Cyclebag realised that they needed a legal arm for their work and so set up Sustainable Transport as a limited company to deal with the leasing of disused railways.

1984 turned out to be seminal year for Cyclebag. The Countryside Commission, now Natural England, asked Sustainable Transport to buy a disused railway from York to Selby with a view to develop it into a cycle path. John agreed immediately and bought the railway that afternoon over the phone. They had to set up a charity in order to manage the land and this event marked the beginning of Sustrans.

By now Sustrans were trying to develop as many cycle paths as possible and were conducting brief studies and submitting planning applications every two to three weeks. By 1985 they had started work in Scotland. The late 1980s however proved problematic, as the Community Programme shut down, leaving Sustrans with a diminished employee base.

The 1990s presented new opportunities. In 1994, Sustrans was granted £42 million of lottery money and was the second biggest project, after the Millennium Dome, in the Millennium Commission. With this money Sustrans built 5,000 miles of cycle paths, which was double their original aim. By the end of this project, 23 million people lived within two miles of the network.

Looking back on Sustrans' success, John Grimshaw says that he feels the most obvious achievement was the National Network, which is over 10,000 miles of signed routes, but that the real achievement was "a bit more subtle than that, because our whole purpose of a National Cycle Network was to be a catalyst for change   by creating something that was national gave the notion or the idea to the general public that cycling was important."

When Cyclebag started 34 years ago, it was in response to the threat of fuel scarcity and the growing domination of the car, which left little or no space for the cyclist and the pedestrian. These concerns are no less relevant today, but Sustrans has provided the nation with an example for change and given the nation over 10,000 miles of cycle routes.

Urban Centre for Appropriate Technology

The oil crisis, concerns about our reliance on fossil fuels and discussion of resource depletion also set the backdrop for another project in Bristol: the Urban Centre for Appropriate Technology (UCAT), which is now The Centre for Sustainable Energy.

In the late 70s Hugh Barton visited The Centre for Alternative Technology (CAT) in Machynlleth and was inspired by their work. He realised however that an urban equivalent was needed in order to demonstrate the realities of sustainable urban living. He worked voluntarily for CAT for a year, exploring possible urban centre options.

Those options did not materialise, but a strange turn of events set in motion the beginning of the urban centre. Hugh and Martin Large, another one of UCAT's founders, were double booked into a countryside cottage on the same weekend with their families. At the local pub they got talking about their ideas and found common ground. Hugh and Martin looked for a suitable city to begin their work. Hugh's home city of Bristol was chosen.

A founding group of five first met in the autumn of 1979. It was decided to use the term 'appropriate' instead of 'alternative' because they decided that they had to "relate to people's normal experience as well as inspiring them. . . Appropriate technology not only meant 'appropriate' to the environmental issues we faced but also the people, the culture, the social scene, the current behaviour of people living in towns." [47]

Their prospectus defined appropriate technology as "the use of tools and physical / social structures that enhance the quality of life, rather than merely increasing GNP, that are conserving in their use of resources, benign in their side-effects, convivial in their social impact." [48]

UCAT began by gathering support from the environmental movement, fundraising and building networks across the city community in order to speak to people who were not already involved in environmental campaigns. Two local MPs, Tony Benn and William Waldegrave, voiced their support.

There was an initially fruitless search for a site for a visitor centre in Bristol docks. Alongside this hard work, the group held barn dances and stalls at fairs to maintain momentum for their work. They wanted to create a 'practical demonstration' house which would bring "abstract ideals of ecologically-sustainable living home to. . . a cross section of the population". Early hopes for an ambitious equivalent to CAT, with people living and working co-operatively in a dynamic visitor centre, including low-energy buildings, craft work, a café, bookshop and exhibition space had to be scaled down.

Two parallel projects were launched – one a demonstration low-energy house, the other a coffee shop/bookshop. Hugh and another core group member, Nigel Heggie, were awarded financial support from Rowntree Charitable Trust to carry these projects out.

The council gave the group a peppercorn rent on 101 Philip Street for the demonstration house. It was a small derelict terraced house in Bedminster, which they used to show how an old house could be renovated to become energy-efficient. It was to be the first low-energy demonstration renovation of an old house in the UK.*

UCAT used Youth Opportunities and Community Programme workers to help renovate the Philip Street site and prepare display and educational materials. The volunteers also ran UCAT's two main community programmes, which aimed to make alternative technologies accessible to people as well as show the environmental, economic and social benefits of energy efficiency.

One programme draught-proofed and insulated houses in the city, especially those of restricted income families and older people. This programme showed how retrofitting made social, economic and environmental sense. People and families saved money, stayed warm and minimised their energy use.

UCAT also ran energy advice and energy training programmes in the Low Energy House. They ran classes which taught people how to draught-proof and insulate their homes as well as displaying examples of retrofitting including draught-proofing, triple glazing, loft insulation, solar panels, under floor heating as well as recycling opportunities and an organic permaculture garden. UCAT wanted to emphasise the cost-effectiveness and practicality of these practices so that no-one was excluded. Their work was about presenting an "integrated picture of sustainable urban life . . . designed to relate closely to people's normal experience".

As UCAT's work progressed they became increasingly interested in dealing with social issues as well as environmental ones. Those at UCAT felt strongly about social issues such as fuel poverty, and found that people in council houses were interested in the benefits of energy efficiency. This in turn encouraged the council to become involved, and Hugh

---

* There was somewhere in Leicester that was not far behind.

Figure 8. Urban Centre For Appropriate Technology: Future City Home (photo © UCAT/CSE Archive)

Barton notes that the council made an 'early move' to insulate and draught-proof more of their houses.

In 1988 UCAT also faced the problematic ending of the Community Programme, which meant they could no longer employ their workforce of over 30 people in Bristol and Bath. With a grant from the Gulbenkian Foundation they persevered with a much smaller workforce. The name 'Bristol Energy Centre' (BEC) was adopted to reflect the main focus of activity.

In the early 90s, BEC worked alongside The Recycling Consortium and were influential in encouraging the council to found the Create Centre. As the organisation continued to grow, BEC became the Centre for Sustainable Energy (CSE) in 1994 to demonstrate their national outlook. In conjunction with its national work, CSE, as we will see, has continued to work closely with the local people, businesses and authorities to encourage sustainable energy use and fuel justice in Bristol.

In parallel with the energy project in the early 80s UCAT was also involved in setting up a series of co-operatives. They began with a bookshop and café and then an energy suppliers and builders. These were designed to be the commercial side of their work and support UCAT's aims of social and environmental equity and responsibility.

In 1981 Hugh approached a local man, Andy King, to support a bookshop. Andy bought 82 Colston Street for this purpose. Irene Galant, who had been working at the Centre for Alternative Technology, was asked if she would like to be involved in setting up the bookshop which would support UCAT's aims by selling environmental books.

The bookshop was formed as a worker's co-op. (The late 70s had been a fertile climate for co-ops and many alternative bookshops, including anarchist and feminist ones, had worked well.) Volunteers renovated the building, and Greenleaf Bookshop opened with a coffee 'corner' selling organic cakes.

They found that the urban setting meant that they did not sell as many environmental books as the specialist bookshop at CAT. The staff decided

Figure 9. UCAT Staff gave energy efficiency advice to householders.
(photo © UCAT / CSE Archive)

> *We were increasingly getting embroiled in the social issues, the fairness issues, the questions of people suffering from fuel poverty. In 1985, we held a seminar which was actually very radical because it was putting together the environmental movement, which was concerned with climate change and pollution and resource management, and the social movement which was concerned with inequity and fuel poverty, poor housing, lack of employment . . .*
>
> *. . . we put these two movements together and said "energy conservation provides a real momentum in both directions [as it] reduces fuel poverty and inequity [and therefore] reduces the need for carbon-rich fuels."*
>
> **Hugh Barton, founder member of UCAT**

to branch out and sell more books about politics, diversity issues, women's rights and psychology. It therefore became somewhat separate from UCAT. Irene notes that since the books often reflected the personal interests of the workers, Greenleaf became seen as a feminist bookshop since it was primarily run by women! [49]

They really tried to reach out into the community and engage people, and had bookstalls at festivals like Glastonbury. While it was not always easy financially, Irene suggests that they had a good following because they provided a personal service and always ordered books in for people. UWE lecturers would also recommend Greenleaf as a good place to go for books.

From the outset it was more than a bookshop because there was the coffee corner where people could sit and chat, exchange ideas and have a cup of tea. The corner soon became a whole café which opened downstairs and was also run as a co-op.

Figure 10. Greenleaf Bookshop (photo © Richard St George)

Both Greenleaf Bookshop and Greenleaf Café became an integral part of the community of the like-minded shops on Colston Street but, like many independent bookshops, they began to suffer in the age of internet shopping and closed in 2005. In the office space above the bookshop, Richard St George ran Low Energy Supply Systems, a renewable energy company which was also linked to UCAT. Greenleaf Builders offered the local area a construction business which considered its environmental impact.

All of these initiatives supported UCAT's overall aims by providing places for people to access appropriate technology information, products and services.

Colston Street was also home to a health food store called Beans and Greens and a shop called Biashara which sold ethical items from developing countries.

Throughout the 80s more and more organisations joined these socially and environmentally-minded organisations, including The Soil Association upon their move in 1985. The local postman called it 'Save the World Street'.

Not long after Greenleaf Bookshop started up, Nuclear Freeze, which was quite a big movement in the United States, wanted to open an office in Britain. They approached us and we said 'Sure, we've got some spare office space above Greenleaf Bookshop, come and join us'. Within a couple of weeks of them moving in the telephones all went cranky and we had a couple of goons in a car sitting outside noting who was coming and going and things like that.

I came into my office one day and I'd obviously got out of bed on the wrong side and I had a load of phone calls to make. I lifted up the phone and it was going "whir click whistle", and I thought 'Oh, I've had enough of this'. I slammed the phone down, grabbed a journalist jotter pad and then stood in front of this car with these two special branch people in, I suppose, and I very deliberately wrote down their registration number and they drove off and we never heard them again. Suddenly the telephones all started working again!

Richard St George, UCAT

Ethical Property Company

These organisations on Colston Street had a lot of help from their land-lord, Andy King. Andy had been interested in co-ops since the 1970s, when there was increasing interest in new business models after a "decade of appalling industrial relations".[50]

When UCAT had wanted to open a bookshop, Andy was able to assist with the purchase of a shop building in Colston Street. This building became Greenleaf Bookshop, and UCAT briefly occupied the rooms above. The bookshop was successful, which attracted other cooperatives to the street. When the neighbouring building became available Andy bought it with Jamie Hartzell to house the fair trade shop, Biashara.

Bristol had a great resource in the form of a local loan fund for co-ops called 'Avon and Bristol Finance Co-operative Finance'. This enabled the city to become quite a fertile ground for co-operatives.

By 1998 there were a large number of co-operatives, both retail and non-retail, in Colston Street and it became clear to Jamie Hartzell and Andy King that there was a role for a property company which let space exclusively to cooperatives and organisations working in the field of social and environmental justice. They founded The Ethical Property Company that year, which incorporated the four properties in Colston Street and one in London that Jamie Hartzell owned. They raised capital by public share issues to expand the company.

The idea behind 'ethical property' was to offer reasonable rent, a sup-portive landlord whose shareholders believed in the causes the organi-sations were working towards, and a well-managed place to work alongside like-minded individuals and organisations. Today the Ethical Property Company has properties throughout the UK, with a growing number in continental Europe.

The Soil Association

'Save the World Street' became home to another of Bristol's biggest organisations. The Soil Association moved from Suffolk in 1985, joining two other small organisations concerned with organic farming and dis-tribution: British Organic Farmers (BOF) and Organic Growers Association (OGF).

The Soil Association (SA) had been founded in 1946 by a group of pio-neering individuals who were concerned at the intensification of agricul-ture: issues such as the use of nitrogen fertiliser on the fertility of the soil, decreased nutritional quality of intensively produced food, and the wider impact of intensive farming systems on the environment and public health.

The organisation was originally based on a farm in Suffolk, and in 1967 the first Soil Association Standards were drawn up which stated that:

". . . the use of, or abstinence from, any particular practice should be judged by its ill-effect on the well-being of the micro-organic life of the soil on which the health of the consumer ultimately depends." [51]

Throughout the 1970s the market for organic food slowly grew, and in 1973 the Soil Association developed their standards for organic food certification. Their location in Suffolk however was quite isolated and in the early 80s they made the decision to move to a city.

Patrick Holden CBE, who was a trustee at the time of the move and later became their Director, suggests that it was thought that "the SA's work needed to become more relevant to people who were urban-dwelling." [52] A city would offer the organisation better transport links and make collaboration with organic producers easier. SA looked for offices in London, Birmingham and Reading, but Bristol became a contender after Peter Segger, another trustee, spoke to a friend who ran the Greenleaf Bookshop.

They were put in touch with Andy King, who secured offices for them on Colston Street. Bristol was also close to their many of the organic farms in the south-west and Wales, where the majority of the new group of younger organic farmers lived. It is also a city that appeals to the environmentally minded; as Patrick Holden states, "you can still see fields even if you are in the very middle of the city and you can very quickly get into beautiful countryside in several different directions."

The move coincided with the growth of the organic market. While the Soil Association had been established for 40 years, the market for organic food had been, in commercial terms, embryonic.

The movement for organic food, as a whole, was also fragmented, which was why in October 1985 the Soil Association, BOF and OGA moved to Bristol together. The move to Bristol, although accidental, marked a new chapter in the organic movement in the UK as they developed new standards and developed a bigger market.

The three organisations grew during their time at Colston Street, and their offices expanded until they sprawled across several first floor buildings. On 24th February 1996 BOF and OGA merged with the Soil

Figure 11. Soil Association on Colston Street (photo © Soil Association)

Association, and at the end of 1997 they moved their 37 members of staff to Bristol House on Victoria Street. During their time at Victoria Street they grew to 135 employees.

The 1980s, however, posed a difficult decision to the growing organic market: should farmers, producers and sellers continue to sell through small, local traders, or should they take organic food to the masses and sell through supermarkets? While supermarkets were able to bring organic food to many people, small-scale producers, whose commitment to the principles behind the standards had led to the development of the market, felt that the supermarkets had no interest in these issues.

Furthermore, these smaller producers felt aggrieved that although could they could less easily afford the certification fees of the Soil Association, they continued to carry the responsibility for innovation and for bringing new ideas and initiatives into the organic movement.

Organic food has found its place in both supermarkets and independent traders, and despite remaining a speciality item to some extent, has become extremely popular. When the Soil Association moved in 1985 the organic food market had been worth under £1 million; less than 30 years later it is worth around £1.5 billion.

The Soil Association's national and international agenda meant that it was somewhat removed from Bristol's environmental movement. It did, however, play a role in encouraging local food projects. Through a link with Alastair Sawday, Eric Booth developed the Local Food Links under the Soil Association. This project looked at the best ways to cultivate a market for local organic produce in Bristol and led to one of Bristol's first veg box schemes.

The Food Links project also developed into a wider initiative called 'Food Futures' which encouraged people in Bristol to work together to develop local food schemes and therefore increase Bristol's resilience in terms of food production. We will look further at the importance of this project in the Food Section.

The Soil Association also launched the Organic Food Festival in Bristol, which is the biggest in Europe, and was involved in the development of Leigh Court Farm, which produces organic fruit and vegetables for a box scheme, in the late 1990s.

The Soil Association's presence in Bristol has been positive, adding to the city's reputation as well as encouraging the development of a local food programme.

Windmill Hill City Farm

In 1976 a local community became involved in Bristol's food movement when they began the first city farm outside London.

The residents of Bedminster and Windmill Hill discovered that a piece of derelict land had been identified as a possible location for a lorry park. The local people did not want a lorry park in the middle of their homes and so appealed to the council to let them develop the land for community use. The council gave them a weekend to prove they could use the land for a good cause. A group of residents organised a two-day event to demonstrate how the land could be used. 1,500 people of all ages turned up, keen to get involved and support a local initiative to create space for the local community to grow food and work together.

Windmill Hill City Farm was founded. The core team of locals, one of whom was Dawn Primarolo, now local MP for Bristol South, set about renovating the derelict building on site, clearing the site, developing allotments and growing food with the many volunteers who had offered their services. The city farm was another project that benefited from the work of the dedicated individuals in the YOPs scheme.

In 1978, ten of the original organising team became directors of the farm and registered as a charity. They found funding and donations of material from local people, trusts and industry. As the work at the farm increased, more local people become involved. The area had been heavily bombed in the war, and this space had been earmarked for the Outer Circuit Road. When the plans for that road fell through, the land was left derelict. So the local people were pleased that it had been taken on for something worthwhile and community-minded – something that fulfilled local needs.

As well as land for growing food and enjoying green space, parents had wanted somewhere for their children to play, grow food and see animals. There were groups set up within the farm, including a playgroup which had its own allotment. The farm also had a woodwork scheme which gave children and young people the opportunity to learn new skills that they were unable to get elsewhere. It became an educational experience for children, both in terms of skills and learning about where their food came from. The young people who visited even built their own adventure play park.

From the outset, those at the farm considered the environmental implications of the work they were doing. People who had allotments were not allowed to use herbicides, and if they did not know how to grow organically then they could attend classes that the farm ran. A tree-planting initiative transformed the farm into a small haven of green amidst the concrete.

Phil Haughton joined the farm in the early 1980s and was concerned that it had become too much like a pets' zoo. He ran a recipe for 'guinea pig stew' in the newsletter and invited people to come and buy a guinea pig. He sold them all the next day to people who wanted to save them from a stew. Phil, like the others, wanted children to know where their meat came from and was keen that Windmill Hill should remain a working farm.

The farm welcomed people with learning difficulties and mental health issues to volunteer there. Local people had found working on the land therapeutic as it had created community spirit and improved their quality of life. They wanted to share this with people who would benefit the most.

In 1986, the farm ran a reunion day for the people who used to live in the houses on the site years ago. Over 100 people turned up, many of whom had not seen each other for decades. The idea was that the people could see what had happened to the land, but the day became more than that. The people who attended set up a community group called 'Memories of Bedminster' to continue to talk about the local area and its history.

Figure 12. Windmill Hill City Farm (photo © WHCF)

John Purkiss, who joined the farm in the late 1970s, suggests that the city farm movement was as much about people developing their community and their local green space as it was about food and the environment.[53] By working together the local people of Windmill Hill and Bedminster had provided a viable and successful alternative to a lorry park.

Windmill Hill City Farm began a movement within Bristol. More city farms began to develop, including St Werburghs, Hartcliffe Park and Lawrence Weston, as well as several community gardens. These farms grew food and had livestock but also provided leisure and learning as well as space for community development and regeneration.

Hartcliffe Community Park Farm developed in the early 1980s and registered as a charity in 1984. It also used volunteers from the Youth Opportunity and Community Programmes. Like at Windmill Hill, there was a piece of land which had been left empty for years and the local community did not want to see it go to waste.

Rocky Pearce, the farm manager, who has been there since the beginning, suggests that the high level of unemployment in the local area meant that creating a farm, which could use the Community Programme, seemed like a good way to create some paid work. The farm also applied for some grants through the council.

Figure 13. Windmill Hill City Farm (photo © WHCF)

> *The story of Windmill Hill City Farm is one of transformation: derelict land developed into an attractive and productive environment, people with nothing to do becoming creative and fulfilled, discarded materials turning into useful articles and buildings.*
>
> **A History of Windmill Hill (1985)**

The farm has recently celebrated its 25th anniversary and has had a difficult time with continuing to find funding as well as vandalism – they have even had animals killed. The farm continues to provide the local community with a place to enjoy green space. They have around 12,000 visitors a year and people use it for birthday parties, school visits and day trips.

Bristol is now home to the Federation of City Farms and Community Gardens, a national organisation that supports community growing and farm projects. They note that these projects are about much more than growing food and keeping animals. This is of course a major part of their work, but the projects' capacity to develop community space which can then be used for a whole manner of activities, including education, skill training, recreation and well-being activities, makes them a valuable resource to the community and to the city.

Avon Wildlife Trust

Unlike the surrounding counties, Bristol did not have a Wildlife Trust for the city in the 1970s. Rural areas had had Wildlife Trusts for many years, but as it became more apparent that urban areas had an abundance of nature, cities were developing their own Trusts to protect this variety of urban wildlife.

In 1980, therefore, Avon Wildlife Trust (AWT) was founded to protect and celebrate wildlife in Bristol. The Trust also wanted to include as many people as possible in this conservation. This is why every nature reserve they have developed is open to anyone, and everyone is encouraged to visit.

One of the Trust's first actions was to set up a nature reserve in Brandon Hill Park. It was the first time in the UK that a formal park was made more 'wild' through two wildlife ponds, a butterfly garden and a hay meadow. This encouraged the flourishing of local wildlife, and Brandon Hill remains one of Bristol's most popular green spaces.

AWT also developed and managed council green spaces as a network of nature reserves. In the 80s and 90s there were many development pressures across the city, and AWT realised that they could not fight every battle alone. They decided to involve local people in protecting their wildlife and green space, as this was the most successful way to preserve these areas.

The campaign in the early 90s at Royate Hill is a good example of this. Royate Hill in Eastville was unusual in that it was a natural green space in the middle of an urbanised area. When developers spotted it as a possible site, AWT decided to fight them. The council refused the developers planning permission and this was upheld by the Secretary of State after an appeal. Yet in May 1991 the developers sent in bulldozers and started demolishing the site. Dozens and dozens of local residents went along to the site to stop this from happening with non-violent direct action. The police had to intervene and stop the work as they thought that it was getting too dangerous.

For the next two years, AWT, the local community and the council worked to put a compulsory purchase order on this piece of land. It was then legally designated as a Local Nature Reserve. This campaign demonstrates the degree of success and change that cross-sectoral support and hard work can achieve. The Trust aimed to engage the public through community work and the development of two local wildlife centres. One of their first projects, Willsbridge Mill, became the first conservation education centre taken over by a wildlife trust in the UK, and in the 90s their regeneration of Folly Farm developed a rural centre for local people to visit, enjoy and experience nature.

AWT have had to respond to changing environmental issues over their 30 years of work. Their recent project, Living Landscapes, responds to a global issue, climate change, at a local level.

Across the county there are 38 nature reserves which are small 'hot spots' of nature and AWT want to make these areas more resilient to the effects of climate change. They are looking to 'join up' these areas so that

Avon County Council carried out the first ever compulsory purchase of a site to declare Royate Hill as a Nature Reserve. Bristol City Council undertook the only ever wildlife prosecution in the country by a local authority.

Avon Wildlife Trust's 20th Anniversary Publication

Figure 14. Protesters abseil off bridge in Royate Hill
(photo © Avon Wildlife Trust Archive)

wildlife can move around more easily. They are working with local landowners and farmers to help them make the most of the funding available to them so they can adopt wildlife-friendly agricultural practices.

Avon Wildlife Trust continues to work in Bristol today, responding to contemporary environmental problems such as climate change through conservation activities and encourages the public to get involved.

Hartcliffe Health and Environment Action Group

Bristol and Avon FoE demonstrate the wealth of grassroots action across the city, but the example of community involvement in Royate Hill shows the importance of community action around issues specific to a neighbourhood or community.

In 1989, a group of local health and community workers in Hartcliffe came together because they were concerned about the health of people living in the area. A social work student helped them to conduct a survey with local people. Local community members in Hartcliffe were asked to fill in questionnaires, which aimed to explore the health needs of the local community. 196 questionnaires were completed, almost three-quarters of which were filled out by women. The survey asked about housing, recreation, play facilities, money, health services, community services, the environment and transport.

From the results, a report entitled 'We live there, we should know. . . ' was written. This report explored the health issues of the area and how these were intertwined with social, economic and environmental injustices. The report concluded that "there is a need to and much value in talking and working with local people".[54]

Two public meetings were called to discuss these results, and a committee was formed that consisted of twelve local residents and three community workers. The group became the Hartcliffe Health and Environment Action Group (HHAEG), and aimed to look at health issues in the area and how to improve the local quality of life.

While the questionnaire had been about just health issues, the group realised that health and the environment were inextricably connected. The group began to tackle issues such as the high incidence of childhood asthma which was linked to housing issues, such as mould and poor draught-proofing, and the group campaigned for council housing to be improved. They also began to look at the high rate of mental health issues in the area and found that these were often related to restricted incomes and the high levels of local unemployment.

The report stated that one woman "summed up what several people described: money problems lead to frustration, short tempers, then that affects relationships between partners and children which leads to depression and then to illness." Another respondent spoke of the stigma attached to living in Hartcliffe and how "if you write a Hartcliffe address on a job application form you don't stand a chance." A mental health group was formed within HHEAG. This went on to become a separate group

Figure 15. Food Co-op (photo © HHEAG)

which looked at how the local environment and social issues such as unemployment contributed to low levels of well-being and quality of life.

Food was a particular issue for the local area. At the time, there was no local large supermarket and so people found it hard to find good quality food at a low price. HHEAG decided that one way to tackle this problem was to set up a food co-op where items were bought in bulk and then split into portions to sell.

While Hartcliffe now has local supermarkets, which have helped the whole community have local, reliable access to food, the food co-op remains popular as it still provides a low-cost way to buy good quality items.

By the mid-90s HHEAG's interest in local food issues had really progressed. At this time however there was little funding for food projects. They managed to find a small grant and set up a cooking programme to teach parents with young children to cook economical, healthy food. The participants in this programme talked about how they would like to be able to grow some of the produce they were using and so HHEAG secured some more funding to begin a community growing project. In 2000, the group began a small community garden at Hartcliffe Community Park Farm and in 2002 they set up a market garden in a disused allotment site.

By this point the cookery courses were so popular that they had to start more for people with diet-related health issues, a course for carers, people who needed help with weight management and young people.

HHEAG have shown that social issues, such as a lack of local facilities like shops, can be aided through developing local resilience. The community growing project not only provided those involved with low cost, healthy food but also enabled people to get outside, reconnect with the landscape.

The work done in Hartcliffe is an excellent example of a community coming together to improve the local area. By noting the way that social and environmental issues affect one another the group developed ways of helping people by improving the local amenity and facilities. Sue Walker at HHEAG says that they are a dynamic organisation which is responding to changing needs in our community and working in the most effective way in the current economic climate.[55]

They have expanded their range of nutrition and cooking courses to address the different needs of the local community as well as offering one-to-one nutritional advice, and a have a library and resource centre where both books and cooking equipment can be borrowed. They have linked up with Positive Minds, which is a support and advice service to help adults with mental or emotional stress. They also have a programme of regular health walks and are linked with the Bristol Walking4Health operation.

There are many other examples of community work which responds to the needs of the local people in Bristol, some of which we will look at later.

Council involvement

Bristol is unusual in that it had been its own county for many centuries. The creation of Avon however, in 1974, brought together Bristol, Somerset and Gloucestershire. But when Avon was dissolved in 1996 Bristol became its own county again.

The city has tended to lean towards a Labour council but in recent years has moved towards the Liberal Democrats. As with any city, there is a certain amount of complaint about council decisions. Bristol's local authorities have made choices that have been recognised as beneficial to the environmental movement as well as ones that have been seen as damaging.

There has always been a lot of political and grassroots activism in the city. From the abolitionist movement to the 1831 riots in Queens Square to the Omnibus boycott in the 1960s, Bristolians have never been afraid of standing up for what they believe in. Bristol's environmental movement is no different.

There are many people in the city who protest against environmental damage, attend council meetings and refuse to give up voicing their opinions. It is noticeable that there have been growing tensions between the council and the environmental movement recently, especially in terms of local planning decisions. Since the late 80s and 90s, however, there have been several sympathetic council leaderships, and Bristol made an early move to be involved with international environmental legislation.

The early 90s saw the council launch the Green Charter. It was a response to calls from Bristol Friends of the Earth and others and was a blueprint for the action the council should take in different areas. These included the built environment, energy, resources and conservation, purchasing power, environmental quality control, the natural environment, and access. Through this charter the council made a series of pledges to improve their environmental credentials and involvement, and to include the 'citizens of Bristol' in this work. Not all aspects of the report, however, showed clearly what actions the council was going take.

After the 1992 United Nations Conference on Environment and Development in Rio de Janeiro, a paper was published called Agenda 21, which was a blueprint for global sustainable development. Within this there was a chapter entitled Local Agenda 21, which dealt specifically with the role of local authorities and municipalities in sustainable development.

The council had a Green Initiatives Team, and a Green Initiatives Joint Sub Committee was formed to oversee progress on the Green Charter. There were concerns that certain areas of the city, specifically the more affluent ones, had better provision for litter-picking and for preventing fly-tipping, and had better air quality. A way of reporting and monitoring these issues was sought.

In 1995 the council developed The State of the Environment report. This looked at local indicators, including air pollution, litter, and satisfaction with green spaces. It covered the quality of the environment in wards across the city. It demonstrated which areas of Bristol needed help and enabled people to campaign with evidence and a better understanding of local issues and needs. Martin Fodor, who was involved in early preparatory work that led to The State of the Local Environment Report 1995, suggests that the ward-by-ward mapping of indicators was an innovative step with political support and enabled the council to "try to even out some of the inequalities, both [in terms of] the conditions people lived in and the services provided by the council." [56]

The initial idea for this came from a report that Bristol had devised a few years earlier to show that there were areas of extreme poverty. This report showed that there was a 'crescent of poverty' through the north and south on the outskirts of the city. These were the areas that were most likely to be subject to poor environmental standards in terms of litter and air, land and water pollution, and so the State of the Local Environment Report was designed to determine the issues of each specific area.

The report was quite revolutionary, as these issues had never been viewed on a ward-by-ward basis. They gave people the ammunition they needed to push for environmental justice. The report was a first of its kind, and showed just how many discrepancies there were between different areas of the city – sometimes areas that were side by side. It was so useful that a form of it remains today. Every year Bristol City Council produces a report called 'Quality of Life Indicators' which uses 60 indicators to determine the quality of life across the city

The council was also involved with the European Sustainable Cities and Towns movement, and signed the European Sustainable Cities and Towns Charter. This was followed by the formation of the Sustainable City Team.

Bristol was one of the first UK cities to become involved with the Local

Agenda 21 process (LA21). The Charter had demonstrated that the council was interested in exploring sustainability, and the LA21 movement encouraged the council to look at Bristol's environmental responsibility and awareness as well as improve the quality of life for people in the city.

The council set up a series of working groups which dealt with different concerns such as energy, food, transport, biodiversity and waste. This demonstrated the level of involvement in all areas across the city and indicated the realisation that, in order to be sustainable, many different aspects of a city system had to be considered. These groups ranged across the different sectors in the city in order to hear different perspectives.

While there is a valid question as to whether the council and local decision-makers have done enough or challenged the traditional way of doing things, the various council initiatives that have been developed over the years have contributed to Bristol's environmental movement by enabling city-wide action for change, and demonstrating that sustainable development is important.

Why Bristol?

Through this early pioneering action in the 70s, 80s and early 90s, Bristol began to gain a reputation for its environmental activities, especially through Bristol Friends of the Earth, which was well known elsewhere. One of our aims is to identify why Bristol has gained such a reputation as a 'green city'. Many theories have been put forward, but it appears that it is a mix of coincidence, critical mass, dedication and geography.

The more 'green organisations' that came here, the more they attracted. Bristol also has the virtue of being a beautiful city set in the heart of the West Country: you do not have to go far to find gorgeous countryside and fresh air. These kinds of attributes probably appeal to those in the population who are 'environmentally minded'. In 1985, Godfrey Boyle stated in *Resurgence* magazine that:

"UCAT's activities, alongside the insulation and recycling schemes of FoE Bristol, the several City Farm projects and the numerous small businesses that are springing up, lend an air of credibility to the optimistic claims of some UCAT people that Bristol is becoming Britain's first Green City – though the fact that the Bristol climate seems particularly favourable to Green experimentation it is probably due in no small measure to the affluence produced by the less-than-green sectors of the city's economy." [57]

Boyle's observation touches on an important aspect of the divided nature of the city of Bristol. Bristol is an affluent city, with one of the highest GDPs outside of London, and much of this wealth has been and is still created through aerospace, automobiles and tobacco. These industries, which were integral to Bristol's economic sustainability, are hard to reconcile with sustainable thinking – but not impossible.

This is not the only way the city is divided. We have already touched on how Bristol has a high level of socio-economic disparity, and how affluent areas of the city can lie next to areas with many indicators of deprivation. These indicators are both social and environmental: they cover items such as high levels of unemployment, lack of local facilities and amenities, poor housing, air pollution and fly-tipping.

The city's high economic disparity shows how the city is not 'fulfilling the needs' of its population. Since 2008, Bristol has fallen from 1st to 4th in Forum for the Future's (FFTF) Sustainable Cities Index, and our lack of social sustainability was cited as explanation.

FFTF reference Bristol's Health Profile for 2010, which states that "life expectancy for men living in the most deprived areas is seven years less than for men in the least deprived areas. The difference for women is over four years." [58] The report goes on to say that "the health of people living in Bristol is generally worse than the England average. Levels of deprivation, and children living in poverty, are both higher than average." Health and well-being are often linked to issues such as housing, access to healthy food, air pollution as well as lifestyle.

It has been suggested that people from disadvantaged areas are less likely to be concerned about environmental issues because they worry more about meeting basic needs, such as housing, food and energy provision.[59] Yet this conclusion can be seen as a generalisation which is in danger of being discriminatory itself. Suggesting that people from disadvantaged or marginalised areas are not interested in environmental issues applies only "when adopting a limited definition of environmental concern". (Burningham and Thrush 2001)

As we will see, there are many community groups in Bristol who have started tackling socio-economic disparity through an awareness of the connections between social and environmental issues. These projects have helped local health and well-being as well as calling for better provision of local services.*

---

* Such as the work of Hartcliffe Health and Environment Action Group, Knowle West Media Centre, the People's Republic of Stokes Croft.

When green things started to take off in the sort of mid-70s, there were a lot of people in London who wanted to do the self-sufficiency thing and up sticks and move to West Wales where land was cheap . . . and I think a lot of people who moved to West Wales then ended up in Bristol. I always thought I was going to move to the South-West somewhere and I got stuck in Bristol, [which is] sort of England's West Coast capital, slightly bohemian, slightly ahead of the game . . . and maybe that's why green ideas are perhaps more in evidence here than in many other places.

Richard St George

There is, however, an unavoidable lack of representation of Bristol's population within the 'core' environmental movement – those who attend workshops, meetings, events, talks and consultations. These are often attended by people who work in the environmental movement or who are already involved with many sustainability initiatives. The term 'greenerati' has been applied to them.

Burningham and Thrush noted that "the language of environmentalism [and] lack of accessible local information" was a discouraging factor for involvement in environmental concerns. A lack of accessibility is a massive problem if we want to include a greater cross-section of people as well as demonstrate the benefits of sustainable thinking.

Ben Barker, a member of Sustainable Southville and Southville Community Development Association, suggested that one criticism of the environmental movement is that at times it has lacked basic community involvement and that people in the environmental movement can appear to think that "they have it cracked, they have secret knowledge that nobody else has", but that this was "no way to sell a message".[60] Ben went on to suggest that the environmental movement is improving on this, but it will become clear throughout the rest of this publication that Bristol has to work hard to engage a wider proportion of the population to truly find out the issues which are concerning everybody, not just a certain section of society – and it must make 'sustainability' accessible for everyone.

The 1970s, 80s and early 90s built a foundation for the many sustainability initiatives that have grown and developed in Bristol. As mentioned earlier, it is worth noting that we are in a similar social and economic position to Bristol in the early 1980s, and that the concerns that people were worried about have not differed in many respects.

It is clear that even as early as the 1980s Bristol had the beginnings of a reputation as a 'green city'. The innovative and creative organisations and initiatives which we have explored in this section, however, are only part of the story.

Bristol's green heritage

Organisations, communities, initiatives and campaigns: 1960-2011

This section is divided into sustainability 'themes' which detail some of the organisations, community and council initiatives, groups and individuals who have developed sustainable thinking, behaviour and change in Bristol. The case studies are not comprehensive, but we hope to give you an understanding of the type of activities that have happened in the city and include the successes, vulnerabilities and achievements, both past and current.

The themes are not exclusive. Many relate to one another: for instance, energy affects both transport and food, whereas the protection of biodiversity and nature often affects urban planning. This demonstrates the importance of recognising the issues individually but also the ways in which they affect one another.

It is necessary to give a bit of background information about each 'theme', but this will not rely on 'doom and gloom' narratives as so many of Bristol's initiatives are about improving the quality of life, increasing equality and creating a society which maximises enjoyment of life for all.

Energy

We have started with the 'energy theme' because so much of our daily life is dependent on fuel. Food, transport, housing and leisure all heavily rely on a steady flow of cheaply priced energy which is accessible literally at the flick of a switch. Yet as peak oil becomes more of a concern, as do the carbon emissions generated from the burning of fossil fuels, energy and how we create it becomes more and more of an issue.

Bristol's recent Peak Oil Report stated that "at current rates of discovery the world is finding approximately one barrel of oil for every three that it uses."[61] Aside from the environmental and social implications of fossil fuel use such as air pollution, carbon emissions and land contamination, it is clear that we need alternative forms of energy.

The oil crisis of the 1970s made people think about the amount of energy they used as well as the way the availability of energy impacted upon other areas of their lives, including transport, leisure and the economy. In 1974, as a result of the combined issues of strikes by coal miners and the oil crisis, the UK had to impose three-day working weeks in order to conserve energy.

These energy shortages coincided with a growing awareness of resource depletion, partly due to a flood of publications about resource use. *Limits to Growth, Only One Earth: The Care and Maintenance of a Small Planet* and *Blueprint for Survival* by *The Ecologist* magazine were all published in 1972. These texts detailed the issues that would arise with a rapidly growing population on a finite planet.

The next year, E. F. Schumacher published *Small is Beautiful: A Study of Economics as if People Mattered*. This discussed how western economics treats resources such as fossil fuels as expendable income; whereas in reality, since they are not renewable, they are "undeniably capital items".[62]

Of course, energy use is connected to one of the most publicly talked about environmental issues: climate change. Reduction of carbon emissions from burning fossil fuels is one of the most controversial topics we have discussed. Most of the organisations, initiatives and community groups that we have examined cite the reduction of carbon emissions as being one of their main aims – but it is often only one aspect of their work. For instance, Sustrans' promotion of sustainable transport not only encourages a reduction of fossil fuel use; it also reduces air pollution and car accidents as well as developing more people-friendly cities. Their work also advocates the bicycle as a cheaper form of transport, and cycling as improving health and well-being through exercise.

The sustainability movement is about changing the way we live, rather than just simply 'reducing' carbon emissions.

Alternative and appropriate technologies

The essential point is that we should consciously choose technologies that increase the enjoyment of life and work with, not against, the environment that supports us.[63]

UCAT's founding principle

The Centre for Sustainable Energy (CSE) is still working on the same issues of energy justice and fuel poverty that UCAT started exploring over 30 years ago. They have also continued to advise people on sustainable energy practices and encourage the uptake of 'appropriate' technologies. In their 30-year celebratory publication, CSE state that since they began they have provided tailored energy advice to nearly 250,000 people as well as assisting more than 60,000 low-income households and reduced their risk of fuel poverty.[64]

At their 2009 celebratory conference, Hugh Barton spoke of the cultural, social and political situations which inspired the founders of UCAT. They were influenced by a situation not unlike the one we face in 2011: economic strife, high unemployment and rising oil prices.

Oil prices have been steadily rising and have hit new highs this year due to the combined issues of tax, VAT and social unrest in the Middle East. This is inconvenient for most, but for some, such as lower-income families, single parent families, the elderly and the vulnerably housed, it makes keeping the house warm, travelling to work and maintaining a comfortable standard of living a continual struggle.

The initiatives and co-ops that developed under UCAT were designed to take the message of 'appropriate' technology further into Bristol's communities. The Low Energy House was the demonstration and the energy advice centre, and Greenleaf Bookshop provided the know-how and information. Richard St George's renewable energy company, Low Energy Supply Systems (LESS), provided a place for people to buy the technologies that they saw in the house. Those involved with UCAT were keen to make low-energy living as accessible as possible. LESS was based in Colston Street and installed its own wind turbine and solar panel on the roof. Although the company did not last, it is an early example of alternative energy options and the development of the renewable energy market.

Figure 16. Wind Turbine and Solar Panel on the roof of LESS offices
(photo © Richard St George)

The consequences of the different kinds of energy production themselves, however, can pose social and environmental issues. Wind, solar and tidal energy have all been subject to criticism.

Nuclear energy probably remains the most controversial alternative technology, and UCAT protested against its uptake in Bristol in the 1970s and 80s. Nuclear power had existed as a concept since the beginning of the twentieth century but it was not until 1954 that the world saw its first nuclear power station. It has become the most prolific alternative form of energy production. As of April 2011, "29 countries worldwide are operating 443 nuclear reactors for electricity generation and 64 new nuclear plants are under construction in 15 countries" and in 2009 "nuclear power plants provided 14 per cent of the world's electricity." [65]

While nuclear power reduces carbon emissions, and is an alternative to generating energy by using the diminishing supplies of fossil fuels, its critics are concerned about the waste it generates as well as its use as a technology for war. There have been anti-nuclear movements around since the technology took hold in the 1960s, with people citing pacifism, environmental damage and health concerns as their motives for resistance.

In 1979 the core meltdown at the Three Mile Island generator fuelled the concerns about its safety. The 1986 incident in Chernobyl, however, has become the focus point for the consequences of nuclear power 'gone wrong'. While estimated deaths from this accident differ greatly,* the impacts of Chernobyl were felt across Europe to the UK, and 25 years later the site is still abandoned. Advocates of nuclear energy, however, point out that other forms of energy production, such as coal mining, have just as high a death risk.

Nuclear power brings about a specific fear which extends into the public consciousness, as accidents impact whole societies. There are also ethical and moral considerations of whether it is right for us to leave future generations with the waste that nuclear energy production generates.

It is understandable that people in Bristol were concerned about nuclear power, as the south-west region at one point had four local reactors: Hinkley Point A and B, Oldbury and Berkeley.** Bristol, specifically, has nuclear waste carriers travelling through it on the railway lines. Anti-nuclear groups pointed to this as a safety hazard in the event of an accident or terrorist-related event.

---

* It is accepted by the UN that there could be up to 9,000 Chernobyl-related cancer deaths but Greenpeace say that this figure is vastly under-estimated and will be closer to 100,000.
** Berkeley was decommissioned in 1989

*Figure 17. Friends of the Earth and UCAT Protest Castle Park
(photo © Richard St George)*

In the late 1970s the government announced that they were commissioning a new batch of nuclear power plants. This led to many national protests, and Bristol FoE was involved in local protest as was Bristol Anti-Nuclear Group and the local Greenpeace Group. Anti-nuclear groups were uniting nationally through the Torness Alliance, which was trying to prevent a nuclear power station in Torness, Scotland. People travelled from all over the UK to help this protest, which eventually became a mass occupation of the site.

The protesters renovated a derelict cottage on the site as a 'symbolic act of restoration' to create living quarters for the protesters. They installed a wood burner, erected a windmill and kept chickens and goats.[66] The cottage was later bulldozed and nineteen members of the Torness Alliance were charged with trespass and a breach of the peace. Direct action, however, was becoming popular as a campaign method.

In 1980, south-west anti-nuclear groups took part in a direct action protest in Sharpness to prevent nuclear waste being dumped at sea. At this time, Bristol's concerns about nuclear power were rising as Hinkley Point was to be expanded. Hinkley Point C was especially controversial as it was to use an American pressurised water reactor – the same reactor that had been used at the Three Mile Island plant. The local anti-nuclear groups joined up as the Severnside Alliance to work together to prevent the expansion.

Trevor Houghton, a member of Bristol FoE, an anti-nuclear protester and employee of Bristol Energy Centre, remembers that concerns about nuclear energy were present in the public consciousness at the time with growing media representation and films like *Silkwood* (1983). In the 1980s UCAT and Bristol FoE held an anti-nuclear demonstration on Castle Park complete with people in Hazmat suits and model nuclear waste containers.

The campaigning against Hinkley continued throughout the 80s, and it culminated in a public inquiry in the later part of the decade. This inquiry not only explored the environmental and health implications of nuclear power but also demonstrated that it was not economically viable. The campaign had support from the council at the time, but in the early 1990s the expansion was approved by the government. The approval, however, coincided with the Conservative privatisation of the electric power industries.

In the late 1980s UCAT (now Bristol Energy Centre) had become involved in the public inquiry into Hinkley Power Station. They did a presentation which showed that improving all the electrically heated homes in the south-west, through insulation, energy management and retrofitting, could displace the demand of the station. Not only would this reduce the need for more energy production, it would save people money. Trevor Houghton from BEC worked with Dr Brenda Boardman, an energy-efficiency research specialist, to develop this presentation into a research paper.[67] With funding from the Joseph Rowntree Foundation they developed this into a bigger national study looking at energy saving in homes and the social, economic and environmental benefits.

Nuclear power did indeed prove to be uneconomical, and so no company wanted to buy the sites without governmental help. All nuclear expansion plans were put on hold.

With continuing concerns about carbon emissions, air pollution and finite resources, nuclear power is often considered a viable alternative for our energy needs. In 2008, it was announced that EDF had bought Hinkley Point and planned to develop Hinkley Point C again. The Stop Hinkley protest has been revived.

In the early 1990s BEC had also became involved in the Bristol Energy and Environment Plan which was EU-funded and looked at the city's energy use and strategies. Out of this plan came the Bristol Environment and Energy Trust, which linked together people across the city in devel-

oping Bristol's environmental awareness and involvement. This eventually became the Western Partnership for Sustainable Development, and
then Future West, which was an early city-wide structure for cross-sectoral collaboration. It set up a series of working groups for different sustainable issues to look at council, organisational, business and
community responsibility within sustainable development, and it
encouraged many projects within the city.

BEC became the Centre for Sustainable Energy in 1994 to reflect its
dedication to national energy issues. Striving for energy justice, however,
remains a large part of CSE's work. It works with organisations from the
public, private and voluntary sectors across the UK but is still involved in
several Bristol-based initiatives and projects.

Closing the gap between the energy use of the rich and the poor is not
just applicable to this country. Energy justice is a prime example of the
interrelatedness of social and environmental issues, and the principles of
Contraction and Convergence provide a framework through which to
address fuel and energy inequalities across the UK, Europe and the globe.

The Converging World

John Pontin OBE, a Bristol businessman known for his work in sustainable construction and property development through his company JT
Group, co-founded The Converging World with Ian Roderick, director of
the Schumacher Institute. Inspired by a local village project, Go Zero in
Chew Magna, which aimed to create a Zero Waste society, The
Converging World is a charity whose mission is to cut carbon emissions
and support sustainable community development across the world.

TCW install renewable energy capacity (wind turbines) in Tamil Nadu,
in South India, with funds generated through donations and investments.
This reduces carbon emissions in India, but in a sense on behalf of Bristol.
TCW use some of the income generated from the turbines to invest in
more renewable energy, and spend the rest on local sustainable economic development in India and back home in Bristol. With two large turbines already turning and two more on order, the charity is set to reduce
carbon emissions and provide income for the next 20 years to spend on
supporting communities around the world.

Bristol still faces tough choices about how to power the city, with
nuclear power being only one of the controversial topics. The recent W4B
campaign shows that renewable and alternative energy can have their
own environmental problems. The proposed plans for a palm oil or jat-

Figure 18. The Converging World Turbine –
Tamil Nadu twinned with Chew Valley
(photo © The Converging World)

ropha oil power plant in Avonmouth are controversial. The people in Avonmouth have stated that they already have too much industry in this area, and Bristol FoE have noted that "this expensive fuel would be sourced in the tropics, funded by our electricity bills in the name of renewable energy, but it would lead to ravaging vast tracts of land with serious human, environmental and negative climate change consequences." [68]

The local and international implications of this power plant show the variety of issues that just one scheme can raise.

Bristol City Council refused the application in February 2010, but W4B appealed to the Government who granted permission in February 2011 with some mitigating conditions, such as that W4B are not allowed to use oils from illegally deforested areas.

Local groups like FoE and ACSEB (Action for Sustainable Energy in Bristol) are still campaigning to have this decision overruled, as they feel that even with these conditions the power plant "would burn 90,000 tonnes of palm oil a year, requiring plantations twice the area of Bristol, and the destruction of that same area of tropical forest".[69]

Biofuel plants and nuclear are not the only alternative energy solutions that are controversial. The Severn Barrage campaign, which we will discuss later, also shows how renewable energy can be environmentally damaging despite the carbon emissions and air pollution that it may be saving.

Council involvement

As Hugh Barton noted, the council became involved with energy justice when it identified the social benefits of retrofitting for council houses. Local authority involvement with sustainable energy increased further after the development of Bristol's Local Agenda 21 strategies.

In 1998, it became one of the first authorities to purchase green electricity and, in 2003 it commissioned CSE to look at the feasibility of using local biomass as a source of renewable energy at Bristol City Council owned or controlled sites (Ward and Holley 2003).[70] The report looked at the viability for biomass boilers at two sites: Social Housing Tower Block in south Bristol and Blaise plant nursery.

In 2008, Bristol City Council commissioned CSE again to perform a city-wide sustainable energy survey, which was then developed into the Sustainable Energy Report 2009. Bristol City Council did this to "look at opportunities and constraints in the city for renewable, sustainable and low-carbon energy supply".[71]

In 2008 Bristol became the first city to have a council commission a peak oil report. The report came about following grass roots awareness-raising by Transition Bristol about the issue, after which Daniel Lerch, from the Post Carbon Institute, was invited by the Green Capital Momentum Group to come to Bristol to give a talk about peak oil. This started a city-wide dialogue between several partners. A diverse cross-sector taskforce, involving the council, Wessex Water, Forum for the Future, Sustrans, GWE Business West and Transition Bristol, was formed to initiate a response to the issue.

The group decided to commission a report to determine whether peak oil was a pressing issue for Bristol and, if so, to assess what the impacts might be and what steps could be taken to mitigate them. Simone Osborn from Transition Bristol was chosen to compile the report. She found that there was a growing consensus among experts within the energy field and the energy industry that "the era of cheap oil is over" and that "An oil crunch in the next decade is highly probable."[72]

In determining what impacts peak oil might have on Bristol, Simone was able to draw on examples from the record oil price inflation of 2008, and also the effects of recent tanker and lorry strikes which had resulted in fuel shortages. Both demonstrated the real dangers that peak oil poses to the economy and its ability to cause dislocation and even social unrest.[73] The research brought in data and input from experts in Bristol, such as the council, contingency planners, health service and utility providers, to hear their concerns and look at how each sector might be affected. It also examined the possible alternatives to oil.

Having found that peak oil was a serious issue for the city, the report looked at what schemes and initiatives that are already active in the city could help with the potential issues of peak oil in Bristol, and explored how these schemes and initiatives could be expanded to improve resilience. It also made suggestions for further action and research.

The report was devised to be accessible to a wide spectrum of people and to provide a platform for action. Simone suggests that the most important lesson the report revealed was that there is a lack of holistic and systems thinking within the city. The report demonstrates how volatile fuel prices and energy shortages will ultimately affect everything from our food supplies and transport system to our ability to keep our houses warm. It concludes that peak oil will have a real and tangible effect upon our economy.

The report is, however, not without hope. It suggests that moving from a cheap oil economy to a low-carbon economy should be seen as an "opportunity for a diverse local economy with a broad range of opportunities which may provide new openings to people who are currently excluded".[74]

The council played a key role in this report, and has begun to include it in its sustainability policy. In February 2010, the council released the Bristol Climate Change and Energy Security Framework which stated that "the Peak Oil Report be welcomed, endorsed and used to inform the development of council services, strategies and plans".[75]

As a local authority the council is responsible for a substantial proportion of the city's energy consumption. It has pledged to cut Bristol's CO_2 emissions by 40% by 2020 and 80% by 2050, from a 2005 baseline. This is an ambitious target. The council had pledged to cut carbon emissions by 10% by 2010 (as compared to 2003/4 figures), and while it only managed 8.8%, this demonstrates a willingness to make changes happen.

Bristol Energy Network

As concerns about carbon emissions, fuel poverty and energy-efficiency have grown, local community groups have become involved in encouraging local and neighbourhood sustainable energy use and production.

Easton Energy Group was one of these. Four friends formed this initiative in order to encourage local people to become more aware of their energy consumption and to consider the energy-efficiency of their homes.

They wanted to explore whether people actually understood why the government and environmental groups were encouraging the minimisation of energy use. They thought an understanding of these reasons and the financial benefits of energy-efficiency would naturally lead to a drop in energy use.

During the course of their work they discovered that there were many community groups across the city working on energy issues, but that there was little or no communication between the groups. This often led to duplication of work and competition for funding. EEG decided therefore to form Bristol Energy Network (BEN), which would provide a framework for these groups to come together and share tips on successes, mistakes and strategies.

This network proved popular. It provided a place for groups which had developed to deal solely with energy concerns as well as the micro-groups within local Transition and sustainability groups that dealt with energy as part of their wider work. BEN provided all of these groups with a place to become part of a city-wide network while remaining connected to their local community.

Dan Narayanan, who was an original founder member of EEG and now of BEN, says that the reception for the network has been excellent and that people have been really supportive. He suggests that because so many people are working in these community groups on top of their jobs and other commitments, the BEN meetings provide a really useful space for collaboration.[76]

BEN prevents duplication of work and enables sharing of resources, as well as developing a city-wide community of people with a shared aim. The network has many partners, and is supported by local organisations such as CSE, The Converging World and the Green Capital Partnership. The Network also run stalls at local events to take energy advice out into Bristol's communities and show some of the innovative ways, such as their bike-powered sound system, in which we can save energy.

Bristol Green Doors

Due to issues of peak oil and climate change, encouraging city-wide reduction of energy use outside of the environmental movement has become more and more important. 30 years ago people at UCAT were keen to show the economic and social benefits of retrofitting and appropriate technologies to the whole of Bristol's population. This desire is just as important today.

Figure 19. Bristol Energy Network bike-powered sound system
(photo © Bristol Energy Network)

In 2010, a city-wide event called Bristol Green Doors (BGD) was launched.* This initiative aims to encourage homeowners to retrofit their houses by hosting a weekend where people who have insulated their houses or fitted solar panels or installed wood-burning stoves 'open their doors' to the public.

Having done a number of retrofitting jobs on his house, Dan Weisselberg found that people were really interested in coming to see it and asking questions. As part of Transition Montpelier, Dan started to discuss the possibility of an eco-open-house day. He was doing a Master's Degree at the time in Architecture, Environment and Energy, and he discovered that there had been similar events in Brighton, Oxford and Norfolk. He began work on the event in February 2010, and Kate Watson, who was doing the same Master's as Dan, joined him in March.

---

* We could have placed this initiative in the Property Section, but since the main remit of the project is to encourage retrofitting to reduce energy use we decided that it was best placed here.

There is a lot of information in the public domain about retrofitting, but Kate suggests that it can be confusing or even contradictory.[77] The idea behind Bristol Green Doors is that it allows anyone to go along and ask the homeowners questions such as how much it cost, how long it took, and whether it was worth it. It was thought that people would rather find out information from their peers than rely on advice given by the government or big business.

By 2050 Britain is committed to reducing carbon emission by 80%. Since 27% of our current carbon emissions come from our homes, we have to make serious reductions in our energy consumption to be able to meet that target.[78] To do this, the benefits of retrofitting and of having more energy-efficient homes need to be demonstrated. Bristol Green Doors allowed members of the public to see that these homes are warmer, healthier and can still be attractive.

At the 2010 event, 52 homes across the city were opened to the public and there were 2,700 visitors. In 2011 the BGD team have decided that they want to hold a series of events, rather than just a single weekend, to keep the importance of retrofitting in people's minds.

Bristol Green Doors is funded by the council and a number of local sponsors, and is run through pro bono work and volunteers. As well as presenting successful domestic retrofitting and encouraging it to become more mainstream, Bristol Green Doors also want to develop the retrofitting supply chain and the green economy, to encourage large-scale community involvement and to serve as a pilot for eco-open door events across the UK.

Redland Park United Reformed Church

One of the local hubs for the 2010 BGD event was the Redland Park United Reformed Church. They became involved with environmental issues in 2009 when they had solar panels fitted on the roof. Rev. Douglas Burnett noticed that several of his congregation were becoming increasingly concerned with environmental issues, and he felt that it would be good for the church to become involved.[79]

Two of Rev. Burnett's church members had already put solar panels on their houses, and he discovered that there were funding streams from the Government to help people do this. They managed to secure some funding, which was then matched by the utility company EDF, and so the church had £40,000 worth of solar panels fitted. Rev. Burnett notes that without funding of this kind it would have been hard for a church to do

this. After the solar panels were fitted, the church continued its involvement with the environmental movement and continued to develop its
green credentials through campaigning.

They have held events to encourage local food growing and cooking,
as well as collaborated with local schools and Sustainable Redland. The
solar panels generated £1,000 in their first year, and the church has
recently had an LED lighting system installed which lowered their power
demand from 8kw to 3kw.

In February 2010 Ed Miliband visited the church to see the solar panels. Local MPs Stephen Williams and Kerry McCarthy have also visited.
The amount of public attention that the church has gained is probably
because they have shown the way that community buildings can get
involved in energy-saving and renewable technologies. Redland Park
Church has become a local landmark for community-led sustainable
energy, and shows that anyone can get involved. Stephen Moore, a member of Easton Energy Group, suggests that:

"Raising community awareness concerning climate change and our
energy use, for me, is not only about sharing information and working
towards a sustainable future but is fundamentally about bringing
communities together to strive towards these goals, as a cohesive
community.

Climate change and rising fuel prices affect us all – empowering
communities to make decisions and create change, both
behaviourally and practically, can shift our attitudes of what it means
to be a community and also create a local energy resilient buffer
against a global energy crisis." [80]

These notions of community resilience and local empowerment are
important to developing sustainable communities, and as energy is such
an important part of our daily life and affects so much of what we take for
granted, local people have seen that is important that we respond pre-
emptively.

Bristol has a long history of involvement with the environmental and
social issues surrounding energy use. Oil crises have enabled us to see
the social and economic effects that peak oil and diminishing fossil fuel
reserves will have. For those who have been struggling with fuel prices
for years, this awareness that fuel poverty is a real and destructive problem has not come too soon.

As noted with the discussion of nuclear power, the debate about energy production can quickly become a conversation about values, ethics and morality. George Monbiot, who has recently become embroiled in a vociferous debate about nuclear power, suggests that:

> "You think you're discussing technologies, and you quickly discover that you're discussing belief systems. The battle among environmentalists over how or whether our future energy is supplied is a cipher for something much bigger: who we are, who we want to be, how we want society to evolve."[81]

Bristol has developed a dialogue about sustainable energy which stretches from the community to the council to organisations and businesses and has raised public consciousness about energy use and production.

The examples of community-led and personal sustainable energy production and retrofitting, including UCAT's Low Energy House, Bristol Green Doors and Redland Park church, show how we do not always have to rely on centralised energy generation. We can begin to develop our own local resilience.

Food

*For Bristol to be serious about being an exemplar of sustainable develop-
ment it would need to have its own food plan – an organised strategic programme for sourcing and distributing its key staple foods from the rural
hinterland of the city.* [82]

Patrick Holden

In the 1960s and 70s the modern notion of self-sufficiency began to
develop. As the desire for 'alternative' lifestyles grew throughout the 1960s
and into the 1970s, the UK saw the rise of 'urban refugees': city-dwellers
escaping the city confines for the countryside and a new way of life. This
cultural phenomenon was portrayed in the mid-70s BBC programme *The
Good Life* (BBC 1975-78), which showed both the positives and down-
sides of shunning the status quo and going at it on your own.

Growing your own food is nothing new, but the post-World War II
drive towards intensive agriculture and the rise of supermarket shopping
has meant that people are ever more distanced from the growing of their
food. While the UK is currently 74% self-sufficient in terms of food that we
can grow in the UK and 60% self-sufficient overall, culturally, we have
become more and more disconnected from where and how our food is
grown. Those who promote local and organic food often feel that this dis-
connection is detrimental to our understanding of food production and its
possible effects on the environment.

In 1946, The Soil Association began to promote organic agriculture as
a way to farm that was in harmony with the land and caused less environmental damage. Since then, organic and local foods have become integral parts of the environmental movement's message about sustainability.

Local and national resilience of the food system is also important in
light of growing concerns about peak oil and carbon emissions, as we
often import food that we are capable of growing in the UK. There are
also social concerns about the treatment of workers abroad who grow
the food that is sold here. Low pay and bad treatment of overseas food
workers, as well as concerns about environmental damage from intensive agriculture, have led to the rise of 'fairly traded' food.

The need for inexpensive, healthy food like fresh fruit and vegetables
in the UK is why supermarkets have become so popular, as they can provide this.

Supermarket dominance is a big concern for many (we will explore later the reasons for this), and therefore many social and environmental justice projects in Bristol look to ways of growing good quality, healthy food that is inexpensive and sustainable.

Organic and local food

In the 1960s, The Soil Association opened a shop on Baker Street in London called Whole Food which sold 'natural' foods such as unrefined grains, beans, fresh fruit and vegetables. The movement marked a backlash against the rise of processed food and the beginnings of the organic movement.

In Bristol, during the early 80s, Colston Street had its own whole food shop called Beans & Greens. The market for organic food at this time was tiny, but was growing steadily as environmental concerns became more mainstream.

In 1985 Phil Haughton, who had previously been the manager of Windmill Hill City Farm, started his first trading operation, called 'Real Food Supplies'. It began as a service where Phil would visit local organic farms, buy produce and deliver it to people's homes. Since the scheme did well, in 1986 Phil opened up a shop on Gloucester Road under the same name.

Real Food Supplies was the first exclusively organic shop in the southwest, and was followed shortly by an organic butchers. Phil remembers having to hunt around for supplies of genuine organic produce, and the excitement of finding new brands.

The mid-80s saw the organic food movement quickly develop: there had been a real growth of organic farming before this, but no real market for the actual produce. The Soil Association's move to Bristol coincided with the growth of the organic food market, and from 1986 onwards there was a real drive for organic food to be in supermarkets. Real Food Supplies, however, did not survive the recession that hit in the late 1980s.

The 1980s and 90s saw the sales of organic food rise. The late 80s had seen two health scares – salmonella and BSE – which led to a massive boom in the sale of organic eggs and meat. This development of sales was perhaps more to do with health concerns than environmental issues. The interest in organic food was genuinely growing, and in 1990 Bristol became home to an annual organic food festival organised by the Soil Association.

Figure 20 Phil Haughton outside Real Food Supplies
(photo © Better Food Company/Phil Haughton)

In the 1990s, Alastair Sawday and Eric Booth became involved in encouraging a local, organic food market by beginning a vegetable box scheme at a local school. While this scheme was not successful, when Alastair found some funding he gave it to the Soil Association to allow Eric to work on the local food market.

Eric researched local food schemes including Community Supported Agriculture schemes in Europe, the US and Japan. CSAs are a form of local growing whereby a community of individuals supports an agricultural project, and the growers and consumers share the risks and benefits of producing the food. He realised that local box schemes, which relied on local produce and were delivered to homes, were a good way to encourage the purchase of local, organic food. The mid-1990s had begun to see a real rise in local box schemes, and Eric began a project to identify local food schemes, producers and consumer groups across Bristol to encourage a market for local food.

This project was called Bristol Food Links and was supported by the Soil Association, local health authority funding and the council. The pro-

> *Perhaps one of the greatest successes of the Soil Association in Bristol is the organic food festival. From my experience, it is the most powerful and best developed specifically organic food festival. There's an atmosphere of wonderful conviviality between all the producers and the visitors.*
>
> **Patrick Holden, former Director of the Soil Association**

ject influenced and encouraged Bristol's local food projects, and laid the foundations for several of them, including the Bristol Sustainable Food Strategy and Bristol Food Network.

Bristol Permaculture Group

Bristol has some pieces of prime agricultural land and a fairly temperate climate which makes it an ideal place for people to start community growing projects. Bristol's city farms, community gardens and orchards, market gardens and permaculture projects have all established creative ways of making the most of the land in the city.

Bristol Permaculture Group started in 1999. Mike Feingold ran Permaculture courses around Bristol and he and Sarah Pugh developed an annual design course for Bristol. The group is practical and hands-on: much of their public work involves demonstration gardens at events and festivals. They have continued to run courses and workshops across Bristol.

The group now has over 500 members in Bristol and has been the catalyst for many other community growing projects across Bristol that look to reclaim derelict or empty land for the purposes of growing food.

Eastside Roots

Permaculture encourages sustainable land use and has become popular within cities as a way of maximising space and minimising environmental damage. In 2000 Sarah Pugh persuaded Network Rail to allow her to use an unused piece of land beside a railway track.

About five years later, a group of people in Easton were keen to start a community garden centre after hearing about a similar project in

Manchester. Sarah Pugh suggested the land next to Stapleton Road Railway Station. It was hard work, but eventually they were given permission to use the land. In the meantime they began a community growing project at the Trinity Centre in Easton, which is still running today.

Before the group started work they held a community consultation to establish what the people in Easton wanted and needed from the project. This consultation decided what form the community garden would take and how it would be run.

Since the beginning of their work the land has been transformed from urban wasteland into a small green space which demonstrates urban organic and permaculture food production. The site now has a covered space, a compost toilet, benches and even a piano. The site has allotment plots for local people, a plant and seed shop, space for community events, and the project encourages skill-sharing.

The project is reliant on funding, and has managed to secure some from Eastside Traders and from Bristol City Council's Neighbourhood Regeneration Fund. This initially paid for a co-ordinator, Nick Ward, who

Figure 21. Schoolchildren at Eastside Roots (photo © James Adamson)

Figure 22. Eastside Roots (photo © Dave Pribelszki)

continued the consultation to ensure that the project was responding to the needs of the community. Nick also developed a programme of events for the project, including a Spring and a Harvest Fair. Since Nick has left, those involved have been running the project co-operatively as well as continuing community involvement.

In April 2010 an official opening of Eastside Roots Garden Centre was held, and during that summer they piloted a café at the site. The Kebele Centre in Easton enabled them to do this, and they are keen to run the café again as it proved so popular locally.

The use of derelict or empty land for growing food is an example of the urban rethinking that is needed to develop the resilience of Bristol's food supply.

The demand for allotments is rising, as in a time of economic recession people are especially keen to grow their own food. The waiting lists for allotments however can be many years long. Projects that regenerate small patches of land are becoming a useful tool to grow food and enjoy time spent in the fresh air.

The development of sustainable agricultural land links with the appropriate use of Bristol's green space. The borders of Bristol are rich with fertile agricultural land, and there are many pieces of derelict land within the city confines which could be regenerated.

Many organisations and community groups in Bristol feel it would be short-sighted to use this land for development rather than food-growing. Allotments, CSAs and other community-minded agricultural projects could use this land for several purposes: to develop the city's self-sufficiency, to create green spaces for community use and to provide habitats for Bristol's wildlife.

One piece of land which has become well known for standing empty is the fertile 'bluefinger' which runs alongside the M32. Richard Spalding, a lecturer at UWE in Human Geography, has been speaking about this piece of land for several years "as a potential site for revitalising the local food economy within the context of peak oil and climate change adaptation." [83]

Sims Hill Shared Harvest

In 2009 James Adamson and Tim Lawrence had both heard that there were smallholdings on a piece of fertile land next to the M32. They each contacted the Smallholdings and Allotments Department at Bristol City Council. At the same time, Avon Wildlife Trust (AWT) had also expressed interest in the 14.5 acre piece of land.

When this land became free, BCC put all three parties in contact with one another, and after discussion it was decided that James and Tim would take one of the fields and AWT would take the other. James and Tim decided that the best use of the land would be to set up a community supported agriculture initiative (CSA). Eric Booth had already looked at CSAs as being a way of developing Bristol's local food resilience and sustainability.

Barbara Janke, in a BCC press release announcing the plans for the Sims Hill site, stated that "Bristol is leading the way in finding opportunities to increase the amount of locally sourced food and maximising the amount of land in food production in the city. These are exactly the type of projects we want to see in the city because [they] are exploring dynamic ways of producing food." [84]

As the model is community-run and owned, it provides a level of resilience and self-sufficiency, in terms of food, for those involved. It also means that those involved know exactly how their food is grown as well developing a community of people with a shared aim who can enjoy the work and celebrate the milestones.

James and Tim began by organising an open meeting at Hamilton House to see who was interested. Six people formed a working group and began to discuss the realities of founding a CSA through participatory workshops. The group, whose ages ranged from 28 to 60, came from mixed backgrounds of skills and experience, and they took time to listen to each other's stories and visited the site to get a feel for the place. The project became known as Sims Hill Shared Harvest.

After four or five months of these workshops and discussions they began to discuss and evaluate the details of their plan for the CSA. In August 2010 they were ready to have another open meeting where they invited Bristol's community to discuss the initiative. Nearly fifty people attended this meeting, and all voiced their encouragement for the CSA. Throughout December 2010 the group held a series of open meetings to recruit more members.

As of January 2011 Sims Hill has 31 members who are ready to break soil on the first working day. The scheme is offering different kinds of membership and they hope to encourage more people to get involved over the next year. The initiative's vision is described as "a member owned and led CSA which will help to reclaim Bristol's historic (and fertile) agricultural land." [85] They also "offer opportunities for education, work and recreation to the wider community, work to include and support people who are socially or economically marginalised [and] build community life."

Tim Lawrence feels that a CSA is quite a radical model for local agriculture as it can respond to social and environmental concerns and injustices.[86]

Asylum Seekers' Allotment Project

The process of growing food is an activity where people can find a common ground, regardless of background, age or gender. One project which has used this to its advantage is the Asylum Seekers' Allotment Project (ASAP), also run by Tim Lawrence.

ASAP began in 2008 and was initiated through Tim's desire to work "with minority groups and people from other cultures and explore with them how all of us could feel more at home and develop our connectedness with Bristol".[87]

Tim found an overgrown plot of land in Barton Hill to begin this project. He wanted to use the land to grow food in an organic and sustainable way and for the project to reconnect its participants, both British volunteers and asylum seekers and refugees, with the local land through a community-led initiative.

The project has become a cross-cultural initiative which grows food and cultivates new relationships. Tim suggests that the project works on two levels. On one level it is about growing food for "asylum seekers who are on £30 weekly Tesco vouchers or no support at all, living in poor accommodation or with host families where they are guests". The individuals donate some of their time to the upkeep and maintenance of the allotment in Barton Hill and in return they can take away food from the allotment every week.

As asylum seekers and refugees are not allowed to work while their application is processed, the project gives them something to do as well as giving them access to fruit and vegetables, which can otherwise be expensive, as well as providing them something to give back to their guest families.

On another level, however, Tim wanted to create a place where his volunteers could feel safe and somewhere "that they could call their own. The work is therapeutic, it builds relationships, and there is space for socialising and sharing food." He feels that the project benefits all the volunteers as the therapeutic benefits of food-growing "brings us all together".

Bristol Permaculture Group, ASAP, Eastside Roots and Sims Hill are only a few examples of the booming food movement in Bristol. There are growing projects across the city, including city farms and community and market gardens, which look to benefit their communities through local food resilience and community development.

Figure 23. Asylum Seekers' Allotment Project (photo © Tim Lawrence)

Supermarkets or local business?

While local food provides a way to encourage social and environmental sustainability, independent businesses, which rely on the local food chain, provide a form of local food resilience. Local businesses keep money in an area rather than it being siphoned out to a centralised company and benefiting shareholders in distant places. For these reasons, some people are understandably upset when a big-name supermarket comes into an area.

In the late 1980s Tesco submitted a planning proposal to develop a store in Golden Hill, Henleaze. The residents protested against this proposal, which was due to be built on a 24-acre green space. The local MP and MEP were both against the proposal, but the government granted planning permission. The protest was one of the first nationally recognised campaigns against a supermarket, and drew support from the whole community, including William Waldegrave, who was MP for Bristol West at the time.

The Independent ran several articles about the campaign, and in one it quoted a local resident, Alison Evans, who spoke about her involvement in the campaign:

> "I managed to get through the Sixties without going to a demonstration or anything like that . . . I never thought in my wildest dreams that I'd one day be dragged away by police . . . but sometimes you just have to take a stand, it's no good sitting at home. There is no need for another supermarket."

In 1992, after several years of campaigning, Alison and 80 other local residents spent 39 days in a round-the-clock vigil underneath lime trees threatened by the development.[88] These protesters, including mothers and their toddlers, pensioners and many other people of all ages and backgrounds, were removed by the police.

The protest continued, however, until August 1992 when the trees were cut down and the new Tesco store was built. *The Independent* stated that "the campaign to stop Tesco developing in the middle class suburb reached an unusual emotional intensity." [89] This emotional intensity and passion to protect local businesses from supermarket dominance and to save local green space continued to grow over the next 20 years.

In 2010, another community in Bristol started the long process of campaigning against a new Tesco store. Stokes Croft has been undergoing a programme of community-organised regeneration in the last few years, culturally, socially and economically.

A social enterprise was formed called the People's Republic of Stokes Croft (PRSC) in 2009 which aims "to help Stokes Croft to recognise its special qualities by improving the streetscape through direct action, by creating a sense of identity, a sense of belonging and of self-worth." PRSC state that:

> "Stokes Croft is the most interesting and culturally diverse area in Bristol, boasting more honesty, beauty and truth than any other part of the city. It is precisely because Stokes Croft has been neglected, that people of all backgrounds and circumstance have learned to co-exist in an enclave of tolerance that few from outside this rich area can begin to understand."

Through the work of this group the local community has tried – and succeeded – to develop the area, making it "more stimulating. Tidier. Safer. Better." [90] Their work has contributed to the development of Hamilton House, a thriving community centre which provides local facilities including gallery space, offices and a bar as well as local events, music, art, film showings and more.

In February 2010 local residents discovered that a site on Cheltenham Road was being fitted out for a Tesco store. The local community had had no idea that Tesco had put in an application for planning permission, as they had applied for permission under an agency name.

PRSC and the local residents were unsure as to whether another chain supermarket would fit in with their desire to cultivate a sense of independence and local economic development. A group of people organised a meeting at Hamilton House, and 200 people turned up to discuss what a chain supermarket would mean for Stokes Croft. An official protest was organised on 13th February, and 2,500 residents sent postcards to Bristol City Council stating that Tesco had not adequately consulted the community.

The campaign had many reasons for 'Saying No' to Tesco. After working to develop Stokes Croft's local economy, it was undesirable to see a shop open which would take money out of the area. Peak oil was cited as another reason: it was feared that as fuel prices rise, supermarkets will no longer be able to provide cheap food. Furthermore, residents were upset that the community had not been adequately consulted about the planning application. Tesco's Corporate Social Responsibility report states that community engagement is important to them: "Any new store is the start of our relationship with a community, and we listen to local people from the moment we identify a site." [91] The Stokes Croft residents do not feel that Tesco did this.

The campaign received support from Barbara Janke, Head of Bristol City Council, who wrote to Tesco stating that "we would like Stokes Croft to become a distinctive destination in Bristol and do not believe another chain store will help achieve this aim." She asked them to meet with the community and urged locals to come up with alternatives for the space. The council had also not been aware the Tesco had been behind the planning application.

Supermarkets do provide good food at cheap prices, and they also cater to those who work during the day. A new store also provides jobs, and some local traders in Stokes Croft stated that they welcomed the store, hoping that it would encourage investment in the area.

The campaigners decided to 'explode' some of the myths surrounding supermarket food and conducted a small-scale study which found that local stores did match prices in Tesco. The campaign also cited a practice called 'price-flexing', where continual offers and 'undercutting' prices keep customers thinking that their prices are cheap.

In 2006, The Office of Fair Trading (OFT) suggested that "aspects of the large supermarkets' pricing behaviour – below cost selling and price flexing . . . provide reasonable grounds for suspecting that competition is being distorted." [92] The OFT requested that an independent audit be carried out by the Competition Commission. While it is obvious that large chain supermarkets will try to undercut each other to attract as much custom as possible, it is also understandable as to why people would be concerned about these practices.

The domination of supermarkets (the four largest chains – Asda, Tesco, Morrison and Sainsbury – own around three-quarters of the grocery market) is a worry to those who feel that local business and independent store shopping is the most sustainable and resilient way for the future. [93] Overall, supermarket domination makes it hard for independent businesses to succeed, which in turn jeopardises local resilience for the future.

During 2010, the 'No to Tesco' protesters continued to campaign, holding vigils outside the Council House, speaking to local residents about their thoughts on a new store and attending council meetings. They started to explore the issues of planning permission. It seemed as though big business and developers benefited from the organisation of the planning system whereas smaller, independent businesses and communities were forgotten.

When it became clear that Tesco was going to open, the campaign decided to seek a judicial review into the way Bristol City Council had dealt with the planning process. The campaign stated that "we are of the firm belief that planning officers failed to follow proper procedure regarding deliveries to the store and subsequently wrongly granted permission for Tesco to open." [94]

The Tesco store opened in April 2011. For the first week of business local campaigners sat outside and offered free home-cooked food to people who were not shopping in Tesco. It was a peaceful protest. On the night of Thursday 21st April, however, 160 police officers raided a squat opposite the Tesco store, which led to a street riot. The Tesco store was damaged in these riots and temporarily closed. 56 people were arrested and many, including police officers, were injured. Stokes Croft became the subject of widespread media attention.

Claire Milne, one of the core campaigners, is quoted in *The Guardian* stating that she does not condone the violence but that it is indicative of the way that "people feel completely unable to influence the day-to-day running of their lives".[95]

Tesco has since re-opened, and the campaigners have been granted a judicial review. Only time will tell whether it was a cost-effective venture for Tesco, and whether the campaigners can continue their fight for local business and sustainable shopping.

Better Food Company

Bristol as a whole is known for its high level of independent businesses, and it is lucky as it has no shortage of environmentally and locally-minded cafés, restaurants and food suppliers including Bordeaux Quay, Folk House Café, Boston Tea Party, Friska, the Thali cafés, Essential Trading Co-operative, local farms like Leigh Court and the Community Farm in Chew Magna and many local food festivals and farmer's markets, like Love Food, Slow Food and St Nicholas' Market.

One of Bristol's most popular local and organic food shops is the Better Food Company. It began in 1992 when Phil Haughton set up a new scheme called Phil's Better Food Campaign. It became the Better Food Company in 1993 and was a box scheme which delivered to homes, cafés and shops – Phil ran it from his house. By 1994 it was doing so well that they moved into a property off Cotham Brow, and by 1996 they had moved again to a warehouse next to St Werburghs City Farm. Over the next few years they kept moving to bigger and bigger warehouses as the company became more successful.

In 2000, the Better Food Company arrived at its current premises, The Proving House in St Werburghs, and it launched as an organic supermarket. In 2001 the Better Food Company bought up Barleywood Walled Garden to grow food for the company and to use it as a demonstration site to show people how to grow organic food.

The combination of the supermarket and the site brought together everything that Phil and those at the Better Food Company felt passionate about: local business, growing local, organic food, and involving the local community in discovering the benefits of growing and eating this food.

When the café opened in 2008 it became a thriving community centre, and the combination of a shop and café provided an alternative to supermarket shopping. Since then the store has gone from strength to strength and in response to this success Better Food Company has opened a second store on Whiteladies Road.

Figure 24. Better Food Company 2000s (photo © Better Food Company)

Who feeds Bristol?

Bristol's recent boom in local and sustainable food initiatives and concerns about our food supply chain show a growing awareness of food issues. In 2009 Bristol Food Network, the foundations of which lie in the 1990s Food Links project, developed the Bristol Sustainable Food strategy. This was in response to the host of increasingly urgent environmental and well-being issues related to food and it aimed to "create a sustainable food system for Bristol".[96]

The Food Network also wanted to provide a framework to link people and groups working on local food issues which were growing in number. In March 2010 Bristol City Council continued its involvement with local food issues by releasing a Food Charter to coincide with a conference held in Bristol by The Soil Association.

Bristol's Peak Oil report in 2009 (mentioned in the Energy section) contained a section which looked at the impact it would have upon our food system. It suggested that the effects would be clear and dramatic:

"Direct Impact: High oil costs would lead to rising pesticide costs. Heavily industrialised farming methods and globalised delivery infrastructures will be affected. In the event of supply shortages food distribution systems would be strained.

Secondary Impact: Rising price of food due to increases in production, packaging and transport costs would affect the public with a knock on effect on the economy and public services as more people fall into food poverty."[97]

The report summarised many of the city-wide concerns about our reliance on food from abroad and lack of local supply. When the Green Capital Initiative asked for recommendations for research on issues raised in the report, Joy Carey, a local food expert, suggested a baseline analysis to understand how the current food supply system for Bristol works and explore what would be needed to increase its resilience in the future.

Building on both the Sustainable Food Strategy for Bristol and the Peak Oil report, Joy and her small research team gathered information to "give people more information about the businesses involved, the way the food system operates, how food makes it onto our plates." This would then "give us a better sense of where the strengths and vulnerabilities lie and what kind of changes need to be made [to our food system]".[98]

The report was entitled 'Who Feeds Bristol? Towards a Resilient Food

Plan'. Joy worked with NHS Bristol throughout the proposal and they commissioned the report with support from the Green Capital Partnership and the council. It looks at the whole food system for the west of England – from production to waste – and includes an estimate of how much fruit and vegetables could be grown on land within the Bristol boundary. It examines how each of the six main components of the food supply system interrelate, the impact the food system has on public health, and the effects, both positive and negative, that it can have on the local economy.

The report presents a holistic understanding of the food system for the decision-makers in the local area. It shows the opportunities for improvement and concludes with nine suggestions for action. By using an approach known as Food Systems Planning, the report aims to encourage Bristol to "build a food culture for the city that has the health of people and planet as its heart".

Joy suggests that while we are "completely dependent on supermarkets . . . they do a brilliant job. They get food to people at affordable prices daily." She also proposes, however, that "there are some consequences due to the way that the supermarket system operates . . . we've lost diversity of food retail. We need to create more market opportunities for producers in and around the Bristol city region and we need to find more ways to produce food closer to the city."

The report found that there was a huge range of food available in and around Bristol, but said that we are not making the most of our potential and that we need to realise that issues of food cut across many other systems like energy, transport, well-being and health. This will enable decision makers and consumers to make informed and systemic changes.

Bristol Food Network is now undergoing a change itself (2011), probably due in no small part to the recent boom in food initiatives. They have recently submitted a proposal to the Lottery Local Food fund for a project called Dig Bristol. This initiative wants to "enable small-scale community groups around Bristol to work together to increase the amount of land and numbers of people involved in growing food across the city".[99]

Food has become a major concern for Bristol at all levels, from organisations and businesses to communities and the council, which is unsurprising due to the concerns about peak oil, environmental damage and the vital role that food plays in physical needs, health and well-being as well as culture and leisure.

Lord Cameron of Dillington, the first Head of the Countryside Agency, reportedly once suggested that we are "nine meals from anarchy". A resilient food chain is of great importance to a sustainable society so that we are not thrown by future threats such as peak oil.

Of course local and organic food can sometimes be more expensive, but the work done in Hartcliffe and elsewhere shows the added benefits that community growing can have, to community development, people's well-being and local food resilience.

Social justice and inclusiveness are key aspect of a sustainable food system, and local food initiatives can provide a community with economic resilience, environmental sustainability as well as a space for community development and improving well-being.

Transport

The vicious spiral of congestion slowing buses, losing passengers, raising fares, losing more passengers, using more cars, creating more congestion must be broken.[100]

Blueprint for Survival, The Ecologist 1972

Many forms of transport rely on oil to function, so our ability to travel easily and cheaply depends on our ability to maintain the availability of fuel at a constant level and a low price. With peak oil emerging as a serious concern, and the continuing issues of air pollution and carbon emissions, fossil fuel use has been identified as unsustainable and a threat to the stability of our climate and our health.

Culturally, we have never been so obsessed with fast and easy travel. We want to be able to move around the UK as quickly and easily as possible to do business, visit loved ones, see the sights. In an age where people are doing business all over the globe and friends and families are scattered far and wide, air travel has also become incredibly popular and 'needed'. This ease of travel and the boom in the number of flights does however cause environmental problems. On a domestic basis, it has also been suggested to be socially damaging.

John Adams, a member of Friends of the Earth's Board of Directors since the 1970s, talks about 'hypermobility'.[101] This is the cultural phenomenon of wanting to travel faster and further than ever before. In his paper for the Royal Society of Arts (RSA), 'The Social Consequences of Hypermobility', he discusses how the ability to travel further in a shorter amount of time does not necessarily make our lives better. He suggests that a hypermobile society will become increasingly less fit and healthy, less community-minded, more socially polarised between those who can afford to travel and those who cannot, and potentially more dangerous for those not in cars, especially children.[102]

The environmental movement promotes walking, cycling and public transport as forms of local transport that are resilient to the threats of oil crises and are more environmentally friendly. Walking and cycling also alleviate the social consequences of travel by car – improving levels of health, fitness and well-being and increasing road safety by lessening levels of traffic. For these reasons the bicycle has become an iconic symbol in the environmental movement as a simple form of transport which

> *My vision for Bristol is to have an integrated transport hub which would be based near Temple Meads station. We should encourage more pedestrian crossings to enable communities to link more easily with local shopping facilities, with green spaces and paths and also public transport so there's far less reliance on and pollution from cars.*
>
> **Elizabeth Ellis, local historian, visual artist and volunteer with Bristol's Ecoshow**

gives you greater freedom than walking but leaves little mark on the environment, other than in its initial manufacturing process.

Cycling has created something of a counter-culture within transport, and can generate a sense of community and shared identity. There are organised bike rides, friends and family cycle together at weekends, and cyclists share tips on maintenance, routes and gadgets. Cycling becomes a way of life, not just a mode of transport.

Obviously, car travel is convenient, gives independence and has made daily life easier. Yet the number of cars that travel every day with only one passenger is worrying for environmental reasons, and the cost of buying and running a car compounds socio-economic problems. Car shares and car clubs, like City Car Club, enable people to share lifts or rent cars when they need them and give a glimpse into a future where cars are just one part of our transport choices, rather than the dominant one.

Sustrans state that a quarter of all journeys made by car are less than two miles long.[103] While for some walking or cycling is not an option for some or for all journeys, choosing more sustainable transport choices for shorter journeys could improve health and fitness levels as well as being better for the planet.

The car has long been a cultural symbol of success and prosperity and is often used as a way of conveying status. While the bicycle is associated with frugality, exercise and, quite often, an alternative way of life, the car is convenient, modern and powerful. In a society concerned with image and economic status the car usually wins in the stakes of cultural perception.

As modern cities grew in the 1960s and 70s, alongside modernisation and the motor car, cycling provision was rare. Urban planning and transport are often linked, as the way we design a city says a lot about how we want people to travel in that city.

Figure 25. The pleasure of cycling

The cycling city?

The Outer Circuit road that was proposed for Bristol in the 1960s is a good example of how cities were becoming car-orientated. There was little or no room for the cyclist. To this day, cyclists have to fight to get space and be respected on the roads.

When Sustrans began (as Cyclebag), it would have been impossible to imagine the extent of the impact that the group would have on Bristol's – and the UK's – cycling. We now have over 10,000 miles of cycle routes in the UK for people to use on their way to and from work, for children to cycle to school and for families and couples to enjoy on weekends and holidays.

While the environmental benefits of walking and cycling are key to Sustrans' mission, the organisation also promotes the health benefits of sustainable travel. They are keen to encourage a greater sense of community spirit and safety, which would allow children to walk and cycle to school without their parents.

When Sustrans became a registered charity in 1984 it began practical action to create cycle paths in the UK. Cyclebag remained as a separate group to continue campaigning to encourage the uptake of cycling within Bristol. Cyclebag's work, however, came to a lull and in 1991 a group of people met at the Youth Hostel Association and Bristol Cycling Campaign formed to continue advocacy and lobbying – to provide a voice for cyclists within the city.

The flyer for the inaugural meeting stated that their campaign methods would be "unashamedly forthright" and that they would be "campaigning directly against the unrestricted use of private cars and for the improvement of cycle and public transport facilities".

Early campaigns included blocking off the M32 with bicycles as Tony Ambrose, a founding member, sat on a throne dressed as King Canute

Hundreds of motorists coming into the city were stopped as protesters stood in the road . . . Some [motorists] sounded their horns while others got out of their cars to complain to the police . . . but police spokesman, PC Sean Dunne, said: "these cyclists are exercising their right to protest."

Bristol Evening Post, **Thursday November 28 1991**

'stemming the tide' of traffic. Fitting to the choice of costume, they only blocked off the road for five minutes. There were also other campaigns across the city including action at Bedminster Roundabout.

The original aims included rolling out 20mph speed limits across the city, a traffic-free city centre and to continue to improve the cycling infrastructure in Bristol. They also wanted to encourage more people to begin cycling and used critical mass-type rides to attract media attention. The campaign suggested that small, but vital, changes within the city's cycling network such as improving 'pinch-points' and danger areas to cyclists on roads around the city were just as important as building new paths.

More recently, they campaigned for the protection of Bristol to Bath Railway Path which was under threat from Bus Rapid Transport plans. During this campaign they joined forces with the walkers who also used the path. They found that they had a stronger voice together.

In 2006 Bristol Cycling Campaign restructured and decided to develop a committee and a constitution. This coincided perfectly with the Cycling City Bid, which we will discuss shortly, as this scheme could only work with organisations that were officially constituted. Bristol Cycling Campaign supported the bid, which demonstrated community support. When Bristol was designated the UK's first cycling city, the group joined the stakeholder advisory panel and helped shape the programme.

As a campaign group they have worked with both the community and council in order to achieve their aims. By encouraging the uptake of cycling as well as policy-making, they have developed the cycling population as well as helped create better infrastructure for cyclists.

The group are about to celebrate their twentieth anniversary and their current secretary, Martin McDonnell, notes that their aims have changed little, as they are still pressing for a traffic-free city centre and to improve the city's infrastructure. In 2009, 20mph speed limits were introduced on all but a few roads in Southville and Bedminster, and then Ashley, St Werburghs and St Pauls. The group, among others, are now encouraging Bristol City Council to do this across the whole of the city.

Bristol Green Bike Scheme

The Bristol Green Bike Scheme was devised in the late 1980s to make cycling more accessible to people, to encourage sharing and to challenge the necessity for private property. Inspired by the 'White Bike' scheme in Amsterdam, a group of cyclists from Bristol, including Ben Searle and

Karen Bell, set up a scheme for people to borrow bikes to be used in the city without any need for payment or ownership.

They advertised for donated bicycles and began organising events where volunteers refurbished the bikes. The bikes were left in specific places across the city, each labelled with the street name of where it belonged. The bike could then be picked up and returned to its original location after use. Volunteers took responsibility for maintaining the bikes. The scheme worked well, but there were not enough bikes for people to be able to find one when needed. Therefore, for the second year of the scheme, the bikes were put in people's houses and a sign was put up in the front window so that people would know where they were. People could then knock on the door, use the bike and return it.

The scheme got quite a lot of media attention, as there had not been a scheme like it in the UK before. It eventually lost momentum, as it was difficult to run without resources and modern communication systems – it was before the days of the internet, mobile phones and the widespread use of computers.

It is an example, however, of the innovative ways sustainable transport schemes can be developed, and these bike schemes are now common in cities across the world. Karen Bell suggests, however, that "with the need for credit cards, payment, access keys etc, these schemes have lost the original anarchist idea of challenging the need for private property which inspired the Bristol Green Bike Scheme." [104]

Council involvement

In the late 1980s Avon County Council, responding to the growing presence of cyclists in the city, set up a small cycling project team within the council's transport department. The first project they worked on was to implement the extension of the Bristol to Bath Railway Path in central Bristol.

Over the next ten years the team simultaneously planned and developed networks and facilities across Avon, collaborated with a range of partners and introduced promotional schemes. The project pioneered the boxes in front of traffic lights and examined alternative road designs in Bristol, such as contraflow traffic. They also tried to influence design and planning decisions by working directly with designers, planners and developers.

The aim was to integrate cycling into highway design, rather than to see it as something separate. For example, many new crossing points were implemented as part of the urban traffic control scheme in Bristol in the early 1990s and cycle/car crashes were substantially reduced at a number of large junctions. A member of this team, Mike Ginger, recalls that they wanted to demonstrate to that with careful planning cycling could become an everyday method of travel.[105] It was challenging, as they had to work within restrictive legal frameworks for different traffic systems and the group had to find solutions for these issues which involved influencing the Department of Transport nationally.

Levels of cycling to and from work depended partly on the provision for cyclists in workplaces, and so the team worked to encourage companies to provide Sheffield stands, changing rooms and cycle routes. In 1996, they managed to get Sheffield stands on platform three at Temple Meads train station after a period of opposition from the station operator. This was a significant step forward, which showed that the demand for provision for cycling commuters was tangible and growing.

They also started promotional activities to get the cycling agenda out into public consciousness. Bike Week and the Big Bike Ride in 1994 got a lot of positive media coverage and helped to raise the profile of cycling in the city. The Big Bike Ride later became Bristol's Biggest Bike Ride, which still happens today. The Portway is closed to become a space solely for Bristol cyclists, and there are a number of rides in and around the city.

In 2008 Mike Ginger was co-ordinating Bristol's bid for Cycling City status. This initiative had developed out of the 'Cycling Towns' project run by the Department for Transport (DfT). Six towns had previously been identified as 'cycling towns' and were encouraged to increase their cycling uptake. When this initiative proved successful, the DfT decided to identify and fund a cycling city and additional demonstration towns.

Bristol already had evidence of a lot of cycling activity, growing levels of provision and city-wide involvement, as well as a passionately dedicated cycling population and a green commuters club. The city also had support from local businesses, organisations and the council.

> *I would like to see whole roads where priorities are given to walkers and cyclists for certain days. For example the Portway could be closed every Sunday all day, not just on the occasional event and that would become a wonderful playground for Bristolians.*
>
> **John Grimshaw, founder member of Sustrans**

Furthermore, the council team and Sustrans had a good track record for examining European cities' cycling provision and drawing on this for new ideas.

Mike and his team had a short period to prepare the bid and were not sure that they would be successful. They were, and Bristol was awarded the £11.5 million grant, which was matched by Bristol and South Gloucestershire councils, to spend over 2½ years.

Bristol therefore became the UK's first 'cycling city'. With the funding Bristol aimed to improve infrastructure, maintain the city's existing network and implement a range of promotional programmes to promote the reasons for cycling and how to get started. The funding also allowed the project to provide businesses, communities and schools with advice, access to maintenance sessions and funding for community projects as well as encouraging young people and adults to cycle through 'bikeability' courses. The idea was to double the numbers of cyclists in Bristol over the course of the project.

The project has had its issues. One year into the project, the *Bristol Evening Post* proclaimed that there was too much talk and not enough action, quoting the Chairman of Cycling England, Phillip Darnton, instructing the Cycling City team to "get on with it".[106] At the close of the

Figure 26. Bristol's Biggest Bike Ride (photo © Tony Smedley)

project, however, it was announced that the scheme had managed to raise cycling levels by a third.

While these results fall short of the original target, the status and funding enabled Bristol to take cycling provision seriously and has added to and improved the city's infrastructure, including over 100 miles of new cycling routes.

Bristol's Transport System

There are times when I feel much less optimistic about the city, and Friday afternoon at 3.30 is a low point. If you ever try and get into the city centre then, it just feels like a great big car park.

Lucy Pedler

Bristol's overall transport system is notoriously bad, and was frequently identified in the interviews conducted for this project as something that needs tackling. Bristol is in the highest 20% for road traffic levels, and 39.2% of the population identify road congestion as something most in need of improvement.[107]

Forum for the Future's Sustainable Cities Index cited, in 2010, that Bristol's residents were "dissatisfied with bus services" and that the city has "a large number of car commuters".[108] It seems obvious therefore that transport is an issue which needs resolving within the city. A more comprehensive, quicker and cheaper public transport scheme is often proposed as a way to improve Bristol's transport. Plans for a tram system and a Rapid Transport Network have been discussed for years, and these delays show how a transport system in a city relies heavily on local authority decisions and urban planning.

In 2005, in response to changes in government funding, Bristol City, North Somerset, South Gloucestershire and Bath and North-East Somerset Councils formed the West of England Partnership and commissioned the Greater Bristol Strategic Transport Study. This looked at the transport needs for the area up to 2026. A Joint Local Transport Plan was then finalised in 2006 which looked to tackle congestion, improve accessibility, improve air quality, improve road safety and improve quality of life.[109]

One of the suggested schemes to improve Bristol's public transport is the implementation of a Bus Rapid Transit network. This has proved a controversial proposal. Bus Rapid Transit consists of dedicated bus lanes which ideally use modern, sustainably-powered vehicles and combine the speed of a train system with the ease of bus travel. The network is designed to be used for short and long journeys and to link up all areas of the city for people to access their workplace, leisure activities and amenities.

In 2008 it transpired that the first phase of Bus Rapid Transit for Bristol proposed running one route along part of the Bristol to Bath Railway Path. This was not a favourable notion for the walkers and cyclists who used the path. Bristol Cycling Campaign and local residents, among others, campaigned for the protection of this path. The plans were eventually shelved.

There could be a whole publication written about the different transport proposals for Bristol and the pros and cons of each scheme, but we want to just touch on two of the proposals which are being discussed at the moment.

West of England Partnership submitted an application for the second phase of BRT (BRT2), from Ashton Vale to Bristol Temple Meads in 2008. In 2010 the construction of a South Bristol Ring Road to improve transport to and from the area was also proposed as part of BRT2.

Transport for Greater Bristol Alliance advocate the development of a light-rail system, stating that they "oppose BRT2 guided bus way in support of environmentally sustainable and more effective alternatives".[110] The concerns about BRT2 are that it will be expensive and that it will damage green space and some of Bristol's historical landscape.

In November 2010 Sustraco, a consortium of Bristol-based and international forms, put forward a proposal for an ultra-light rail system to Bristol City Council. The scheme is supported by 'Trams for Bristol', an offshoot of Transport for Greater Bristol Alliance, and the plans gained favourable attention in the *Bristol Evening Post* ('New tram vision for the future', May 4th, 2011). It would use existing rail corridors, thus minimising environmental damage, and according to the study would also be cheaper than BRT2. The Sustraco Consortium proposal states that "it combines the best elements of proven bus and tram technology".[111]

Our transport choices determine so much more than how we travel. They determine the green space of the city, access to local amenities and other aspects of urban planning, local noise levels, levels of pollution, the cost and accessibility of travel as well as the role of community and local authority in public transport.

Freebus

When public transport is privatised it can become a commodity rather than a community-orientated service, and this can exclude people as transport prices rise.

In 2011 a free bus scheme was launched. The scheme began life as a campaign group who decided that "Bristol would benefit from a non-profit, community run transport operator to provide low cost services and stimulate discussion of transport issues in the city".[112] In the 1970s Bristol Friends of the Earth had run a free bus scheme on a Saturday through the city centre to highlight Bristol's transport issues. Thirty years later, Bristol is still calling for better public transport provision to alleviate both social and environmental issues.

This scheme answered these calls. Freebus is non-profit and runs on donations and membership. The initiative is solely owned by its members, with decisions made on a one member, one vote basis. It is an example of practical action (like the FoE scheme but on a bigger scale) aiming to stimulate debate. By running a free bus, the initiative is encouraging local people to ask why this could not be done more often.

The Freebus Team state that by using the service the public can contribute to the development of a "new paradigm" by showing that they "want to contribute to quality public services". The scheme is dependent on public uptake, but the pilot weekend had an average ridership of 53 people, showing that they are not short of support.

Community involvement within a city's transport system highlights how people are becoming more and more concerned about the issues of the privatisation of public facilities and amenities. Gus Hoyt, a member of the core team of the Free Bus scheme and the newly elected Green Party Councillor for Ashley suggests that "if Bristol is going to lead the way as a green city, we must take back ownership of our transport system."[113]

The Freebus scheme is about more than the price of transport. It is about creating transport schemes which put the community rather than profit first.

Streets Alive

There have been other campaigns within Bristol that have concentrated on making the city more community-minded and people-friendly. Streets Alive began through the European Car Free Movement in 2001 and was formally constituted in 2003. The organisation realised that by closing roads and holding street parties in local communities, they could show the environmental and social benefits of car-free areas.

Again this initiative is about more than reducing car use. Chris Gittens, Director of Streets Alive, suggests that they are essentially a community capacity-building organisation that wants to build local community spirit in order to build local resilience. Streets Alive want communities across the UK to be able to respond to concerns as diverse as climate change, economic recession, social cohesion and well-being.

Car use can divide neighbourhoods by roads, deny children the safety to play outside and prevent the development of community space. Streets Alive work across the UK with a range of different neighbourhoods to help communities create more opportunities for 'social connection and inclusion' in their street. While street parties are now only one part of the work that Streets Alive does, the closure of a local road for the community is a powerful tool to fostering a greater sense of community spirit and resilience. They also encourage a range of other environmentally and socially beneficial community capacity activities including skills-sharing, 'collaborative consumption' of items like books and the development of local exercise groups.

Front Garden Award

Walking when everyone else is driving is not a pleasant experience. The noise, the pollution and the danger can put people off walking or cycling, even in their local area. Southville Community Development Association (SCDA) thought that one reason that people did not want to walk around the Greater Bedminster area was because it was not always aesthetically pleasing.

Figure 27. Easton Street Party (photo © Streets Alive)

> *Bristol is the UK's capital of street parties. In 2010 there were 150 street parties with 8,000 people taking part.*

They decided that one way to improve local amenity was to give awards to people for having nicer front gardens. This led to the development of the surprisingly simple 'Front Garden Award', which was designed to encourage people to take care of their front gardens and thus encourage the community as a whole to walk around the local neighbourhood.

The scheme aims to encourage people to walk around the local area rather than getting in their cars. SCDA have found that the scheme also encourages a sense of local community as people will help others who cannot garden.

Ben Barker from SCDA and Sustainable Southville Project states that the scheme only costs a few hundred pounds, and that "people producing nice front gardens, some really good ones, is a great example of volunteering. When you ask people . . . 'do you volunteer?' no one says 'yeah actually I do my front garden.' But it is a sort of volunteering, it is a . . . contribution to the community because it just makes the place more attractive to wander round and explore." [111]

Bristol Bike Project

In December 2008 two friends set up a community bike project which also demonstrates the potential of sustainable transport to alleviate social issues. James Lucas and Colin Fan were keen to begin a socially inclusive initiative which would have tangible effects for those who took part.

James had been volunteering at Bristol Refugee Rights and realised that the process of asylum application was incredibly demoralising and could take years. This was also compounded by the prejudice and marginalisation that asylum seekers and political refugees face. Since asylum seekers are not allowed to work, they have to depend on a voucher system run by the government and are given around £30 of vouchers a week. This means that they have no actual money which would enable them to use services like public transport. Individuals often have to walk for hours to get to important meetings for their applications, classes or to meet friends.

James and Colin saw the need for a cheap, reliable form of transport for those going through this process. They started a project where they refurbished donated bikes that would otherwise be thrown away and passed these bikes onto people at the refugee centre who had expressed interest. They began working in a garden shed but as the project grew more successful they moved into a space in Hamilton House.

James and Colin soon realised that they did not just want to be giving out bikes. They wanted the people involved to feel part of a process and to take ownership of the bikes. They developed a system where they fixed bikes to a level where they still needed some work and held sessions where people would come along and finish fixing the bikes themselves.

Each participant, therefore, felt responsible for the bike as well as learning the necessary skills to maintain it in a way that was inclusive and empowering. The sessions also provided time for socialising and opportunities for skills-sharing. The project also has long-term benefits, as if and when the individuals are granted asylum and are allowed to look for jobs, their bike allows them to travel to the job centre, training classes and job interviews.

As the project has grown it has begun to work with other marginalised and disadvantaged people in their community, including young offenders, people recovering from drug addictions and those with mental health problems. It was felt that these groups would also benefit not only from cheap transport and the skills to maintain it, but also from the sense of community and responsibility that the project creates.

Cycling is a great form of cheap exercise and also provides people with independence and the ability to travel freely around the city without having to rely on expensive public transport. The project has practical social and health benefits as well as tackling the environmental impacts of waste. The donated bikes are not left to rust away unused or at the tip; they are reused for a worthwhile cause. James says that he loves reusing something that other people consider to have no worth, and making it into something which has the capacity to transform someone's life.[115]

The project has now been running for over two years. It has been run and developed entirely by volunteers and sustained through selling the more valuable donated bikes. They are, however, restructuring because they feel it has gone as far as it can with just volunteers. They would like to find funding to pay a core team to make the project more sustainable in the long term.

John Adams, in his discussion of hypermobility, suggests that "the increase in the mobility of the average Briton . . . conceals a growing gap between the mobility-rich and the mobility have-nots." [116] Many of us will not give a second thought to being able to pay for the bus when our jour-

Figure 28 Bristol Bike Project, left to right: Aziz, Colin (co-founder), Abraham, Daahir, James (co-founder). Photo © Paul Blakemore

ney is just that bit too long to walk, but for those unable to do so, a city suddenly becomes a much 'bigger' place; the transport freedom that we take for granted is denied to them. The Bristol Bike Project shows the transformative quality that something as simple as a bicycle can have for people's lives.

In 2009, a lecturer in film-making from UWE called Alistair Oldham made a short film about the work at Bristol Bike Project. He concentrated on two individuals whom the project had helped, Dahir from Somalia and Aziz from Afghanistan. Dahir says in the film that his bicycle makes him feel free: "I'm not worrying about anything else. It's me, the road and my bike . . . I have the freedom of riding to where I want." Aziz also talks about the freedom his bike has given him: "When I ride the bike I feel like an eagle, like a bird, like myself." [117]

Bristol has a long history of involvement with sustainable transport through work done at a community, business, organisation and council level. But the city has a reputation for failing the general public over public transport.

Bristol has far to go before its transport problems are solved. Over the last 40 years the different organisations and initiatives in the city have tried to show the benefits of an improved traffic system and a move to a more people-orientated, rather than car-dominated, city.

Cars will undoubtedly still form a part of the transport system of Bristol and the UK. The organisations and schemes discussed have shown, however, that different forms of sustainable transport can come together to provide a way to improve city-wide mobility for all, especially for those on lower incomes.

Recycling and resource management

If we squander our fossil fuels, we threaten civilisation; but if we squander the capital represented by living nature around us, we threaten life itself.

E. F. Schumacher

While the modern kerbside collection schemes are a fairly recent phenomenon, reusing resources has been a necessity for centuries. During World War I and II thrift, frugality and recycling became a way of life, but since then our society has become stuck in a 'take-make-waste' model where we mine the earth for material, make it into something and then throw it away. Resource management is an integral part of sustainability as so many areas of daily life rely on the use of natural resources including food, energy, transport, property and green space.

As the environmental movement got into its stride in the 1970s, the work of the Club of Rome, alternative economists like Schumacher and The Ecologist's *Blueprint for Survival* raised concerns that our rising levels of consumption were "undermining the very foundations of survival"[118]

Schumacher suggested that "modern economics does not distinguish between renewable and non-renewable materials, as its very method is to equalize and quantify everything by means of a money price."[119] He also stated that we treat the Earth's resources as expendable income when we should view them as natural capital.

The fact that our economy relies on finite resources means that their long-term management is often thought about in economic terms rather than thinking about the needs of future generations, or the need to maintain ecological sustainability at a planetary level. Sustainable resource use and recycling initiatives, therefore, have played a vital role in the environmental movement as a reaction against mining the earth, making items and

The worldview of the economy as a machine unprejudiced by ethical questions led logically to the belief that nature exists for the unbridled use of humans. From this way of thinking emerged what is often called the 'take-make-waste' economic system.

Bob Doppelt

throwing them away. When resources are recycled rather than thrown away, fewer natural resources have to be mined from the earth, which reduces pollution, soil damage and carbon emissions from production.

Consumerism advocates the rapid and ongoing development of the new, which replaces the old. The environmental movement has encouraged the creative reuse of resources, the development of markets for recycled materials, and the valuing of used resources as more than something to be 'thrown away'.

Bristol has an impressive history of recycling through modern kerbside collection schemes and the tireless work of community recycling initiatives. Bristol's recycling may have looked different today if it were not for the work done by Bristol and Avon FoE in the 1970s and 80s. As previously mentioned, Bristol FoE began recycling in the 1976 when Bristol City Council reduced their collection service. Alastair Sawday then began Avon FoE in the early 80s, which developed their series of community enterprises which encouraged the local market for recycled materials.

Arboreta Papers also emerged from the work of Avon FoE. In 1982 Richard Walker, who was the Chairman of Avon FoE at the time, realised that there were not many recycled paper products available.

Figure 29. Bristol FoE 'Tins for No. 10 Campaign.' Sent tin cans to No. 10 Downing St to highlight recycling issues (photo © Ray Smith)

Most waste paper was made into packaging material, as there was little market for other commercial products. Richard wanted to expand this market so that recycled paper was seen as a valuable resource. In May 1983, he and others founded Treesaver Paper Products and decided to risk having products specially made, including office and photocopy paper and envelopes. This was expensive, and difficult to finance.

In late 1983 Treesaver Paper Products teamed up with Birmingham FoE, Paperback in London and a few others, and each contributed 20% to have 10 tonnes of recycled paper processed. The groups then formed a partnership called ARPS (Association of Recycled Paper Suppliers) who worked together for the next few years to pool their resources.

ARPS worked for several years as the member groups developed. In the late 80s Treesaver Products started to work on their own, and in 1986 they became Arboreta Papers. Richard remembers that over the next 10 to 12 years there was an increasing interest in recycled paper products, but that it was still a struggle to encourage the paper industry to expand the range of products they would make. It was often the smaller paper mills who would become involved.[120]

The importance of business involvement in the environmental movement is clear: in order to make sustainable living possible, we need large and steady markets for sustainable products, such as recycled materials.

The relationship that both Bristol FoE and Avon FoE developed with a local paper merchant, Nick Francis, enabled their success. Nick's waste paper business, Clarfield's Waste Paper, provided Bristol and Avon FoE with a guaranteed market and price for the paper they collected. Nick says that he is "very firmly of the conviction that business is important to the environmental movement".[121] The work of FoE, with his help, made local sustainable waste management a realistic option for Bristol by giving recycled materials a market.

The scheme continued for several years, and was extended to collect other materials including textiles, glass and cans. Harris and Co, who have been recycling locally since the nineteenth century, accepted the textiles. The local network of recycling initiatives, including Children's Scrapstore, SOFA Project and another recycling programme, The Recycling Collective, worked in Bristol and enabled a wide variety of resources to be recycled.

When in 1988 the Community Programme shut down, a guaranteed workforce was no longer available to Avon FoE's various community enterprises. The contemporary recession made finding funding hard. The

late 80s and early 90s, however, had marked a shift in the UK's awareness of environmental issues.

Local Bath MP Chris Patten was the Secretary for the State of the
Environment, and he had guided the Environment Protection Act
through into legislation in 1990. This Act stated that local authorities had
the duty to collect recycling in their local area.

The emergence in 1988 of global warming as a serious concern was
followed closely by the Rio de Janeiro conference in 1992 which released
the Agenda 21 and the Local Agenda 21 strategies. From here on, Bristol's
involvement with sustainability, including recycling, grew in all areas of
the city, from community groups to the council.

The council launched its own series of recycling initiatives. Penny
Gane, a member of the council's recycling team at the time, says:

> "The oil recycling project that I led was before we really had proper
> oil recycling facilities in the city. I was able to go into partnership with
> Texaco UK, and we put out a system of oil recycling bins in the Texaco
> garages in Bristol. The idea was that it would stop people putting their
> waste oil down the drain. At the time it was the first comprehensive
> oil recycling system in the country."

Penny went on to give talks across the UK about the oil recycling
scheme. The council continued to improve recycling facilities in the city
with the black box kerbside scheme beginning in 1995. In 2006 Bristol
became the first UK city to offer food waste recycling to all residents. In
2011 the council have pledged to send zero waste to landfills by 2014; in
2010 Bristol managed to recycle, compost or reuse 37% of its waste.

The Create Centre

As already mentioned, The Create Centre (originally called the CREATE
Centre) developed through a partnership between the council, Recycling
Consortium and Bristol Energy Centre. It was supported by Bristol
Energy and Environment Trust (BEET). B-Bond, the tobacco warehouse
in the Cumberland Basin, was not suitable for the practical operations of
the recycling organisations and so Resourcesaver, SOFA Project and
Children's Scrapstore went to other council sites for their work.

Jane Stephenson suggests that this was incredibly useful while "they
were embryonic social enterprises [as] having that security of tenure of the
premises they were occupying made a big difference to their development."

Figure 30. The Create Centre 1990s (photo © Bristol City Council)

The above organisations worked together to transform B-Bond from a derelict warehouse into a centre for environmental action which included offices, community facilities and exhibition space. B-Bond, however, was not in any fit state to be used; it was dirty, there was no lighting, and the council had no funding to begin renovation. The council's environmental team managed to secure some funding and began to develop plans for the centre. A community consultation was run by Jeff Bishop of Bristol Bridge Consultancy, who used participatory workshops to encourage community involvement in planning.

The name, CREATE, stood for Community Recycling Environmental Action Training and Education, which showed the importance for the centre to be a hub of environmental action and learning that engaged communities.

Robert Lambourne, the director of Health and Environmental services at the time, suggests that a turning point for the project was when local design and build company JT Group, who we will discuss later, became involved.[122] JT Group surveyed the building and with their help the Create Centre began.

The first step was to put in a Portacabin and power wash the floor. The development was split into two phases. Phase One was to develop the downstairs into the café and gallery space. Phase Two began work on a cinema, a presentation room and office space. A project called 'Lifeskills', which dealt with community safety and health issues, joined Bristol's Recycling Consortium and Bristol Energy Centre. They were also joined by community art projects and the council's own sustainable department, the Sustainable City Team.

> *The idea [for Create] was to bring people together from the council with the community sector, the voluntary sector and business. The idea being that there would be a synergy of things when people got together so although they were perhaps working on different projects they would meet informally, socially in the workplace and things would start to buzz off each other and you would get ideas generated and that one group would be able to see and have ideas about how to help the others. It turned into a very unique local authority building with all sorts of functions including a lecture theatre which people could rent very cheaply for presentations, an art gallery and display space for events, talks and presentations on a whole range of issues.*
>
> **Robert Lambourne, ex-Director of Health and Environmental Services, involved in the beginning of the Create Centre**

The centre therefore began with a varied mix of organisations who dealt with a whole host of environmental issues. The centre also provided space for community, organisation and business use including exhibition space, a library, adult learning courses, conference and event space which allowed the Create Centre to host special events.

The centre's original mission statement was "to reduce energy and water consumption; to reuse, repair and recycle resources in Bristol to improve the quality of life for its inhabitants; and create the framework for sustainable development in the City of Bristol".[123] We will talk further about the centre during discussion about the positives of 'shared space' between cross-sectoral organisations and initiatives.

It bears mentioning that rethinking and reusing buildings is a form of recycling – one that in Bristol has had some amazing results. The Create Centre, for example, is a perfect example of this: a tobacco warehouse, a trade that once dominated Bristol's economy, now an environmental hub representative of Bristol's new reputation.

Bristol had become a fertile ground for recycling initiatives. Another of these was The Community Recycling Network, which began in Bristol in 1990 as an exit project for an initiative called UK 2000 which looked at sustainability in the UK. It was hosted by Avon FoE to begin with, but then went on to become a separate organisation. The project looked at developing community recycling initiatives nationally, and helped groups who were smaller, had less experience and needed some sup-

Figure 31. Recycling at Glastonbury Festival 1998 (photo © Network Recycling)

Figure 32. Resourcesaver Truck (photo © Resourcesaver/CRN)

port. CRN also developed Network Recycling, which is responsible for the recycling at many of the UK music festivals.

It is not an exaggeration to say that these initiatives, which started so small, have been essential to Bristol's recycling movement. The variety of materials and items that these schemes recycled and the innovative ways that they reused them, or the funds that they generated, showed the vast potential and opportunities that recycled materials offer.

By creating and providing a market, specifically a market which can benefit local people, Bristol and Avon FoE and their offshoot projects demonstrated that recycling was making not only environmental sense, but also social and economic sense.

Bristol Wood Recycling Project

Bristol Wood Recycling Project (BWRP) is another example of an initiative which has created a market for recycled materials as well as offering social benefit to the community. This not-for-profit initiative collects scrap wood from around the city, working with the help of volunteers. This wood is then sorted, de-nailed and, if appropriate, refurbished and sold on or recycled. When they began, they just cycled onto building sites and asked them where they sent their scrap wood.

The initiative began in 2003 when Ben Moss and Nicola Padden, both volunteers with the Community Recycling Network, heard a talk at a conference given by the man who ran Brighton and Hove Wood Recycling Project. They were inspired by the idea and intrigued by the possibilities for a Bristol version, so they attended a day workshop together. The workshop, run by Richard Mehmed from the Brighton and Hove project, demonstrated that it was fairly straightforward to develop a business model that generated income as well as fulfilling social and environmental objectives.

The project, however, needed a site before it could start its work. In a stroke of luck, Ben had an email from the council who were advertising an ex-council building which would be empty for a few months and could be used free of charge for that time and would be good for a community group. Ben and Nicola submitted a proposal for the building and were given the ground floor and outside space in the building on Cattle Market Road, near Temple Meads.

The project's initial financing was from the founders rather than a funding stream, as they did not want to have to 'dance to somebody else's

Figure 33. Bristol Wood Recycling Project (photo © BWRP)

tune'. With this initial investment they bought a van and began work.

As their service was cheaper than a skip, Ben and Nicola found that people were keen to use them. As shown by the project's success, this kind of enterprise can offer a valuable resource to both businesses and homeowners who have scrap materials as well as those who need these materials. Any profit is put straight back into the project in order to provide their volunteers with training and work experience. BWRP invite people from all backgrounds to help them. The project therefore is a recycling initiative and a community enterprise as it provides opportunities for training, work experience and social inclusion.

The wood collected, from both businesses and private residences, is sorted into different categories. Wood that is reusable is de-nailed, cleaned up and sold to the public. This accounts for about a third of the wood they collect. Wood which is recyclable is mechanically recycled, which accounts for the rest. A tiny 3% is not reusable or recyclable, because it is made of chipboard or MDF, and this has to go to landfill.

BWRP is another initiative that has benefited from council tenancy. Later we will talk more about the potential for empty buildings for community initiatives, but it is worth noting the positives of allowing not-for-profit organisations to use and manage empty space across the city. Not only do the initiatives gain benefit but also the building is improved as the organisations develop the facilities within the space. The BWRP building, however, was only going to be available for a short time, as the Bristol Arena was due to be built on the other side of the river. The building was on land for a planned bridge to the site. When the plans for the arena folded, BWRP's lease was extended by three years.

As the project grew it attracted a lot of media attention, including coverage in the *Bristol Evening Post* and on HTV news and Points West. Ben suggests that the project has worked well in Bristol because the local people want to become involved through donating and shopping in a place that is not-for-profit and helps people gain experience and training.

BWRP want to be able to reach both their financial and social capacity through volunteers making products using the recycled wood. This develops more training opportunities as well as creating products which can then be sold to generate more funding. The project also hopes to run classes out of these workshops for the wider community.

The recession had an interesting outcome for the project. While their levels of collection reduced, they found that they had more people from the general public coming to buy wood. People were doing more DIY themselves to save money, and their wood was reasonably priced. This shows how recycling and rethinking waste can provide a certain amount of resilience in times of economic problems.

The land that their building is on has been sold, but they are hoping for their lease to be guaranteed so that they can continue their work, as the project has proved popular and useful to many, including Bristol's businesses, communities and people.

Fairtrade

Resource management, however, is not just about recycling. It is also about looking at the resources we use and the way they are grown, processed and manufactured. Food, timber, fossil fuels, textiles, minerals and metals are all vital to daily life. It is not feasible to stop importing resources from abroad, but as environmental and social concerns develop it has become more important to know about where they have come from or how they were extracted from the Earth or grown. Textile use, for example, has become controversial in recent years as 'fast fashion' has been pinpointed as damaging to the environment and to people.

The fashion industry is dependent on fast-moving shifts in 'style' and taste, and on vociferous appetites for the latest look; this means a high turnover of production and a lot of waste. It is estimated that in 2005, 1.2 million tons of clothing went to landfill in the UK alone.[124]

The environmental issues of clothing manufacture are visible at every stage of the supply chain: the pesticides used to grow the raw material, the energy used in manufacture and transport of raw material and finished product, the use of chemicals and water in the dyeing process, and the disposal of the finished item.

Waste and environmental damage are not the only issues. As the materials and labour used are often sourced in developing countries, workers' rights and exploitation of resources abroad have become concerning aspects of fashion and other industries. There are many businesses that have looked at the environmental and social implications of their use of natural resources and overseas workers. One example of this is the Bishopston Trading Company (BTC).

In the late 1970s Carolyn Whitwell, who had been interested in international development work from her time with VSO, wanted to set up a link between Bishopston and a developing country. She started by canvassing all the communities in Bishopston and found others who were also interested. Carolyn met a doctor from South India who was visiting Bristol, and through this exchange Bishopston formed a link with the community of K. V. Kuppam in 1978. Over 500 people pledged to support this link, and they started to have street fairs to raise funds for this community. They continued this fundraising in their community for the next seven years.

In 1985, however, they received a letter saying that the K. V. Kuppam community was thankful for their help but what they really wanted was work, not charity. Carolyn decided that she could propose a trade link where K. V. Kuppam would provide a product which could be sold in Bristol. She communicated with K. V. Kuppam to discuss the development of this trade link, and it became clear that they could provide skilled craftsmanship in clothing and the Bristol side of the partnership could deal with the marketing and selling. Carolyn visited India with her family, and met with four tailors to start the business.

By providing a fair price for the skills that the Indian community was providing, Bishopston Trading Company developed an equal business partnership. The Bishopston-K. V. Kuppam link remained as a charity, and was separate from the trading company.

Bishopston Trading Company bought a shop on Gloucester Road with a 21-year lease, and K. V. Kuppam provided the raw materials of Madras cotton and the workers. Carolyn also wanted the clothing to be environmentally sustainable and to use organic cotton. Unfortunately it was not easily available, as this was before the organic industry had become well-known. BTC actually sent somebody out to India to grow organic cotton, but unfortunately they could not grow enough for the weavers to do their work.

Five years ago, however, Agrocel, a large Indian business, started producing organic cotton and BTC became their first commercial customers for this product. Everything they sell is now Fairtrade and organic.

The business itself grew organically, as there was never any injection of capital or funding. As it grew, so did the community in India. The business link had visible results for K. V. Kuppam and for Bristol; the employee base in K. V. Kuppam has grown from six to 100 people, and Bishopston Trading

Fairtrade is about giving workers better prices, decent working conditions, local sustainability, and fair terms of trade for farmers and workers in the developing world. By requiring companies to pay sustainable prices that must never fall lower than the market price, Fairtrade addresses the injustices of conventional trade, which traditionally discriminates against the poorest, weakest producers.

Company now have four shops in the south-west.[125]

The workers in India are paid above average wages as well as receiving a healthcare allowance, an on-site crèche for young children, a provident fund and gratuity. BTC also has a charity, The South Indian Rural Development Trust, which supports social development projects in the area.

The growing demand for Fairtrade and organic clothing around ten years ago added to BTC's success. They expanded, and built a factory in India for their workers which opened in 2005. They have, however, been hit hard by the recession, and while they have always tried to provide competitively priced clothing, this has become harder due to the rise in cotton prices.

The rise of 'ethical' fashion is just one example of a wider under-standing that we need to think about the way we source and manufacture our goods. It is clear in Bristol, shown by the growth of 'make do and mend', vintage fairs, charity shopping and 'clothes swap parties', that issues of sustainability and economic downturn have combined to form a movement of innovative clothing choices.

The success of Bishopston Trading Company shows the rise of Fairtrade goods. The term 'Fairtrade' has been officially used since 1988 under the initiative of the Dutch development agency Solidaridad.[126] In the last ten years the term has spread, and is now widely understood. When something has the Fairtrade mark it tells the consumer that the people who were involved in the growing, production, manufacture or development of that product were paid a fair price and treated fairly.

In 2001 Garstang in Lancashire became the first Fairtrade town in the UK, as they had been actively promoting and encouraging the local pur-chase of Fairtrade goods. They had been working on this since 1992, and in 2001, when the Fairtrade Foundation launched the Fairtrade Town pro-gramme, Garstang was presented with the first Fairtrade Town Certificate.

In 2003, Bristol began its campaign to become one of the first Fairtrade cities. The council's Sustainable City team took a lead in developing a net-work of organisations, businesses and volunteers who were interested in and involved with Fairtrade, and in 2005 their bid was successful.

In order to achieve Fairtrade status, a city has to achieve five goals which include council support, a range of Fairtrade products available in local shops and catering establishments, Fairtrade products in local workplaces and community organisations, as well as developing a local steering group and ensuring that there is media coverage and popular support for the campaign. 'Fairtrade status' has to be renewed every two years, and Bristol has never failed to achieve this.

Figure 34. Fairtrade Celebration on SS Great Britain 2011 (photo © Jon Craig)

In 2006 a co-ordinator was employed to manage the Fairtrade network, and since then Bristol's Fairtrade Network has built itself up through encouraging more organisations to get involved and concern themselves with Fairtrade issues. In the most recent renewal (2010) the Fairtrade Foundation commented that: "Without a doubt, Bristol City Council continues to be one of the pioneer authorities in terms of promoting and adopting Fairtrade and in offering genuine support to the wider network as it seeks to take this commitment out across the wider community." [127]

Bristol is now one of the leading Fairtrade cities, and was awarded the Outstanding Achievement Award in the Fairtrade Foundation Awards 2011.

Food and fashion have been two industries in which Fairtrade has had a visible impact. Bristol's Fairtrade Fashion show has tried to bring issues of fast, cheap fashion to light as well as demonstrating the variety of Fairtrade fashion available. The network has also encouraged local schools to discuss the reasons why Fairtrade food is important.

Jenny Foster, the co-ordinator of Bristol's Fairtrade Network, wants to make sure that Fairtrade is promoted as an essential part of Bristol's sustainability movement. Fairtrade is not a separate agenda from the environmental movement. Much of what Fairtrade does encourages both social and environmental justice, as one of the certification targets for Fairtrade is to be environmentally aware and responsible.

Forest of Avon Products

In the late 1990s Forest of Avon Products was founded as a co-operative to develop a local timber supply chain and promote sustainable woodland management in and around Bristol. The co-op encouraged a local market for products created by local crafts people using local timber. Jim O'Shaughnessy, the Project Manager, was employed by Forest of Avon to deliver community forestry in and around Bristol.

Woodland serves many purposes, including the preservation of wildlife, a space for recreation and an economic resource through the timber. The management of all this also creates jobs. Jim wanted to get the woodlands around Bristol into better management so that this variety of opportunities was conserved and extended.

The co-op's main aim is to "to promote local timber and woodland crafts in the local economy, so supporting the sustainable management of woodlands in the West of England". By bringing together woodland owners and a variety of craftspeople, the co-op have created a local supply chain and market for woodland products and services.

Jim suggests that "Forest of Avon Products Cooperative is a great example of a sustainable business, providing jobs, utilizing a renewable

Figure 35. Forest of Avon Products visited by pupils of Wood School (photo © FOAP – Jim O'Shaughnessy)

resource and improving wildlife and recreation opportunities. It's very much been a win-win scenario, with nature and humans for once both on the winning side." [128] This holistic understanding and community involvement means that people are more likely to get involved in protecting and using their local woodland.

Wessex Water became involved in Bristol's sustainability movement through committing to several practices to minimise their environmental impact as well as sustainably managing water use in the local area. They have pledged to control leakage and manage demand for water while protecting the water environment and wildlife. They have also promised to look at the ways in which sludge from treated sewage can be used on the land and as an energy source, as well as encouraging their customers to reduce water use. The involvement of local service providers is important as there is only so much that customers can do themselves.

Resource management is not just about recycling. It is about considering what we need, what we use and where it is from, as well as noticing innovative ways to use items which may have been discarded as 'useless' without a second thought. The way we feel about the items we use in daily life is indicative of our attitude towards our natural resources; once something no longer performs its intended function, it is quite literally 'rubbish'.

This section has shown some of the ways in which Bristol's recycling has developed to give new life to these items, as well as developing models of employment and volunteering that can provide people with new skills and training in order to refurbish and revamp these materials.

Bristol's environmental movement also shows an awareness of where our resources come from and who is involved in their growth, manufacture or mining. Fairtrade may not immediately be recognisable as part of the environmental movement, but its message of treating other countries' people and environment with the same respect we demand for our own encourages a global sustainability.

We should not be depleting other countries' natural resources at an unsustainable rate to give ourselves an unfair share of the Earth's abundance. We should also be developing our own resilience through encouraging the sustainable management of local resources, which in turn develops the local economy.

Wildlife, biodiversity and green space

Climb the mountains and get their good tidings. Nature's peace will flow into you as sunshine flows into trees. The winds will blow their own fresh-ness into you, and the storms their energy, while cares will drop off like autumn leaves.[129]

John Muir

Possibly the most famous side of the environmental movement is nature preservation. Dating back to Muir's work in the late 1800s, conservation and protection of the natural world remains at the heart of sustainability. Bristol has a reputation for engagement with wildlife preservation and exploration which pre-dates many other forms of environmental involve-ment and includes organisations, campaigning, community involvement and, more recently, digital media representation.

Bristol Zoo Gardens were founded in 1836, and it is the fifth oldest zoo in the world. While some zoos have a less than salubrious reputation, Bristol Zoo Gardens have become involved in conservation education, the breeding of endangered species and environmental advocacy. Their cur-rent vision is to "create a sustainable future for wildlife and people". They have also successfully bred and reintroduced two native species to the UK: the Barberry carpet moth and the water vole.

One of Bristol's longest standing community wildlife preservation groups is the Bristol Naturalists' Society, which was founded in 1862. They documented "detailed summaries of the geology of the region and its plant life, its birds, its insects, and the wildlife of the shores and estu-aries". The society still works in Bristol, and observes and documents changes in the natural environment of Bristol.[130]

In 1957, the Natural History Unit was set up in the city by the BBC, and remains here to this day. While the unit has no direct link with the envi-ronmental movement their work, through exploring the amazing wildlife that our planet has and how people affect that wildlife, has inspired peo-ple to be aware of the incredible richness of the natural world.

John Muir's quotation above touches on an important aspect of Bristol's environmental movement. There are organisations, community groups and initiatives in the city which promote the benefits that we can get from experiencing wildlife and the natural environment.

Bristol is incredibly lucky to have such beautiful green spaces within the city. These spaces benefit both us and the wildlife that lives there, which is why Bristol's communities and conservation organisations have worked so hard to protect them.

Bristol's wildlife conservation

In the late 1950s the Conservation Corps started in London to provide a free labour workforce for practical conservation activities. The idea was incredibly popular, and the London group was joined by others across the UK over the next ten years, including a Bristol operation.

The Bristol volunteers often worked in conjunction with local naturalist trusts in the south-west and travelled at weekends to visit nature reserves. The activities differed from place to place, but a common activity was managing woodland through coppicing and tree-felling. The wood would then be used to build fences around nature reserves. The volunteers also worked on footpath construction and scrub clearance. The work was practical hands-on action that helped conservation, rather than campaigning action. While the Bristol Conservations Corps team worked all across the south-west and into Wales, they also did work within Bristol at Ashton Court and Brandon Hill.

The volunteers provided a conservation labour force, but one member, Susan Carter, remembers that it was also about having fun and enjoying the natural environment. Susan, who became involved during her Duke of Edinburgh Award, suggests that the work came alongside an 'alternative' value choice; moving away from materialism towards spending time enjoying nature.[131]

The British Trust for Conservation Volunteers (BTCV) grew out of this work and was founded as a national organisation in 1970. An office opened in Bath, which then moved to Newton St Loe (between Bristol and Bath) several years later. In 1979 the local BTCV got involved with the Youth Opportunities Scheme (later the Community Programme), which gave them an increased workforce as well as providing the volunteers with new skills.

Mark Durk, then Projects Manager, remembers that the Newton St Loe office expanded, taking on increasing numbers of staff:

"I moved from Avon County Council to work full time for BTCV managing the YTS scheme. I don't think the locals in Newton St Loe were

Figure 36. BTCV Volunteers (photos © BTCV)

Figure 37. Stone walling (photo © BTCV)

too keen on groups of surly youths wandering about, but the village shop did a good trade in fags, crisps and coke." [132]

BTCV moved into the Create Centre in 1995 and remain there today. During their time at the Create Centre they developed a tree nursery on the top floor under the skylights. This was known as the Forest Floor project, which moved on to Blaise Castle and became the Tree Life Centre. BTCV also formed a partnership with the Forest of Avon and worked together on local conservation projects with local people.

BTCV's work brings together conservation and enjoyment of the natural environment. Over the last 20 years their volunteer base and operational programmes have steadily grown, and they run conservation activities almost every day in and around the city. The Downs Wildlife Project protects "the dramatic landscape that is home to an astonishing diversity of plants and animals".[133] The Gorge is recognised both as a national Site of Special Scientific Interest (SSSI) and internationally as a Special Area of Conservation. It is close to Leigh Woods and the Downs, beautiful woodland and green space respectively.

The "stunningly beautiful" aesthetic qualities of the area have been under threat in the past.[134] In 1971, an extension to expand the Grand Spa Hotel was proposed, but there was a large-scale campaign against the develpment run by local residents, who formed the Save The Avon Gorge (STAG) group.

This campaign not only received attention locally; it became a concern of national proportions that this extension might affect an area so renowned for its natural beauty and wildlife. The extension was eventually denied, even though it was initially suggested by a planning official that it should be approved.

It is not just the areas of beauty, however, that people want to protect. In the 1980s a proposal for the Severn Barrage was put forward. Ideas about damming or barraging the Severn Estuary had been considered since the 19th century, but had never come to fruition.*

While the barrage would provide a source of renewable energy, which was (and still is) increasingly needed, it would also jeopardise the area's ability to provide a habitat for its wildlife, including the 69,000 migratory birds which journey there every year.[135] The barrage proved an interest-

---

* This campaign could go in the energy section as well. We have chosen to put it here because the overwhelming concern of the campaign was for the preservation of the Estuary's natural habitat.

Figure 38. The Avon Gorge

ing dilemma for the local environmental movement.

Bristol Friends of the Earth held a symposium to debate the merits of the barrage versus the environmental implications. The overall conclusion seemed to be that the environmental consequences would be too great. Mike Birkin and Paul Glendell, both Bristol FoE campaigners, put together a case for the Severn Estuary as an important habitat.

Mike Birkin remembers that the estuary "didn't have a good reputation. It was something that was seen . . . quite widely as a muddy, polluted sort of place." Mike and Paul developed a 20-minute presentation which discussed the threats to wildlife that the barrage would pose, to encourage this natural habitat to be seen "as a real asset for the area and an important natural site that really merited protection".[136]

It was not just Bristol that was concerned about the implications of the barrage. Friends of the Earth Severn Estuary Network was founded, which

The government was dragging its heels about designating the Severn Estuary [a special protection area]. We found out that the paperwork was all on the Minister's desk and it was just waiting to be processed and signed off and this had been sort of languishing there for a couple of years or more. So we looked for an anniversary event and eventually we figured out that we were coming up to the time when it was a thousand days since the paperwork had been with the Minister and not been acted on. So we got a Severn Estuary mud cake made . . . it had a blue outline of the Estuary in icing on top of it and we said 'A thousand days and still waiting' in lettering on the top of the cake.

We took it along [to] the Department of the Environment [as] the wildlife division that was responsible for the designation was actually based here in Bristol. The security staff had absolutely no idea what to make of this when these people turned up with a chocolate cake. So the shutters came down and nobody could get in or out of the building for about 20 minutes while the security staff tried to decide what to do. But eventually somebody came round and took delivery of the cake from us and we got a letter from the Minister expressing appreciation for the chocolate cake, saying how much it had been appreciated by the staff, but much more importantly saying the government recognised that the Estuary merited designation as a European site of wildlife importance and should be treated for planning purposes as if it was already designated.

Mike Birkin

linked together the various environmental groups around the Estuary including Friends of the Earth Cymru. The network decided that the Estuary needed official protection and began to campaign for it to be deemed a 'Special Protection Area' in European Law. The Estuary was designated as an Area of Special Protection in 1995, but the idea for a barrage is a continuing proposition. It was raised (and rejected) again in 2003.

In 2007 the UK's Sustainable Development Commission (SDC) published a report looking at the potential of tidal power in the UK, including proposals for a Severn barrage. This report stated that:

> "A barrage in the Severn Estuary could supply 4.4% of the UK electricity supply (17TWh) from the second greatest tidal range resource in the world, generating electricity for over 120 years. However, it would have a major impact on the local environment, with the loss of up to 75% of the existing intertidal habitat, which is internationally protected. In light of this and other concerns, the report lays down a series of tough conditions which a Severn barrage would have to meet in order to be considered sustainable." [137]

Both the RSPB and Avon Wildlife Trust voiced their concerns about the proposal.[138] In 2010 Chris Huhne dropped the proposal, citing the expense as "excessive". The area is still pinpointed as a potential site for renewable energy schemes in the future. The positive and negative environmental implications of this barrage demonstrate the difficult choices that we face in the light of growing concerns about the forms of energy generation that we are going to use in the future.[139]

Bristol's green horizon

Bristol is renowned for its green space, and the city's 'green horizon' has been commented on throughout the project as a defining attribute. The city is "blessed with over 450 parks and green spaces, proportionately more than any other UK city".[140]

There are communities across the city working to protect these valuable inner-city spaces. Bristol Parks Forum is an online space for these groups to link up, share advice and discuss threats to local space. The forum is supported by Bristol City Council, but it is an independent group.

Bristol's parks are officially managed and maintained by the council, but these groups organise events and activities in the space, encourage sustainable use of the parks, including wildlife conservation, as well as responding to possible development plans which would affect the space.

Figure 39. Beauty and tranquillity

For example, the Northern Slopes Initiative was set up in 2001 to protect the slopes in Knowle from a proposed housing development. The group, however, expanded into an ongoing group to protect the slopes from development, vandalism, fly-tipping and littering as well as encourage use of the space for community activities.

Parks and green space have a number of uses, including space for recreation, exercise, community events, experiencing wildlife and even growing food. Often they quite simply provide a green oasis in the middle of a concrete jungle.

Ashton Court Quarry campaign

The Ashton Quarry campaign in the 1990s demonstrates the level of commitment that Bristol's people have shown to protect local green space and to maintain its multiple uses.

In the mid-1990s Pioneer Aggregates submitted an application to extend the nearby quarry by 34 acres into Ashton Court's Top Park Meadow.

The loss of this meadow threatened the wildlife that lived there, as well as the enjoyment of Ashton Court by the people of the city. Bristol's residents, organisations and communities, including Bristol Friends of

> *Top Park Field was a tranquil place, full of meadow flowers and but-*
> *terflies, home to nesting skylarks and enjoyed by the many visitors to*
> *the estate ... to our surprise and disappointment, and despite the out-*
> *standing wildlife value of the field, in 1997 North Somerset Council gave*
> *permission for quarrying to go ahead.*
>
> **Avon Wildlife Trust, 20th anniversary publication**

the Earth and Avon Wildlife Trust, were involved in protesting against this planning application. In their 1994 summer edition of InFoE, Bristol FoE stated that the plans meant that the "the meadow would be stripped, top soil bulldozed and the whole area gouged out into a massive, cliff-faced void, 150 metres deep. It will then never be backfilled but will be left as a gaping wound in this most beautiful of Bristol's landscapes." [141]

Pioneer Aggregates stated that they would "translocate" pieces of the land to continue to provide a habitat for the species that lived there. This, however, was a controversial move as this process had been unsuccessful in the past.

The people of the Ashton Quarry campaign began by attending council meetings in order to voice their issues with the proposed plans. The council decided in favour of Pioneer Aggregates.

A group of campaigners launched a judicial review into the decision. The court told them that "since they were merely citizens of the city they had no clear property or financial right over the area ... they did not have sufficient legal status to object to Pioneer's proposal." [142] This campaign highlights some of the political issues that environmental campaigners can face, including a lack of voice when compared to big developers and businesses.

In his paper 'Spatial Politics in Practice: The Style and Substance of Environmental Direct Action', Jon Anderson quotes a local resident who stated that:

"The on-going battle to save the Top Park field has thrown up a whole range of issues, one of which is the rights of the public in a supposedly democratic society. It would seem that the planning system and the legal system have evolved with the rights of business, landowners and developers in mind. The rights of the population seem to be of mini-mal importance." [143]

Figure 40. Ashton Court 2011

The role of the local population in decision-making is an ongoing issue in the environmental movement. The way that people often have little say in what happens to their local area can culminate in a sense of powerlessness and often anger about the fact that their views about their city are not always taken into account.

Calls for community consultation and involvement in urban planning have grown as people become more and more determined to have a say in what their local space is used for.

Whether community involvement can be truly achieved is unclear. As the campaigners discovered, 'ownership' is a key tenet of being able to determine the use of a piece of land, and communities can find themselves coming up against companies with a lot of finance and power. When it became clear to the protesters that they were not being heard, some campaigners staged a sit-in on the Ashton Court site next to the meadow. This lasted for months, and employed tactics such as tunnelling underneath the meadow, without damaging it, to try to prevent the work from taking place.[144]

The campaign came to a dramatic finish in 1999 when two of the protesters were arrested for aggravated trespass after abseiling into the quarry five minutes before a blast was scheduled. The beginning of the quarry blasting marked the end of the occupation and of the "pixie villages in the woods". The occupation cost Pioneer Aggregates £4 million in security.[145]

The rise of direct action in campaigns where people felt disempowered by local decision-making is an example of people finding innovative ways of reclaiming their voices. While direct action can involve 'civil disobedience' it does not always do so, and it can show the strength of feeling about a local, national or global decision.

Bristol Natural History Consortium

In the early 2000s many of Bristol's conservation organisations came together to promote city-wide involvement in conservation action.

In 2002, Harriet Nimmo, CEO of Wildscreen at that time, wanted to create a public face for her organisation. Wildscreen uses wildlife imagery to promote an appreciation of biodiversity and encourage wider involvement in the preservation of the natural environment. At the same time Jo Gipps, the then Director of Bristol Zoo, and Keith Scholey, Head of the Natural History Unit at the BBC at that time, were talking about how to link up the various Natural History 'goings-on' around the city.

These two conversations connected and led to the first Festival of Nature which took place in October 2003. It consisted of a three-week schedule with events held across the city. In 2004 the festival became more centralised and was indoors at L-Shed, a Harbourside warehouse.

Over the next few years an outdoor event in Millennium Square was added, followed by events at Waterfront Square and the Amphitheatre. The festival has taken place at all four locations since then, and has become one of Bristol's most popular annual events and is the biggest festival of its kind in the UK.

Alongside the development of the festival, Bristol Natural History Consortium began in 2002 as a network and space for collaboration for the different wildlife and natural history organisations across the city. To begin with there were six consortium members who were loosely bound together by a memorandum of understanding.

On May 1st 2008 they officially became registered as a charity, and there is now a steering group which consists of one member from each consortium group to discuss strategy and projects. By 2010 there were 11 members including Avon Wildlife Trust, the BBC, Bristol City Council, Bristol Zoo Gardens, the Environment Agency, DEFRA, Natural England,

Figure 41. Unnamed Bristol Resident (photo © Bristol Natural History Consortium)

the University of Bristol, the University of the West of England and Wildscreen. Their objectives are to stimulate public interest in conservation through entertaining events and innovative communication and to support research that will explore how to communicate conservation.

In 2004 the consortium added another strand to their activities in the form of the Communicate Conference, which centred on communication issues in the environmental and nature preservation sectors. This annual conference provides a space for discussion about environmental communication for those in the sustainability movement.

In 2009, BNHC piloted Bristol's first Bioblitz at Ashton Court. This was an idea which had started in the USA and aims to get a large number of people engaged with biodiversity by surveying and monitoring wildlife in a certain area over a 24-hour period.

Bioblitzs have become a good tool for public engagement with the wildlife and nature in a local area, and they emphasise the importance of scientific recording. BHNC ran another at Blaise Castle in 2010, and were also responsible for co-ordinating the National Bioblitz programme to celebrate 2010 as the International Year of Biodiversity.

2011 is going to be a busy year for BNHC as they are involved in the

Cultural Olympiad for the 2010 Olympics. They are involved in the running of a programme called 'Meet the Species', which is a series of events across the UK in the spring and summer of 2011 to discover 2,012 species in the run up to the 2012 London Olympics.

At each event experts will identify animal and plant species and 'tick' them off the list. The programme of events is designed to inspire people about their local environment and find out more about the wildlife with which we 'share our lives'.

Green space, wildlife and social justice

While Bristol is known for its high level of green space, there are issues with the quality of these spaces across the city. The 2010 Quality of Life report stated that:

> "Geographically, higher satisfaction was recorded in the more affluent leafy central suburbs. Some wards with a high proportion of open green space recorded lower satisfaction, particularly Stockwood, Avonmouth and Whitchurch Park (all 69% or below)." [146]

This disparity is probably due to a complex mix of factors including

Figure 42. Bristol Bioblitz 2011 (photo © Bristol Natural History Consortium)

levels of investment in different areas, the distribution of funding, the maintenance and treatment of the space among others. A disparity in quality of green space is an issue, because it can contribute significantly to a community in a number of ways by providing space for community activities, play space for children, the appreciation of wildlife and exercise.

While Avon Wildlife Trust's work on public engagement aims to encourage wildlife conservation, they also cite research which suggests that experience of the natural environment can aid a sense of well-being as well as helping those with mental health issues.

The Quality of Life survey says that "a high or increasing value can indicate improvements to park facilities, cleanliness and attractiveness." A park or green space that has facilities, is clean, attractive and safe is much more likely to be used by its community, and thus it is important to ensure that green space across the city is equally developed. Furthermore, social and economic issues can prevent enjoyment of the space outside of the city.

AWT suggest that people, especially children, are much less likely to experience wildlife and nature than they were 30 years ago. AWT want to make local green space in and around Bristol much more accessible to everyone within the city. Steve Micklewright, the current Director of Community Programmes, at Avon Wildlife Trust, suggests the barriers that prevent people from being able to visit the countryside are often quite simple, such as the childcare that a teenage mother needs or the transport that refugees and asylum seekers would require to get outside the city.[147]

Their heritage lottery-funded project tries to move these barriers and enable more people to visit the green space in and around the city that other people take for granted.

Bristol City Council has also launched a wildlife project, the Wild City Initiative, to include a wider proportion of Bristol's population in discovering the city's wildlife and green space. This three-year project is funded by Big Lottery and Natural England and aims to meet the needs of the most deprived urban communities in Bristol" They also want to work with a range of priority groups, including older people, young people, disabled people, people with physical and mental health issues and adults with learning difficulties.[148]

Their plan is to increase involvement with eco-teering trails, guided walks and wildlife encounters, practical conservation programmes and community river festivals, and to improve signage and accessibility. They hope that this will encourage more people to use their local green space

Figure 43. View from Perrets Park 2011

and feel more involved with both wildlife and their communities. There are seven key sites that have been identified, including the Avon New Cut and the Northern Slopes. This initiative will be officially launched late in 2011.

Friends of the New Avon Cut, or FrANC, was formally established in 2006 by local people who wanted to promote a "greater understanding and appreciation of the Cut – including its history, geology, wildlife, bridges and its role in making Bristol work".[149]

The Cut has had a significant effect on Bristol as a city. Not only did it allow the city to develop the floating harbour which allowed travel in and out of the city, it also gave the city centre a unique quality. In an article written by Richard Bland from Bristol Naturalists Society, the Cut is described as "a genuinely wild, untamed habitat, not neat, not pretty, a sharp and brilliant contrast to the human technology of the city".[150]

It is this "brilliant contrast" of an urbanised area with swathes of green space and wildlife that Bristol's people have protected. Bristol's areas of wildlife and green space provide the city with natural beauty, wildlife, 'green lungs' and havens away from bleak concrete and main roads for individuals and communities alike.

While the preservation of these areas will need to be balanced with the needs of the future, such as the development of renewable energy, housing and local amenities, it is clear that they provide many of the city's needs themselves and we need to recognise their inherent – rather than purely monetary – value.

Construction, property and urban planning

Management of the land must be primarily orientated towards three goals – health, beauty, and permanence. The fourth goal – the only one accepted by the experts – productivity, will then be attained almost as a by-product.
E. F. Schumacher

[We need] to create an environment which is really healthy for people to live in, which is really community-orientated, which is low-carbon, much more inclusive [where] everyone has the opportunity for doing things, for getting places, for meeting, for doing everything that those who are rich and mobile take for granted. Only when we really plan for those who are less mobile, don't have vehicles, can't drive . . . and those who are poorer in terms of housing, jobs . . . will we begin to think 'yeah, we're getting there'.
Hugh Barton on Sustainable Urban Planning

Developing and regenerating the city through building new homes, facilities, roads and leisure areas is an important part of improving quality of life, especially in areas that have not had much investment. Construction, however, can be an environmentally damaging process through the energy used, carbon emissions, drainage impacts and waste generated. Sustainable construction, as well as the creative reuse and redevelopment of derelict buildings, has therefore become an essential part of sustainable development.

The development of new facilities and housing, within and beyond the city confines, can also jeopardise local green space and wildlife. While this is needed, especially in areas in need of regeneration, loss of green space to new developments is a major concern. Furthermore, ensuring that all neighbourhoods have good transport links to and from their community and have local amenities like health centres, grocery shops, community centres and green space makes the city an easier and more pleasant place to live in, as well as reducing the need for car use.

As Hugh Barton suggests, sustainable urban planning is therefore needed to develop Bristol as a sustainable and resilient city for all. Clever and innovative urban planning can minimise the environmental impact while maximising social benefit.

Demand for community consultation has grown as local people note that the layout and development of a city can help or hinder the environmental and social sustainability of Bristol. The Civic Society in Bristol has worked since 1905 to preserve Bristol's historical buildings, spaces and landmarks and discourage "dull, monotonous building in the future".[151]

After the world wars, the city's landscape was in ruins. The 1950s saw a determined effort to regenerate and redevelop, but the country was economically crippled by the war. The city in the 1960s still bore the visible marks of the damage done to the beautiful architecture and houses lost in the bombings.

The Civic Society was concerned by the plans proposed by the local authorities and urban planners. They felt that "the new planning structure . . . resulted in charmless environments that replaced ones that many people remembered with affection." [152] These development plans were characterised by the drive for modernisation, and it appeared that Bristol was in danger of losing some of the landmarks, buildings and areas which made it unique and special in the eyes of its residents in favour of 'super' highways and large shopping malls modelled on the USA.

In 1980 Bristol Civic Society published *The Fight for Bristol*, which looked at the actions taken by the city's communities through the 1960s and 70s. It details how "a local community fought not only against insensitive planning but against what was increasingly seen as the undemocratic character of the planning system." [153] This documentation highlights tensions which have since characterised urban development: the different priorities and motivations of local authorities, big developers and local communities.

In the 70s, in response to plans released in 1969 which left sections of Floating Harbour available to be 'filled in' to create more land for commercial development and for roads, people in Bristol came together to show the value of this area.[154] The plans for the Harbour coincided with the proposal for the Outer Circuit road, and it was clear that areas of Bristol were under threat. The Bristol City Docks Group (BCDG) formed in the early 70s and worked alongside other community and amenity groups to ensure that the floating harbour was not lost.

Between 1974 and 1977 the Bristol City Docks Group released a series of seven reports which looked at the facilities that Bristol needed and how the Floating Harbour could fulfil these while remaining a unique and beautiful setting. The public were encouraged to get involved, and suggestions for the area were displayed at the exhibition 'Twenty Ideas For Bristol'.

Figure 44. Narrow Quay in 1960s (photo © Arnolfini Archive)

The move of the Arnolfini Art Gallery into Bush House in 1975 showed "the potential in the Docks for cultural purposes and the value of old buildings in that setting", and in 1978, showing their own commitment to the regeneration of the harbour, the council opened the Industrial Museum in another disused shed opposite Bush House.[155]

In the mid-70s the cranes outside of the Industrial Museum were being auctioned off. These cranes gave the docks a unique character and the City Docks Venture Group, whose members included John Grimshaw and George Ferguson among others, formed to generate funds and buy two of these cranes back from the scrap merchant.

There was money left from the fundraising, and in 1977 CDVG used this to found Bristol Ferry Boat Company, which still runs today. George Ferguson suggests that the ferry was "not just [a form of] sustainable transport but [a way of] sparking interest, public interest, in the possibility of the docks being a real resource for leisure, for play, for culture."[156]

While the recession played a major part in the cancelling of the plans for both the Outer Circuit Road and the changes to the docks, the local campaigners and organisations involved in the regeneration of the Harbourside had demonstrated the potential of the area culturally, socially and economically.

Figure 45. Bristol Ferry Company and the Cranes 2011

In his book about the JT Group, *A View to the Future*, Roland Adburgham cites the JT Group as vital to this regeneration, saying that "Bush House was to prove the first revival of Bristol's desolate dockland, and one of the first examples of how the arts could stimulate economic as well as social regeneration." [157]

The JT Group was founded in 1961 as an innovative construction company. John Pontin and Tim Organ had become disillusioned with their work in the building industry, and felt that the divide between 'building' and 'design' had become too apparent.

They felt that this 'divide' was damaging to the quality of the work offered to clients, and wanted to create a company which provided a 'one-stop shop' for design and build. This service would not only be good value; it would also tackle the wasteful and inefficient nature of the construction industry. JT started life in the first floor bedroom of Tim Organ's rented house; their only equipment was a phone, a ladder and van. They began with just a few hundred pounds and by the end of the first year, their turnover was £50,000.

JT Group became involved in the Harbourside regeneration through the development of Bush House, a derelict warehouse on the Waterfront. John says that when they began work on Bush House, "the building was stripped down to a shell . . . we started the new concrete frame from literally the mud just below the ground floor." [158]

Bush House became a pioneering 'mixed-use' scheme through integrating arts and commercial space to give new life to a derelict warehouse. The Arnolfini moved into the lower two floors and was made economically viable through the development of the upper four floors into offices.

JT Group went on to develop the waterfront 'E' and 'W' sheds which were mostly occupied by the Watershed Arts Trust. They also helped to give Leigh Court a new lease of life in 1992 when JT completed the purchase and renovation works on the grade II listed building in 1992.

In 2000, JT helped bring back Leigh Court's derelict Walled Garden into use in conjunction with another local charitable trust. This on-site

> *Tim and I, in August 1960, said 'why don't we start our own business. Let's design and build, let's be the architect and the builders and let's offer a one-stop-shop.' This was new thinking in those days."*
>
> **John Pontin**

Figure 46. Bush House during Renovation 1970s (photo © Arnolfini Archive)

organic garden was used for educational and demonstration purposes. This repair and regeneration has demonstrated the importance of rethinking derelict or empty buildings for modern-day use, and JT Group have developed "an imaginative concept of mixed-use sustainable developments to benefit local communities".[159]

JT Group, and John Pontin himself, have contributed to the development of sustainable construction. In 1992, John was introduced to The Natural Step, a Swedish-based environmental initiative. The Natural Step's principles of practical application of sustainability gave John an important framework to implement these principles at the core of JT's work. John attributes much of his interest in the sustainability agenda to his role as Chair of Dartington Hall Trust (1984-1997). During his time at the Trust they were responsible for the creation of Schumacher College under the direction of Satish Kumar, President of the Schumacher Society.

In 2004, John Pontin founded a not-for-profit company called Under the Sky. This social enterprise has been developed out of JT's work and John's dedicated support to issues of social, economic and environmental sustainability. John says that Under The Sky's principal objective is "to provide development expertise and assist with the transformation of neglected buildings and sites for the benefit of the community as a whole, but which are outside the normal scope of private developers, housing associations or other organisations".[160]

As mentioned earlier, derelict or empty buildings can be of great use to community groups and initiatives, and rising housing shortages suggest that we need to be continually rethinking potential new uses for local buildings rather than allowing them to stay empty.

Sustainable urban planning and regeneration

Decisions about urban planning and local development have been an issue in Bristol. In the 1980s the Concept Planning Group was developed as a partnership between three architectural companies, Bruges Tozer, Ferguson Mann and Alex French Partnership. They wanted to challenge 'standard' planning decisions around the city and to encourage planning that supported Bristol's residents, local businesses and historical architecture, rather than cars and chain stores.

One of their example sites for sustainable urban planning was Canons Marsh. The area, near the Harbourside behind the cathedral, was dominated by car parking. In the late 1980s, the Concept Planning group suggested that it could become "a focus for leisure activities, a place for the whole family to stroll, look at exhibitions, take part in sports, and to eat" (from Canons Marsh Development Leaflet).

They suggested that the site could still be used for car parking, but that this could be underground. The space could then be pedestrianised and housing, small-scale units for shops and cafés and leisure facilities could then populate the space above ground.

This development was designed so that "at least one part of the city is free from the danger, noise and smell of cars". They also wanted to give the cathedral more appropriate surroundings. Bristol Cathedral's riverside setting is unusual, and the group felt that it should be better exploited; its location as it stood was seen as "a pretty dire setting".[161] The plans were designed to encourage local entrepreneurs and businesses. The housing and small-scale units for local businesses would be combined with shops at street level and housing on the first floors. George Ferguson conducted a study which concluded that encouraging small businesses would actually bring in more revenue than chain stores, as it would keep money in Bristol.

The space remained a controversial site throughout the 1990s, as Concept Planning Group and local people challenged proposed developments on the site which threatened to dominate the space with housing and large-scale leisure units.

The site does now have underground parking, and is pedestrianised to an extent through the £90 million Bristol Millennium Project by the Concept Planning Group, also responsible for @Bristol and Wildwalk. The Group also proposed a development of the walk between Temple Meads and the city centre over Bristol Bridge. James Bruges, of Bruges Tozer Architects, took inspiration from European towns like Vittoria in Italy, and designed a pedestrianised route lined with small shops, cafés and trees known as the 'Millennium Mile'.

James suggested in his publication *Sustainability and the Bristol Urban Village Initiative*, that "the harm caused by failure to consider this site holistically will be a permanent blight on the city, particularly apparent to visitors who arrive by train." [162] It is hard to disagree when you consider that the first experience of Bristol as you leave the train station is the four exits Temple Circus Gyratory. This roundabout dominates the route with its time-consuming and stressful road crossings, and leaves little space for community space and local businesses.

The Bristol Urban Village Initiative (BUVI) was launched in 1998 and was an initiative of James Skinner. It explored the concept of an 'urban village'. This would be a people-centred development, which would implement socially mixed space (combining living, work and leisure facilities), technology and designed for environmental conservation, integrated transport systems and urban farming.

Sustainability and the Urban Village Initiative examined the ways in which urban planning affects local transport, resource use, pollution, the local economy and quality of life, as well as how the concept of an urban village could be introduced in Bristol. James identified two areas, Redcliffe and Hartcliffe, which would benefit from the ideas behind the urban village. These areas were different from one another in many respects but were both in need of regeneration.

James discusses how Keith Hallett, a Bristol architect, had become interested in the development of Redcliffe in the 1980s. He wanted to encourage the city council to help regenerate the local area to reawaken its former 'glory' and end the dominance of cars. Keith felt that a lot of this could be achieved just by allowing buildings to "expand into the excessively wide roads which at present are appropriate for lorries and hostile to pedestrians".[163] James and Keith suggested that this would encourage the local economy through providing more space for local businesses and make the space more community-minded by developing more housing.

The second area that BUVI looked at was Hartcliffe. James suggested that the area "lacks facilities that are necessary for convivial urban living". The case study suggested that the area would have to balance between keeping areas of open and green space with developing more housing, shops and other facilities.

The BUVI suggested that self-build and co-housing, and improving transport links, would develop the area's economic resilience.

James's examination of two different areas showed that looking to develop mixed-use spaces can provide a variety of benefits to an area, and that these developments should be tailor-made to tackle specific concerns, whether social, environmental or economic.

Shared space

The sustainable use of derelict buildings and the rise of mixed-use space in Bristol have shown to be amazing ways of developing resilient space for community enterprises and initiatives, as well as small businesses and ventures. As the Arnolfini demonstrated, multi-use space can make a venture more economically viable. Sharing space can also facilitate partnership, as different organisations come together. This is especially important in the environmental movement, as cross-sectoral collaboration can generate new ideas, support and different perspectives.

Keith Hallett's interest in the regeneration of Redcliffe came partly from that fact that he had co-founded two shared office spaces in the area. In 1977 Cyclebag, Avon FoE, Architecton, Artist Constructor, Hallett Pollard Hilliar (an architectural and urban planning firm) and CoExist moved into 35 King Street. It was Bristol's first serviced shared office space. The property was owned by the council, and these organisations developed the office space as well as beginning a gallery on the ground floor where they displayed architectural work, bike shows and art.

Keith remembers that it became a space for "a new way of working. . . there was cross-fertilisation – professional, visionary and even marriages and babies." [164] Wool Hall was opened in 1981 in a similar format, and both spaces are still going today.

Avon FoE were involved in several other shared spaces, including the Cameron Balloon Building in Bedminster with Children's Scrapstore and Treesaver Products (now Arboreta Papers). In the 1980s they moved to the Avon Environment Centre with Children's Scrapstore, SOFA Project, Community Recycling Network and Resourcesaver.

As mentioned previously, the end of the Avon Environment Centre marked the start of the Create Centre. As Create progressed it developed ties with local communities and encouraged partnerships between sec-

Buying the Tobacco Factory was a piece of chance really. Two young women came to me when I lived in Clifton overlooking this area. I looked down, and there was W D and HO Wills written up in the sky above these buildings. They were nearly a million square feet of grand brick build-ings and I was very fond of them. [The women] said 'there's a plan to demolish them' and to cut a very long story short . . . in a cheeky moment I made an offer to buy this site which was on the market for four hundred thousand pounds and I said 'well, I'll save you demolishing it'.

I offered them 180 and they accepted 200. So for the price of what is now a small terraced house in this area I bought this great lump of building. My reason for doing so was because I thought it was a criminal waste of a really good building but [also] because I saw it as a way to demon-strate to my clients, as an architect, that there is another way of doing things and that the more uses you mix in a building, cultural, business, recreational, the more value you bring, not just to that building, but to the area that surrounds it.

So the Tobacco Factory in the last fifteen years has become a piece of 'slow architecture'. It has demonstrated to me that sometimes it is not best just to hit these things with big expenditure. There's something to be said for feeling your way with a project so 'slow architecture', as with 'slow food', I think can be really good for the environment.

It enables us to think as we go.

George Ferguson on The Tobacco Factory

tors. We have already talked about how the centre developed, but it is important to emphasise how it began as a place for shared collaboration.

In its most recent branding the centre has dropped the capitalisation of its name to become the Create Centre. The acronym stood for the cen-tre's original aims, Community Recycling Environmental Action Training and Education, but it was also a clear nod to what the centre was doing; *creating* something new where new partnerships would grow.

The Centre for Sustainable Energy has since left, but Create is still home to Resource Futures, Lifeskills and the Sustainable City Team, and these have been joined by Alive!, Avon Gardens Trust, Bristol Fairtrade Network, BTCV, The Green Register, Pickard Garden Design, The Real Ideas Organisation, Retired and Senior Volunteers Programme,

> *We were particularly lucky that there was the Avon Environment Centre which was the converted warehouse in Brislington ... it attracted volunteers, it attracted projects, it had accommodation facilities. Campaign groups met there as well as it being a space for businesses and non-profit organisations. It was a thriving place.*
>
> **Martin Fodor, Bristol environmentalist and campaigner**

Schumacher Institute, The Travel Foundation, Voscur and City Car Club.

In the mid-90s the centre held a competition to build an Eco-home on the site. The contract was won by Bruges Tozer Architects, and it opened in 1997 as a demonstration of different environmental technologies and building techniques. The centre is still run by the council and hosts events, exhibitions and is open to the public as well as housing conference and office space.

Another organisation which we have already touched on is the Ethical Property Company, who developed on Colston Street throughout the 80s. Andy King helped UCAT's various co-ops, The Soil Association and Biashara to begin by renting them properties for a fair price. This amalgamation of third-sector organisations and sustainably-minded businesses grew on Colston Street throughout the 80s and into the 90s.

The Ethical Property Company is still going strong today, and has centres across the UK including four in Bristol. The Colston Street site remains and is home to a range of organisations including Streets Alive, *The Spark* magazine and City Car Club. Their aim is to make the best use of property for society and the environment.[165]

Bush House has also remained in the city as a mixed space development, home to the Arnolfini and with shared office space. These offices house some of the most important environmental and social organisations in Bristol including Business in the Community, The Converging World, Mowgli Foundation, Forum for the Future, Sustainability South West and the Energy Saving Trust.

Sustainable construction

Reusing and redeveloping buildings however is only part of the story. The construction industry can be wasteful and energy-intensive, and so sustainable construction has become a key phrase in recent years.

Figure 47 Create Eco-home (photo © Bristol City Council)

> *Bush House is extraordinary . . . possibly one of the best things, in development terms, that JT Design and Build have been associated with.*
>
> **John Pontin, co-founder of JT Group**

Sustainable construction minimises waste, energy use and carbon emissions as well as designing buildings that will be sustainable in the long run through fitting them with good insulation, triple-glazing, solar panels, ground-source heat pumps and other environmental technologies.

One of the co-ops that UCAT set up was Greenleaf Builders. Bill Flinn, a Bristol University graduate, volunteered for UCAT to start a 'green' building company. This eventually became a paid role. Greenleaf Builders were also based on Colston Street in the 1980s, and were one of the first of their kind in the UK.

In 2002, Bristol City Council, under Diane Bunyan's leadership, became involved in encouraging environmentally responsible building practices. The council released its own guide to sustainable construction, entitled 'Bristol Sustainable Development Guide for Construction'. The guide was designed to "assist all developers (big and small) to adopt more sustainable approaches to how they plan and build".[166]

The realisation of the need for sustainable building was also demonstrated through the development of The Green Register that started in 2000. This is a not-for-profit organisation which aims to promote sustainable building practices across all disciplines of the construction industry. The organisation relocated from London to Bristol in 2005 when the Director, Lucy Pedler, and her family moved.

The Register began because Lucy noted that the term sustainable was still on the 'sidelines' within the construction industry, and that there was a lack of information about sustainable building practices. There was, however, a thirst for independent information about sustainability. To encourage sustainable construction to become the mainstream, The Green Register (TGR) provides information, guidance and training about sustainable, low-carbon and efficient practices which are free from agendas and sponsorship.

TGR achieves its aims by running training courses across the UK. The people who attend these courses are then placed on their register of members. This register is accessible to people who are looking for professionals who are committed to sustainable building practices. TGR also provides space for networking across disciplines.

Lucy says that she "cannot overemphasise the importance of sustainability in construction", as much of the energy in the UK is used to heat, light and cool houses. Lucy suggests that the construction industry "has an enormous potential to reduce environmental degradation . . . It's not an alternative. It's not a choice. If we want to keep living the way we do . . . we have to build sustainably." [167] She feels that TGR's greatest success has been in raising awareness about the importance of sustainability within the construction industry. She notes that "every one of the thousands of people that [they] have trained goes back into their office and hopefully affects change in the wider construction community."

There are many architectural and building firms in Bristol who have become involved in sustainable building, such as Archipeleco Architects, White Design, Ferguson Mann, Bruges Tozer, Quattro Design, Greenheart Builders, Urbane Building and JT Group. Furthermore, places like the Architecture Centre and the Create Ecohome engage people and to think about how sustainable construction can benefit us, the city and the environment.

Bristol Green House, an online blog by Rik Lander, documents his own construction journey as he builds a workshop in his back garden. Rik's construction techniques demonstrate the principles of reuse, recycling and low embodied energy.[168] Rik says that:

"My inner city garden studio built from straw bales, car tyres and garden rubble is an interesting experiment in eco-building methods – not only in the use of materials, but also the use of volunteers and information sharing. As far as I know it is the first building in the UK to combine straw bale methods with 'earthship' style rammed earth tyres as well the first straw bale building with an entire wall of glass.

To build in this way I needed to do a lot of research and found that the web is full of dubious advice and unsubstantiated opinion. The website of my experiences offers a personal perspective based on actual experience. It continues to get around 1,300 visitors from all parts of the world each month. This sharing of information is important; some things worked really well, others less so. There's no need for the next person to make the same mistakes as me.

I'm pleased that some of the people that helped me are now doing their own builds and are themselves empowering the next generation of volunteers. As well as helping to keep costs down, this cycle of exchange and inspiration will aid the evolution and refinement of the building methods and ensure that these home-grown learnings will be passed on." [169]

People across the city, from organisations, businesses, council and individuals alike, are becoming involved in sustainable construction, showing that it is both a pertinent issue but also that it can be done.

Ashley Vale Action Group

In 1999 a former scaffolding yard in St Werburghs came up for sale. A community meeting was held as there were concerns that the space could be bought by a big developer. Over a dozen people attended the meeting, and they decided they should create their own plans for the space. They discussed many alternatives, but it was decided that the development of a 'self-build site' was the best option.

Ashley Vale Action Group was formed as a not-for-profit initiative and organised the purchase, the community consultation and development of the site. They were concerned with sustainable housing, community development and improving the area to benefit the local people.

In order to determine whether the self-build site was a popular and viable idea, AVAG asked local residents whether anyone would like a self-build plot. It became clear that the local community were interested, and so AVAG began work to explore the realities of this scheme and to try to secure the land.

In May 2001 AVAG managed to buy the land for the self-build plots, and named it 'The Yard'. The site was designed to contain 20 self-build plots and six housing association units. There was also a derelict 1960s office building on site, which was identified as a space for offices, art studios and a community centre.

The plots were sold with the idea that everyone would build 'sustainable' homes, and it was written into the contracts that the houses had to be built out of materials rated 'Category A' in the BREEAM Guide. The design of the houses also had to be approved by AVAG, and all local community members were welcome to have their input. This was to ensure that local residents were happy about the development, and they were encouraged to be involved at every stage of the consultation.

This self-build site is, as The Housing Minister Grant Shapps describes it as "a great example of a self-build community".[170] The community-run project shows the way sustainable construction and development can benefit people socially and economically.

Jackson Moulding, self-build homeowner at The Yard, describes the development as follows:

"There are many areas of the development that could have been done differently which would have brought different results. Some better for the self-builders and those living on site, some better for the wider community and some better for the planet. The size of some of the homes has been questioned, particularly in relation to the pre-existing Victorian terrace houses. In hindsight, the self-build homes close to the Victorian terraces could have been smaller, which may have improved the visual transition from the pre-existing homes to the new houses.

However, the plans and designs of the homes were in public access for a long time with models of the site available for all to see, and each of the designs had to be signed off by the local community group which consisted mainly of residents living in the surrounding houses. So we all need to take some responsibility for the size of the homes, including those who have since expressed their opinion believing that the self-builders got involved to build big homes to make huge profits. Only one home along Mina Road has been sold in last 10 years, which demonstrates that the majority of those that got involved wanted to live in the area, and weren't out for speculative gain.

With hindsight, some other areas which could have been done better, such as setting up a site-wide communal heating system. However, this may not have worked as well as the theory states it should and it's impossible to now know. Personally I believe more people could have installed solar thermal hot water systems to reduce their gas consumption for hot water. This would have benefited the occupiers, and would also have had a wider impact on reducing carbon emissions.

However, overall the site has evolved as it has, lots of people have learnt new skills and trades, a strong community has grown, and there is good sense of empowerment within the local area. The question is do we want to be involved in how housing is delivered or have it done for us? And if we do want to be involved, then it's not necessarily going to be an easy ride.

I'm sure if you ask anyone that has been involved with the project, they will have their own list of what works and what doesn't, and how the project could have been done differently."

In 2005, the Housing Association that owned six of the plots got into difficulty and had to get rid of some of its assets. These plots were almost sold on to a private developer but AVAG managed to buy them and build 'self-finish' units instead.

In 2009, AVAG set up a sub-group to develop the derelict building. It had the objective of creating community space and work space, but two external feasibility studies demonstrated to AVAG that renovating the whole building for work space was not financially viable. However, adding another storey to the building using a glulam timber frame structure so that six apartments could be developed enabled the project to work financially.

The ground floor was then developed into offices, workspace and community space. The six groups of individuals who bought the flats were involved in the design and formed a commonhold group with AVAG to take responsibility for the renovation and future maintenance of the building. The apartments were self-finished to the design and budget of the future occupants.

The derelict building was designed to be as environmentally sound as possible, with extra thick external wall insulation, new smaller windows and a communal heating system which consists of 2 x 26kW wood pellet

Figure 48. The Yard (photo © Bristol City Council)

burners and 27m² of solar thermal panels. Due to this, and the fact that the building was developed as a co-op, Jackson Moulding feels that it is probably the most sustainable building on site.[171]

In 2009 the renovated office building won Regen South West's Best Housing Scheme, and in 2010 the whole site gained the accolade of being first self-build project to receive a Building for Life award.

Ecomotive

As the self-build plots began to take shape, Ecomotive (a social enterprise) grew out of the project to encourage further self-build schemes across Bristol and the south-west. Ecomotive facilitated, alongside others, the creation of the National Self Build Association (NaSBA) which aims to raise the profile of self-build in central government and local authorities. NaSBA aims to show that self-build is viable and exciting way of developing community-led housing schemes.

Ecomotive aims to take the lessons and experiences gained at Ashley Vale, and explore how the process could be fast-tracked for other communities, so that they too can deliver successful and sustainable self-build plots in an affordable way.

Through input into NaSBA a number of reports have been produced, and the Government has created the Government-Industry Self-Build Working Group to look at barriers to self-build across the UK. The Housing Minister is now looking to have the number of self-build projects doubling in the UK over the next ten years.

Ecomotive have also recently set up a 'Community Build' social media platform to bring together like-minded individuals around potential land sites for self-build and community-led housing. Ecomotive and AVAG have therefore dealt with sustainable construction as well as issues of community empowerment. Self-build can deal with issues of social justice through collaborative approaches with housing associations, community land trusts and co-housing, and can create a cheaper way to get onto the 'property ladder'.

In 2010 Ecomotive was a member of a partnership, including Bristol City Council and Wessex Community Assets, which put forward a proposal for an umbrella organisation to promote community land trusts in Bristol.

A community land trust (CLT) is a non-profit, community-run organisation which develops housing or other assets at permanently affordable levels for long-term community benefit. It does this by separating the value of the building from the land that it stands on and, in the case of shared-equity homes, fixing the resale percentage. The CLT holds the asset in trust for long-term community benefit.[172]

A CLT not only provides affordable housing; it can also empower communities by allowing them to determine how the land around them is used. The model also allows people to determine the practices used to build their houses, making it a perfect way to build in an environmentally friendly way.

While this model is designed to allow people on restricted incomes to secure fairly priced housing, you may still need, at the moment, a large amount of money to attain the land in the first place as well as to fund the building. Perhaps, however, the involvement of local authorities, funding partners and others could provide ways of developing pieces of land to be guaranteed as housing and community space for people now and for future generations.

Hamilton House

The involvement of businesses can also lend a hand to the development of sustainable use of buildings. Hamilton House in Stokes Croft had lain empty for several years. When the People's Republic of Stokes Croft (PRSC) began, with the initiative of local resident Chris Chalkley, it became clear the empty buildings were not helping Stokes Croft's local economy or amenity.

Chris and the work of PRSC caught the eye of Connolly and Callaghan, the business that owned Hamilton House. They realised that by developing the building to be used as shared workspace it would contribute to the work of regenerating the local area.

The building is run by Co-Exist, a community interest company which began in order to manage the space in Hamilton House so that 'people can coexist (verb – to exist in harmony) with themselves, with each other and the environment.' [173] The building opened to tenants in 2008 and proved so popular that by June 2009 the back block was full.

Co-Exist then turned their attention to the development of the front of the block. This, however, did not develop as quickly as hoped. When The Canteen bar opened later in 2009 it acted as the catalyst, and the space is now thriving with a successful bar, shop and exhibition space.

Co-exist at Hamilton House try to respond to the needs of the local community. The success of the studio space, the shop and The Canteen demonstrate the way in which Hamilton House has managed to combine in one shared space many of the facilities that Stokes Croft needed.

Sennen Timcke, a member of the Co-exist team, notes that the ethos behind Co-exist is interesting in that the initiative deals with 'space management' but is not interested in this itself. Those at Co-exist are more interested in what shared space offers in terms of collaboration, playfulness and partnership. The initiative has grown organically, and they are still developing systems of management.[174]

It is important to remember that Hamilton House could have easily been used as something else with a sole purpose – a supermarket, a bar, standard office space or flats – but through the partnership of business and community it has managed to become something truly special which gives back to the community as well as sustaining itself.

Bristol's landscape is part of what makes the city so special. The iconic images of the Suspension Bridge, the higgledy-piggledy coloured houses on the hills, the swathes of green space, the Gorge, the Docks and the hot air balloons which float over the city every summer, all instantly evoke a sense of 'Bristol'.

We are lucky to have a city with so much green space visible on the horizon and lucky that we have so many people willing to work so hard to protect it. It is undeniable however that the city needs more housing, better transport links and more facilities. This raises an interesting tension between environmental protection and social responsibility.

There are many organisations, community groups, initiatives and people in the city who have shown that a balance between these and maintaining green space can be found. The social, environmental and economic benefits of sustainable building, retrofitting and the reuse of buildings are also clear, including the positives of cross-sectoral space, and hopefully these spaces and initiatives will continue to grow.

Thinking about the city:
top-down and bottom-up actions

*We will become a sustainable city if we're intelligent about what we know
. . . and apply what we know.*

Alastair Sawday

*If we cannot achieve a real 'meeting of the minds' with the people nearest
to us in our daily lives, our existence becomes an agony and a disaster.*

E. F. Schumacher

*I'm no more an environmentalist than anyone else. I'm just somebody who
cares about the future of Bristol, about fairness and equality and everybody
having a decent standard of living. We need to say 'let's build the future we
want'.*

Angela Raffle

Throughout the other sections of this book we have talked about the different organisations, businesses, community groups and council initiatives
which have shaped Bristol's environmental movement. It is this top-down
and bottom-up action which has enabled many things to happen in Bristol
as a wide section of the city's population share a common aim.

There is a lot of work across the city that deals with the issues of
behaviour and policy change and engages with the general public, businesses, local authorities and NGOs. The different sectors in the city, which
are working to encourage sustainable behaviour change, often come
together to work in partnership.

Bristol has a strong grassroots movement of people across the city,
from different backgrounds, working to protect and improve the city.
There are hundreds of community groups in the city, dealing with a range
of issues including social deprivation, youth engagement, women's
rights, BME inclusion, racial, sexual and social discrimination, local
regeneration and, of course, sustainability and Transition groups.

As environmental issues become more prominent, more communities
are adopting sustainable thinking alongside their other work. While we
cannot discuss all the community groups in the city who are tirelessly

working to make the city a better place, we hope to give a sense of the range of people involved.

The organisations who began small but are now national, like Sustrans, Resource Futures and CSE, have remained dedicated to sustainability issues within Bristol – encouraging local initiatives and contributing to local events, research and community work.

The council has had a vital part to play in the city's environmental movement. There are a lot of complaints about how the council deals with certain issues, and it can be frustrating to see decisions made that are not in-keeping with what is considered 'sustainable'; yet it is also evident that having a council that has incorporated concerns about sustainability into policy-making has made a positive impact on Bristol's ability, at times, to make good, sustainable decisions.

We have seen some of the many tensions within the city that result from the differing priorities of Bristol's council, communities and business people. These tensions often lead to polarisation of standpoints where compromise is hard to reach, because of the feelings of betrayal that communities can feel and the frustrations that businesses and planners face when their developments are met with opposition.

This section will look at the organisations, community groups and council initiatives that deal with both policy and behaviour change across the city. We will also discuss the importance of cross-sectoral partnership and inclusion from all areas of the city.

There has been little mention of politics specifically, but it is important to note that there are many local MPs and councillors involved in Bristol's environmental movement through supporting environmental legislation through to voicing support for local community groups and campaigns.

We are going to mention The Green Party, as they have obviously worked within Bristol with a specifically sustainable or environmental agenda. The Green Party began life in 1973 when five people founded a political group called 'People'. The party was founded as the Ecology Party in 1975 and became known as the Green Party in 1985. In 1975, they adopted the 'Manifesto for a Sustainable Society'.

J. K. Ingham stood as the first Ecology Party candidate in Bristol in 1979, gaining 1,154 votes in Bristol West. In the early 1980s an Ecology Party was founded in Bristol South by Glenn Vowles and a few others. Geoff Collard stood as the Ecology Party candidate in 1983 in Bristol South, gaining 352 votes. Since then the Green Party have had a visible presence in the city, with both candidates and members of the party speaking about local and national environmental issues.

Glenn Vowles became the first Green to sit on a council committee in Bristol for 2000-2001. In 2005, Bristol South Greens saved their election deposit for this first time with Charlie Boulton as the candidate in the general election. In 2006, Charlie was the first Green elected to Bristol City Council, as councillor for Southville Ward.

In 2011 Bristol has two Green Party Councillors: Tess Green in Southville and Gus Hoyt in Ashley, meaning that the party now have a visible presence in both the north and the south of the city. Tess Green feels that the importance of the Green Party in Bristol is quite simply that they take environmental issues into the political realm and push for sustainable change: Green Party politicians and councillors can take environmental issues straight to the decision-makers. Without this ability, change at a national and local level will be slow to happen.

Tess says that there are not as many people in Bristol involved in the Green Party as you would expect, and that people shy away from political involvement and have become disillusioned with party politics and the lack of community voice, especially in local planning. The role and position of councillors is often confused with that of MPs, which means that after the recent expenses scandal people can be wary and mistrustful of anyone connected with politics.

The Green Party in Bristol is keen for more people, especially younger people, to become involved with local politics and show that councillors from all parties are trying to make the city and their local communities a better place.

Local political parties can lend their support to environmental campaigns, much as Bristol Green Party has done with the campaign to protect the Bristol to Bath Railway Path from the Bus Rapid Transport Plans. They have also condemned the plans for the W4B biofuel plant.

Tess also notes that it is somewhat of a fallacy that middle-class people are the most concerned about the environment. She says that while canvassing she meets people from all walks of life and backgrounds who support the Green Party.

Bristol FoE

Bristol Friends of the Earth have played a pivotal role in Bristol's environmental policy and behaviour change within the city. Throughout the 1990s, as we have mentioned, Bristol FoE continued to campaign for local and national sustainable decision-making.

They were influential in encouraging the council to become more involved with environmental issues, and were involved in the development of the Green Charter which Bristol City Council released in the early 1990s.

Their work to protect the Severn Estuary was only one of their more recent campaigns. They have also become involved with local food issues, transport, campaigning against the airport expansion and the W4B bio-fuel plant in Avonmouth. They ran a campaign against the transportation of nuclear waste through Bristol.

Their work is incredibly varied, but often responds to local and national issues as they arise. The group do this through lobbying, attending council meetings concerning decisions that may affect Bristol's sustainability and organising awareness-raising events, discussions and practical actions.

Lobbying and examining local policy and planning are not Bristol FoE's only way of raising awareness and challenging 'unsustainable' decisions. During their campaign against the Ikea store some volunteers ran a small recycled furniture shop nearby to show the alternatives to the superstore.

Jane Stevenson, the Bristol FoE Co-ordinator from 2006 to 2011, notes that FoE is a useful group because it allows people to contribute even in the smallest way. Fundraising, involvement in campaigns and signing petitions all add to their overall effectiveness. She also notes that recently it has become more popular to work in alliances with other like-minded organisations.

It used to be that if you were an environmentalist then you belonged to either Friends of the Earth or Greenpeace, but the recent proliferation of sustainability groups and the Transition movement means that groups have formed in specific communities in the city. It means that people are more spread out, which make partnerships vital.[175]

Greenpeace Bristol

Greenpeace are also active within Bristol. Greenpeace Bristol is linked with Bristol Permaculture Group, Transition Bristol and local students. They were also involved in the beginnings of the Organic Food Festival. Historically the actions of Greenpeace have been characterised by non-violent direct action, and Bristol's Greenpeace group has co-ordinated many protests.

In 2006 Greenpeace Bristol protested at the city's largest McDonald's to highlight the environmental issues of soya. Soya is fed to much of our livestock but is often grown on deforested land in the Amazon.

Protesters, dressed as chickens, chained themselves to chairs at McDonald's to highlight this problem.

Greenpeace Bristol, like Bristol FoE, do not restrict themselves to any one issue, choosing to get involved with protests and campaigns for all aspects of environmental issues including Trident, the extraction of oil from tar sands and the protection of the rainforest.

Both organisations, locally, nationally and globally, empower people to get involved in determining decisions about the environment, and thus our future, and encourage people to take an active role in talking to local authorities, national government and decision-makers.

Project Agora

Project Agora is a small charity which seeks to encourage people, particularly faith communities, to take an active role in citizenship. Chris Sunderland began Agora through teaching notions of 'citizenship' to school pupils by using storytelling with themes such as success, power and trust.

Over the last six years Project Agora has become increasingly involved in local environmental issues, and they have encouraged faith communities to become active in the sustainability movement. Chris also started Earth Abbey, which is a space for people of faith who have a spiritual interest in the environment.

Both Agora and Earth Abbey are involved in local food issues, and are keen to explore the ways a renewed relationship with the land can help a wide range of people to become better involved in community life as well as improve their well-being.

Project Agora is responsible for a recent project in Barton Hill called The Walled Garden. It works with several other growing projects from across the area, including the Asylum Seekers Allotment Project, to develop a space to grow local food for generations to come. As many people in Barton Hill live in tower blocks, the garden also provides space for those who have nowhere to enjoy the benefits of growing food.

The Walled Garden is based at a former vicarage, now licensed by the church to Agora, to develop as a community garden. The project works to encourage community integration as it brings many different local groups together.

Transition Bristol

The Transition Movement was a powerful impetus for the growth of specifically local environmental groups. It was founded in 2006 in the light of growing concerns about peak oil, climate change and environmental degradation.

The Transition Movement links with the 'prepare for change' mentality as it concentrates on developing resilient communities which share and celebrate the move towards a more sustainable society.

The earliest Transition Towns were in Kinsale in Ireland and Totnes in Devon. Rob Hopkins had been inspired to start the movement when he was running a permaculture course in Kinsale. He showed the film 'The End of Suburbia' to his students and invited the peak oil expert Colin Campbell, who lived nearby, to talk to them about peak oil. He then worked with his students on an 'energy descent plan' which detailed how a community could move to a low-carbon economy. This developed into the Transition Town concept, which has proved popular with people concerned about the environment and looking for a different way of life.

In 2006, Sarah Pugh attended a talk by Rob Hopkins discussing the Transition Movement. Sarah had been working with permaculture for several years, and was inspired by the concept. She and a few others set up a one-day event in St Werburghs which hosted around 20 workshops including talks on peak oil and permaculture. By the end of January of 2007 there were several people interested in what 'Transition' would mean for Bristol, and a steering group was developed. They began by encouraging local groups to take part in Transition activities through holding events like tree-planting days, workshops about energy descent plans, film-showing, exhibitions about sustainability and other awareness-raising and networking activities.

In June 2007 Transition Bristol formally registered as a Limited Liability Company, and a year of events culminated in The Big Event which took place at the Council House in November 2007. The Big Event asked 'Can you imagine Bristol after oil?', and had a range of speakers, workshops, films, open space and a bookshop in order to unleash "the collective genius of the community".

Rob Hopkins attended, and spoke about the progression of the Transition Movement since its beginnings in 2006.[176] Bristol became the UK's first 'Transition city', and so encouraged other cities to do the same.[177]

Ciaran Mundy, one of the current directors, suggests that since The Big Event, Transition Bristol has been less about promoting the various envi-

Figure 49. The Big Event 2007 Council House (photo © Transition Bristol)

ronmental issues and more about "bringing together a lot of people who are already doing amazing work . . . the knowledge and creativity is out there, especially in Bristol which is full of amazingly capable people." [178]

Angela Raffle, another director of Transition Bristol, also suggests that the Transition movement is about the opportunities to create a better future for Bristol, rather than campaigning against things.

In 2011 Transition Bristol has a massive network across the city. There are official Transition groups in Barton Hill and Redfield, Bishopston and Horfield, Easton, Hotwells and Cliftonwood, Henbury, Knowle, Montpelier, St Werburghs and Westbury-upon-Trym. The network is also linked to other sustainability groups and activities in the city, and encourages different events across the city.

Ciaran says that Transition Bristol "don't have a controlling influence over the activities, we just try and support and bring people together and do some signposting to ensure that the 'wheel isn't constantly reinvented'."

She touches on an interesting issue here. The number and diversity of environmental groups within the city is a blessing but, at times, can be a problem. The incredible energy and dedication of people in Bristol is admirable, and we have been impressed time and time again by the variety of hard-working people in the city. However, it has been suggested that at times there is not enough communication and collaboration between groups. For instance, groups with similar aims can find themselves holding similar events or fighting for the same funding. In order to make sure that work is not repeated, it seems as though we need to promote an 'Act Neighbourhood, Think City' mentality within Bristol itself.

The rise of the Transition Movement in Bristol followed on from an increasing number of community groups who had already begun to engage with sustainability. There were already examples of community work that was tackling environmental concerns while developing social cohesion or social equity.

As we have seen with Hartcliffe Health and Environment Action Group, there have been people working to improve the quality of life and standard of the environment within their area since the early 1990s.

In 1999, a group of people was concerned with the levels of unemployment, especially for young adults, in Knowle West. This group of Knowle West residents came together to cook shared breakfasts and invite unemployed people to join them. They were then asked if they would like to do some community work. This marked the beginning of Re:work, and the group started a formal programme where people were encouraged to take part in volunteering projects including regeneration, gardening, furniture restoration, retail and construction.

This project has steadily grown, and people are now referred to them by schools and colleges. While part of the benefit of this project is the training, activities and community benefit the work provides, eating together is still a big part of the initiative. Mary Smith and Rose Manning, two of the original founder members, have gone on to be awarded OBEs for their community work in the area.

Community development is an important part of creating local sustainability and resilience and many groups have noted this. In 1991, the Southville Centre opened as a community building for the local people and home to the Southville Community Development Association. The centre aims to encourage financial, environmental and social wealth for the local area. They worked steadily to improve the Greater Bedminster area throughout the 1990s. In 2000 the centre was awarded £4,000 through Bristol City Council's Sustainable Neighbourhood Fund. The council had £1 million to give to local communities to enable local social and environmental action.

The Southville Centre used this grant to develop the Southville and Bedminster Community Resources Bank, which would lend pieces of equipment, including a camera, display boards, laminating machine etc

> We've put in half a dozen or so metal benches in different parts of the area and we see that as a public service but also as an aid to encourage people to use local shops rather than jump into a car and drive somewhere else. Somewhere to sit down and be in a community space seemed to us to be to be quite important.
>
> **Ben Barker**

so that community groups did not have to spend their limited funds on items they may only use once.

The Sustainable Southville project started in 2002 and built on the work of the Green Team which had been around for a few years. An audit consultation with SCDA and The Southville Centre made it apparent that the local community were increasingly concerned about environmental issues. Mo Mulligan, a member of the Western Partnership for Sustainable Development, conducted this audit and became involved in Sustainable Southville Project (SSP).

The group began by looking at the area's recycling facilities, and created a cycling map to encourage sustainable transport. They wanted to improve the quality of life for local residents through looking at environmental and social sustainability. The group also became involved in the Local Exchange and Trading System (LETS), which allows a trade of skills, items and expertise without the need for money. This was especially useful for people on restricted incomes. The group also developed a green guide for the local area which listed 24 sustainable actions as well as a directory of local businesses and organisations. A green map for the area also contained listings as well as walks, cycle routes, green spaces and public transport.

SSP, like many neighbourhood initiatives, is made up of small working parties that focus on different aspects of the local environment, including energy, waste management, green space and transport. It has spawned many other initiatives such as Dame Emily Park Group, Friends of the New Avon Cut and The Patchwork Group, who improve small run-down patches of green space. The group also secured funding for more benches to make shopping easier for older people. SSP have also published, through the Neighbourhood Partnership, a 'toilets and benches map' which shows the benches in the area as well as places where the owners of the buildings have said people can go and use the bathroom facilities without purchasing something.

Ben Barker suggests that all of these initiatives are to do with "people being part of their community and being able to use their community – and that seems to us to be a very important part of sustainability." Community groups, environmental and others, often provide a support network as well as encouraging development of the local area.

In 2005, another neighbourhood sustainability group began. Hamish Wills, who lived in Redland, found himself asking "why isn't anyone doing anything about all these environmental issues?" He realised, however, that he should be doing something himself. He delivered a letter to 400 houses in Redland, asking "Is anybody else feeling like me?".

From the respondents, Hamish organised a meeting that around 12 people attended. Their first activity was simply to write on post-it notes what was worrying them and what they would like to see change. It became clear that people felt confused as to whether personal lifestyle change made any difference, and they were overwhelmed by advice and information in the media. They also discussed whether there would be any merit in forming a group and ultimately decided that having a group to discuss these kinds of issues, their thoughts and perspectives was important and so Sustainable Redland was formed.

They had a copy of Sustainable Southville's guide, which helped them see what another community in Bristol was doing, but like Southville they were concerned about the specific issues and opportunities for change within their own neighbourhood.

The group discussed and researched all the issues that had been worrying and bothering them. They invited people to come and talk to them about personal lifestyle change such as car use, energy consumption and recycling, and they started a popular local farmer's market. They aimed to build links with local businesses, and have developed a good relationship with their local MP, Stephen Williams. SusRed have also collaborated with other groups such as Sustainable Westbury-on-Trym and are connected to the Bristol University Sustainability Team.

Street Parties and film nights have proved successful in bringing the community together and spreading information. In 2010 the group organised a walk from Redland to Hartcliffe through Redcliffe. Angela Raffle, a member of SusRed and director of Transition Bristol, says that "walking through the city can generate a sense of 'place' and belonging in Bristol which can be lost when everyone travels by car." [179]

SusRed have started a number of practical initiatives. These include a CRAG (Carbon Reduction Action Group) where they shared their quarterly energy figures, which was run for two years. They set up a gardener's club for those interested in local growing, and they have installed solar water heating in at least 20 households – helped by a group purchase deal. They have planted 99 apple trees as part of the Transition Fruit Trees project, joined in with the Metford Road Community Orchard, and become actively involved in their local Neighbourhood Partnership.

SusRed have also been involved in helping set up The Community Farm in the Chew Valley. Dave Hunter, a member of SusRed, is chair of the Community Farm board and has worked on the legal structures for the farm. The Community Farm is a not-for-profit community supported agriculture project (CSA). Local people were invited to become members through buying shares of the farm. Members then volunteer and receive discounted produce from the farm. Angela Raffle, who is on the steering group of the community farm, says that "400 people believed it was an investment in the future. Just going out there and volunteering is the sort of thing you cannot put a value on."

These community groups have, with or without planning, developed a holistic sense of the sustainability issues within their area. As well as encouraging sustainability as a whole, these groups appear to create a support network for those involved, which allows them to respond rapidly to specific issues within their areas, such as HHEAG's work on food or Sustainable Southville's work on local transport.

During the course of the Bristol's Green Roots project we held a community workshop where we invited people from different groups across the city to come and discuss the role of community work in Bristol's environmental movement. We discussed the positives and drawbacks of the community led initiatives with people from different community groups across the city.*

One thing that became clear was that they felt that these groups offer a level of involvement and hold tacit knowledge that outside organisations or the council will not have. Community groups are formed with the people from that local neighbourhood, and so know the needs and perspectives of a particular area.

Those at the community workshop also noted that the innovative and imaginative nature of community work is a fantastic resource for Bristol and stems from the fact that community groups bring together a range of different people who really want to be involved.

---

* There were 15 people in attendance from Bristol Ecoshow, Eastside Roots, Bristol Friends of the Earth, Sustainable Southville, Sustainable Westbury-on-Trym as well as those had taken part in community work across the city and had no affiliation to one specific group.

The participants also suggested that community work is more democratic than business-led or council-led initiatives, as it grows from grassroots action, and that community groups may be more trustworthy in the eyes of the public as there is a lot of mistrust of large corporations trying to become involved in the environmental movement. The involvement of community groups in city-wide initiatives could help more people feel that their concerns were being heard.

However, the group raised some issues. They suggested that at times community work can be dominated by 'self-selected voices' as certain people are more likely to become involved and those who are more assertive, established or confident can, often not beneficially, dominate the discussions and the action that takes place. They also spoke of the rivalry that can stem from community groups doing the same thing, which is not conducive to partnership, especially when you note that they all have similar aims.

The group suggested that city-wide problems need city-wide strategies, and often community groups do not have the resources for that kind of work. Community group work provides a local support network and brings imagination, freedom and dynamism to Bristol environmental movement, but we need city-wide structures to support and link up this work.

We have already seen the beginnings of this. Bristol Energy Network responded to a need for city-wide links, realising that there was not enough communication between the different community groups in the city.

These kinds of networks can also work with local organisations, businesses, NGOs, the council and, recently, the Green Capital Partnership which we will discuss shortly. This again shows the recognition of the importance of partnership and collaboration for city-wide action. Community, organisations, businesses and the council all have a role to play, as all have their own strengths and vulnerabilities.

One hope for the future, referring back to issues of representation, which those at the workshop expressed emphatically, was that a wider proportion of Bristol's population need to be engaged. Those at the workshop expressed their concerns that the majority of environmental action, discussion and involvement that takes place in Bristol can be limited in terms of representation of minority groups.

Community engagement offers huge opportunities for sustainability thinking in Bristol to encompass the perspectives of everyone who lives in the city, but efforts must be made to make that inclusion happen.

This is hard. Community consultation and engagement can be used in a huge range of ways, including in the discussion of urban planning and

> *We use different words for the same thing and we spend a lot of time fighting over that language, instead of saying 'actually language isn't important. It's the outcome.'*
>
> **Darren Hall, Bristol Green Partnership**

decision-making about local services. There are issues, however, about what constitutes community engagement – just because it is being used does not mean that a wide representation of people will necessarily have their views heard or appreciated. True community consultation means looking to involve the hard-to-reach households and developing meetings that everybody, no matter what their mobility, work schedule or childcare situation is, can attend.

Of course, not all people will want to be involved in community consultation, but there are people in Bristol from all backgrounds who are keen to have their say in how the city, and their local area, is developed.

The number of people who have attended council meetings, discussed local decisions on online forums and formed local community groups show only a few of the many ways that Bristol's residents try to get involved in neighbourhood and city-wide sustainable choices and decisions for Bristol.

There is no one easy answer on how to achieve community consultation which includes the widest possible representation in the city, but responding to local needs and perspectives seems like an obvious first step for developing Bristol's fairness and resilience for the whole population.

The Schumacher Society

Bristol has a number of 'think-tanks' or groups which encourage change through engagement with all sectors of society including communities, businesses and the council. They provide research activities, lectures, talks and workshops.

Ernst Friedrich (Fritz) Schumacher died in 1977. He was an eminent economist and a radical thinker concerned with the way our systems dehumanise people and destroy the very environment on which they depend. He was the author of the famous book *Small is Beautiful*, a title phrase that has entered into the lexicon of environmentalism.

The Dr E. F. Schumacher Society was formed in 1978. It objectives are to build on his work and through public education to promote the ideas of others who share his holistic thinking about the nature of our social and environmental problems. Known commonly as The Schumacher Society UK, it organised its first Bristol Lecture in the year after his death, at which the keynote speakers were Ivan Illich, the radical social critic and author of *Deschooling Society*, and R. D. Laing, the controversial psychologist. These two names set the style of Schumacher Lectures in the city: radical, and unafraid of taboo subjects.

There has been a Schumacher Lecture in Bristol every year since. They have brought world-renowned people in the environmental and social movements to the city and drawn in audiences of up to 500 people for a full day of lectures and workshops. Speakers have included Lester Brown, Wangari Maathi, Arne Naess, Anita Roddick, Vandana Shiva, Fritjof Capra, James Lovelock and Amory Lovins, and many other influential thinkers and 'do-ers' have joined them.

In 1991, under the presidency of Satish Kumar, the Society was involved in setting up Schumacher College in Dartington. In 2005 the Schumacher Society, led by Richard St George, formed an independent research organisation known as the Schumacher Institute for Sustainable Systems. The Institute is now well established, conducting research at the highest level and offering its own MSc course in Managing Sustainability and Uncertainty.

Figure 50. Satish Kumar speaking at a Schumacher Lecture
(photo © Schumacher Society UK)

Forum for the Future

Forum for the Future, a non-profit organisation working with business and government, originally began in London in 1996. The founder members were Jonathon Porritt CBE, Sara Parkin OBE and Paul Ekins.

FFTF primarily focuses on three areas which underpin our lives and prospects for sustainability – food, finance and energy – but it also works on issues in other areas such as health, transport and ICT. By working with different organisations, NGOs, businesses and the government, FFTF brings together different specialities and experiences to try to adapt these areas to protect them from sustainability issues such as climate change and resource depletion.

In 2007, when they decided to develop an 'example city' for sustainability, Forum for the Future chose to set up a second office in Bristol. In 2008 they launched their sustainable city region initiative which was "an ambitious 10-year programme to help make the greater Bristol area the most sustainable city-region in the UK".[180] This looked to make housing more energy-efficient; help organisations cut their carbon emissions; reduce dependency on private cars; encourage local food; and raise awareness of sustainability.

While FFTF is a now a global organisation with a new office in New York, their Sustainable Bristol programme has added a level of support to the local area. They work with local authorities, decision-makers, businesses and organisations to try to create an understanding and visible example of what a sustainability city will look like and what it needs to contain. Paul Rainger, Head of Sustainable Bristol City-Region Project, suggests that "the battle for sustainability will be won or lost in our cities. By 2050, seven out of ten people on the planet will be urban dwellers. Bristol's ambitions to become a leading European Green Capital is an important showcase for how we will can live and work together in new ways in those eco-cities of the future." [181]

Sustainability South West

Sustainability South West is an independent charity that encourages sustainable behaviour change within the city and the south-west region. The organisation began in 1998 to create a regional forum to accelerate the development of sustainable action. Its roots lie in a New Labour Initiative that tried to make sure that regional decisions were in line with sustainable development. This led to the foundation of Regional Round Tables, which were forums for the discussion and encouragement of sustainability between different sectors of the city.

This initiative, however, had no core team. It was decided that there was a need for work to be done between these forums, and so Leslie Watson was employed as the Director for Sustainability South West. The first task was to produce a framework for regional sustainable development through consultation. This framework contained a vision for sustainability as well as a set of principles and themes important to the region.

SSW are an independent body and now offer guidance for key sustainability decisions in the area as well as developing projects where they feel that things are not moving quickly enough. They have started projects on sustainable construction, tourism in the south-west and packaging. They advise local authorities, and their SusNav programme provides guidance to any organisation or group that want to move toward a more sustainable way of working.

BETS and Low Carbon South West

On April 27th 2006, Bristol City Council invited people to an evening event at Explore-At-Bristol to "help inform the development of the Bristol Environmental Technologies & Services Sector". The aim was to raise the profile of the sector and promote its growth. This was an area that the council had recognised was nascent, offering many opportunities but probably needing some support.

By September 2006 a small group of people drawn from business, the council, the universities and various other bodies met to continue this initiative and create an informal partnership board. This initiative was called Bristol Environmental Technology Sector (BETS).

Bristol City Council gave much support in time and resources led by Robin McDowell, and BETS soon found a chairperson in the shape of the businessman Richard Hogg – a longstanding champion of environmental issues. Over the next few years BETS pressed on with many areas, looking at skills, eco-technology parks, encouraging collaboration, and commenting on strategies and policy in the Bristol region. It organised many events to share knowledge, and put on trade exhibitions like the Sustainable Business in Practice Expo in July 2009.

The intention for BETS was to become a trade association: membership was free, and by January 2007 over 300 companies had joined. Following the tragically early death of Richard Hogg in late 2007, the chairmanship passed to Alan Bailey of ABS Renewables and Rob Enticott of Sustainability Solutions Ltd., both of whom had had a long association with environmental businesses in the city.

By April 2010, with membership rising, plans to incorporate BETS properly as a community interest company were well under way. It was a good time to consider merging with a similar network called Low Carbon South West, a brand developed by the University of Bath. Initial funding came from the local authorities, with membership remaining free until April 2011.

Low Carbon South West (LCSW) is active in such enterprises as setting up a renewable heating grid at Avonmouth. It aims to be the largest environmental technology sector (ETS) trade association in the country. A trade show is planned for October 2011 with more than 200 stands for exhibitors. Amy Robinson, LCSW Network Director, says: "We want to create a resilient low-carbon business community. . . we want to make low-carbon business the only way to do business." [182]

Business in the Community

Business in the Community is a business-led charity that brings together a network of businesses who are concerned with social, economic and environmental responsibility and sustainability. They work locally, nationally and internationally to "advise, support and challenge [their] members to create a sustainable future for people and the planet and to improve business performance." [183]

The charity began in London in the 1980s after there were riots in communities across the capital. Business leaders began to realise that they had a role to play in community regeneration and cohesion, and had a responsibility to their their local communities. BITC began life with a handful of business members. Over the next 10 years they grew by organising a network of enterprise agencies across the UK for those who were interested in being involved in community development.

Their agenda developed into wider concerns of corporate social responsibility. They continued to look to contribute to the regeneration of deprived communities, but began to look at workplace issues including diversity, health and well-being, skills training as well as environmental responsibility and responsible business practice in the marketplace. BITC therefore seeks to show the benefits that responsible business practice can bring and to develop a solid and reliable view of what a responsible business looks like.

The Bristol office has been here since 1985, and works to better both

Bristol's business practice and the opportunities for people in the city. The Bristol office has an education programme which includes a specific strand to match Black and Minority Ethnic (BME) students with BME business people to encourage aspirations. They also run a successful employment programme which helps homeless people to find jobs through a 'back to work' scheme which includes training, mentoring and support. These programmes are run with the support of their business members, and aim to encourage their members and other businesses to see the benefits that responsible and sustainable business practice brings, both to their business and the city.

BITC also run an environmental programme called 'Mayday', a collaboration of businesses who share advice and solutions to the environmental challenges we face and try to support, inspire and challenge one another. BITC see that engaging with environmental sustainability is a way in which businesses can become more resilient in the face of future problems.

Local authorities and sustainable development

Bristol's early involvement with Local Agenda 21 (LA21) meant that many council-led initiatives included thinking about sustainable development in city-wide policy making throughout the 1990s and 2000s. A series of working groups were developed to push sustainable development in all areas including food, biodiversity, waste, transport and energy.

In October 1999 BCC launched the Sustainable Neighbourhood Fund which was run by Wendy Emmett from within the Sustainable City Team. These grants came at a time when Bristol City Council was engaging heavily with sustainability issues, especially through LA21 strategies. The fund had £1 million to be awarded to voluntary or community organisations that were looking at social, environmental or economic sustainability in their local communities.

In 2002 *The Guardian* ran a piece on Bristol's involvement in sustainable development and quoted Diane Bunyan, leader of the council at the time, as citing this fund as an important way to "carry the benefits of sustainability into communities, particularly the most needy . . . the sustainable neighbourhood fund [is] weighted towards projects in the most deprived areas." [184]

The Bristol Partnership

The Bristol Partnership is another initiative which has linked together environmental and social concerns as well as cross-sectoral collaboration to try and develop Bristol into a better place to live.

The Partnership is a Local Strategic Partnership (LSP) that started in the early 2000s as the result of a drive by central government for developing local partnerships for regeneration. The Partnership links agencies or organisations from business, the public sector, community, voluntary sector and higher and further education in order to develop Bristol into a more 'successful city'. It responds to local concerns, but is also determined by central government initiatives and targets.

In 2003 the Partnership developed Bristol's first 'Community Strategy', which examined ways to improve the social, economic and environmental well-being of Bristol. This 68-page document detailed five aims: Achieving lifelong learning, Building a thriving economy, Strengthening local communities, Promoting health and well-being, and Investing in a sustainable environment.

The Bristol Partnership's more recent 20:20 plan, developed in 2009, aims to put Bristol in the top 20 cities in Europe in 10 years by making our prosperity sustainable, reducing health and wealth inequalities, developing strong and safe communities, and raising the aspirations and achievements of our children, young people and families. The Partnership's Community Strategy contributed to a more recent initiative dealing specifically with Bristol's aim to be a 'green capital'.

Bristol Green Capital Partnership
and Momentum Group

In 2003 The Bristol Partnership published their 'Community Strategy 2003' which contained a vision entitled 'Bristol: a green capital in Europe – creating sustainable communities and improving the quality of life.' [185]

Dr Jo Gipps from Bristol Zoo saw this vision, and organised a conference at the zoo about a 'green Bristol'. At this time there was also a series of World Cafés at Bristol University organised by Professor Vala Ragnasdottir at which people discussed possible ways of stimulating sustainable behaviour.

Bristol, of course, already had a number of influential and involved environmental organisations. Bristol City Council had also become steadily more involved, and had become the only organisation based in

Bristol (and one of the few councils in the UK) to take part in the voluntary Eco-Management Audit System.

The notion of Bristol becoming a 'green capital' was powerful. At the initial meeting it was decided that there should be a launch event. Some of the various environmental initiatives across the city came together at a 'Green Capital' launch on the 2nd March 2007 to pledge their dedication to making Bristol a 'Green Capital'.

The first organisations to sign up for the launch were: Bristol City Council, Knowle West Media Centre, Environment Agency, Cater Business Park, Bristol Primary Care Trust, Luckwell Primary School, University of Bristol, Bart Spices, DAS, Safer Bristol (which no longer exists) and The Care Forum. The Soil Association, Sustrans, Project Agora, Colliers CRE and Bordeaux Quay also signed up at the launch.

The first official meeting was in June 2007, and coincidentally in August 2007 the EU launched the Green Capital Award. Bristol's Green Capital Group, therefore, was set up before the drive to have Bristol recognised as an 'official' Green Capital. Their aim is to encourage the collaboration of the private, public and voluntary sectors across the city and the initiative is supported by the Bristol Partnership.

After the launch, some funding was found through the council and Catherine Bailhache was employed as the Green Capital co-ordinator within the Sustainable City Team at the Create Centre. Alex Minshull and Steve Marriott were also (and continue to be) involved.

During the time that Catherine was the co-ordinator, the group went from having 12 pledgees to 90, and Daniel Oliver, another member of the Sustainable City team, organised many business events which stimulated interest and involvement with the sustainability movement in Bristol.

In September 2007, Alastair Sawday and Dan Green were elected as Chair and Vice-Chair, respectively, of this Green Capital Momentum Group. Alastair and Dan provided leadership from outside the council and worked closely with Catherine to create an effective partnership between Bristol's organisations and the council.

The Bristol Green Capital Partnership is run through the council and the Momentum Group is made up of representatives from some of the organisations, initiatives and community groups who have pledged to support the aims of the Green Capital Partnership. The Green Capital pledge states that those who sign it will help make Bristol "a low-carbon city with a high quality of life" and that they will "develop and deliver an action plan, regularly report progress publicly and work with others to make a real difference".[186]

Figure 51. The signing of the Bristol Green Capital Pledge. Left to right: Gene Joyner (Bart Spices), Helen Gunn (DAS), Professor David Clarke (Deputy Vice Chancellor, University of Bristol), Cllr Barbara Janke (Leader of Bristol City Council), Miles Ford (KWMC), Jim Flory (Environment Agency), Emily Stokes (KWMC).
Photo © Bristol City Council

The idea of public, private and voluntary sector collaboration was to stimulate discussion and action to make Bristol a low-carbon city. The obvious differences in approach and mindset between the public and private sectors could be viewed as a hindrance to progress, but Mark Leach (Green Capital co-ordinator 2008-2010) believes that it has added value through the three sectors working together in order to become "greater than the sum of their parts." [187]

In 2010 the Community Challenge Fund was created to fund community-led initiatives to help them further Bristol as a Green Capital. The fund both recognises the hard work that Bristol's communities do as well as contributes to this action by making money available. The fund was piloted with awards to four projects to generate interest. When the fund processes were finalised, the panel convened in August 2010 to award half of the annual budget of £75,000, and they have met biannually since. To be eligible the projects have to be community-led and align with the Green Capital Partnership's vision.

The Momentum Group holds regular meetings to discuss issues which affect Bristol's development as a low-carbon city. The regular contributors provide continuity to the discussions, and occasional attenders can add fresh perspectives.

The Green Capital Partnership and Momentum Group were also influential in both the *Peak Oil* report as well as *Who Feeds Bristol? A Resilient Food Plan for Bristol.* Darren Hall, the current manager of the partnership, suggests that ultimately the partnership aims to make Bristol a "city that lives up to the idea of one planet living . . . a city that doesn't take more that it gives".[188] By mixing the energy and ideas of grassroots action in the city with the expertise, structure and funding that the council and business sector can provide, the partnership has developed a support network for those who want to do something about the environmental issues we face.

Darren also suggests that "we are at a moment of choice. We can learn from the banking crisis and say 'let's not go back there. Let's look forward to a [model] that's not oil-based, that's not consumer-based' . . . we need to be talking about a well-being model."

Sustainable economies

The recent economic crisis in 2008 has shown that we may not always be able to rely on money or economic growth to keep us going. Bristol people have tried to make the city more resilient to financial failure. Informal trading of skills and goods has taken place alongside the money system for centuries – but at a low level. These ideas have had a recent revival through fears of economic instability.

Throughout the 1990s, Bristol's communities developed a more formal scheme for this called a Local Exchange Trading System (LETS). A LETS is a way through which a community (whether it be a neighbourhood or a whole city) can trade skills, services or goods without the use of the local economy. It can be likened to a barter system, but is not always a direct swap.

The scheme develops a form of alternative currency, which can be exchanged using an agreed hourly rate for work done. Not only does the model allow the sharing and exchanging of skills and time but it also creates community ties between people and groups. In the 1990s Bristol had several local LETS schemes including ones in Bishopston, St Werburghs and Southville. Local groups including Bristol Friends of the Earth became involved, as did people such as Phil Haughton and John Dawson (founder of *The Spark*). Bishopston LETS became Ashely LETS, encompassing members in Montpelier, Bishopston and St Werburghs.

As a LETS currency is tied to the local area it means that the exchanges stay within the region and develop local community ties as well as providing people with a model to enable them access to services and work without having to rely on money. This is especially useful for people on restricted incomes but can prove a useful tool for everyone in the current economic climate.

The LETS scheme in the 1990s in Bristol went from strength to strength as groups publicised their work at local events, developed ties between groups and applied for funding. In 1999, three LETS groups in the south of Bristol (Totterdown & Knowle, Southville and Hotwells) set up the LETSwork South Development Project with funding from the Sustainable Neighbourhood Fund. They encouraged the involvement of socially excluded people such as older people, young people, ethnic minorities and disabled people.[189]

A network called Interlets was also developed with funding from Bristol City Council with the aim of linking the LETS groups in Bristol. Their work continued throughout the 2000s but at a quieter level, and Interlets suffered a cutback in funding. In 2010, however, Southville and Ashley LETS merged to form Bristol LETS, an online service for the city's LETS members.

The recent relaunch of Bristol LETS as a city-wide scheme shows the importance and validity of the idea for a city that wants to encourage economic as well as social and environmental sustainability. The scheme not only provides an alternative to money exchange but also promotes local services, goods and skills. The scheme also relies on goodwill, trust, sharing and it values all contributions – whether it be plumbing, dog-walking or massage – at the same rate, as all are needed.

Informal schemes provide incredible local resilience, but there is a need for larger frameworks of sustainable economic thinking. Bristol is the home of the UK branch of Triodos Bank, which opened in 1995. Triodos is a bank which only finances enterprises that have social or environmental benefit. They were founded in 1980 as a move away from standard 'banking' to a model which manages money sustainably. Triodos works with organic food and farming, renewable energy, social housing and fair trade ventures, and demonstrates that investment does not have to be at the expense of people or the planet.

Another scheme which has recently been launched to develop Bristol's economic resilience and sustainability is the Bristol Pound. This initiative, developed through Transition Bristol, supported by the Green Capital Momentum group and following on from similar schemes in Brixton and Totnes, is again looking to enable a move away from the dominant economy to a more community-minded model which promotes local resilience. The concept was proposed by Chris Sunderland of Agora Project at the Transition Bristol Money and Economics Forum in 2009. The Bristol Green Capital Partnership supported the idea, and a feasibility study of the concept was done in 2010.

Ciaran Mundy, one of the scheme's directors, says that the main aim is simply "to keep money locked into the Bristol economy. . . we need to build local businesses and the connections between them and the way to do this is to have a local regional currency for Bristol." [190]

The scheme is non-profit, and is a Community Interest Company. It was developed and is run by a mix of people, including James Berry from Bristol Credit Union, Ciaran Mundy, Director of Transition Bristol, Chris Sunderland, Director of Agora, Stephen Clarke, a solicitor, David Hunter, a consultant lawyer, Mark Burton, a lecturer at Bristol University in social equity and economic resilience and Owen Davis, an ex-Friends of the Earth Communications Director and IT and marketing expert.

The initiative states that "the Bristol pound will be spent very like pounds sterling and is backed pound for pound by sterling deposits. However it is different to sterling in that the money will typically be accepted only within the region so will continue to be spent in the region. Bristol Pounds are purchased for sterling and then can be spent with other trader members in the region." [191]

The scheme will use paper notes which will have imagery celebrating Bristol's cultural history, as well as introduce a new mobile phone text system as a form of payment.[192] Those behind the scheme anticipate that "many people will simply prefer to use Bristol or Bath pounds because they will tap into the strong sense of identity people have, enhancing their sense of belonging to their home town. In addition, many will enjoy the positive role they are playing in helping improve and maintain a vibrant local economy." [193]

The pound will be launched in 2011 to not only create a resilient local economy but also build better community and independent business relationships as well as relationships between businesses. It is hoped it will also reduce pollution from supply chains by developing a strong local network and reducing social inequity by developing local economies in neighbourhoods as well as the whole city. While these may seem like ambitious targets, it is clear that people are in the mood for change when it comes to our economy and similar schemes elsewhere in the UK have been well-received and supported by organisations like the New Economics Foundation.[194]

The sustainability movement's call for a move away from the modern economic system is also visible in a call for a concentration on well-being, rather than using economic growth as a measure of 'success'.

This concentration on well-being and 'happiness' has become more popular, perhaps most visible in the recent attempts by the coalition government to emphasise the development of a 'Happiness Index' to measure the nation's satisfaction and overall happiness with their lives. This can also be linked in with the work done by the authors of *The Spirit Level*, a study which showed that a wide inequality between the affluent and the deprived is damaging to everyone, and that a model of consumerism is not what ultimately makes people happy.

An initiative in Bristol has tapped into these issues of encouraging well-being and happiness and combined them with engaging people with sustainability. In 2009, Mike and Liz Zeidler founded The Happy City Initiative to develop a sustainable culture centred on positivity, happiness, community and relationships rather than on consumption, fear and bad news.

Mike and Liz decided that they could utilise their 15 years' experience in the public and private sectors. They thought that the action of bringing people together under the notion of happiness would work well as a community engagement tool, because 'being happy' is something with which everyone identifies and aspires to achieve. Another positive aspect of identifying 'happiness' as a unifying element is to rid the environmental movement of the negative connotations it has such as frugality, 'going without', and pessimism about a future with no resources or energy.

Through the concept of 'happiness' Mike and Liz wanted to discover what matters to people, and from this create ways of genuinely appealing to and getting through to people in order to encourage sustainable modes of living. The Happy City Initiative employs a method called appreciative inquiry which focuses people away from blame and fear towards solutions and positivity. They do this through a mix of events, communication campaigns and an online community hub. They say that the events are designed to encourage people to "explore their visions of a happier community, discover the things that are already happening to increase happiness in their neighbourhoods, enable and inspire each other to come together to support and cultivate success to build happiness." [195] The online hub is a place where people can develop networks for support, inspiration and resources for their projects and share experiences, contacts and knowledge.

> *The contrast between the material success and the social failure of many rich countries is an important signpost. It suggests that, if we are to gain further improvements in the real quality of life, we need to shift attention from material standards and economic growth to ways of improving the psychological and social well-being of whole societies.*
>
> **from *The Spirit Level: Why Equality is Better for Everyone*
> by Richard Wilkinson and Kate Pickett**

Rather than talk to people solely about the environment, the HI team discuss many issues with Bristol's communities, but concerns about environmental issues do often arise in these conversations. Mike Zeidler says that it is important to make people feel that there are other people out there who feel the same so that people do not feel alone, and to remind Bristol's communities that the solutions are out there. We have to link up with others and discuss the various issues that we are facing together.

Mike feels that Bristol is a positive city, and that there are many fantastic initiatives going on across the whole of the city ranging from community-driven campaigns to work done by the council.

Lifestyle, leisure, learning and play

We want to briefly continue to discuss well-being and give a flavour of the different things that happen across the city which demonstrate the rise of demand for sustainably-minded activities, facilities and spaces in Bristol.

The *Guide to Good Living* published in 2010 by Sawdays Publishing details these comprehensively, and so we just want to indicate the different areas in which sustainability has become a foundation for the development of businesses and facilities within the city.

The city also has a variety of places to shop, eat, play and learn that are concerned with sustainable issues. For eating, drinking and relaxing we have The Harbourside on the Waterfront and The Canteen in Stokes Croft. We also have publications which engage with the 'green' and sustainable goings-on in the city such as *Venue*, *The Spark* and the online 'green scene' Ecojam.

The success of *The Spark* Magazine and Ecojam shows a strong demand for information about environmental and social issues, campaigns, local events, community opportunities and jobs in the local area.

Figure 52. Easton Road Show (photo © Happy City Initiative)

The Spark's history began with the Avon Health Directory in 1990, a publication which featured listings for local alternative, complementary and traditional health practitioners. John Dawson, the instigator of the directory, felt that Bristol needed a more regular publication that highlighted these issues and so *The Spark* was born in May 1993 as a quarterly magazine. Their summer 2011 edition marked their 18th birthday.

The Spark is a magazine which promotes positive change through showing different activities across the south-west that people can get involved in. They state that they "cover a whole range of ideas, activities and behaviours that make up personal, social and global change for the better. We're pro-green, pro-bike and pro-gress." They printed 10,000 copies of the first magazine. They now print 34,000 copies every quarter. Their growth has been an organic process, and they distribute the magazine themselves.

Darryl Bullock, who now runs the magazine, suggests that this gives them a unique contact with their readership and distribution points. They take the magazine to places where they know it will be read and appreciated.

This free publication has remained popular with its readership: the BBC said that *The Spark* was "at the heart of the alternative West country". The rise of the internet has meant that they have found it harder to secure adverts but they are responding to this through developing their online presence. The fact that they are a niche publication also helps as their main advertisers know their readership will appreciate their products.

The magazine has recently taken over the distribution of *Bristol – A Guide to Good Living* (a Sawday's publication), and in light of their 18th celebration, Darryl aims to make sure that the Spark continues for many years to come.

Ecojam.org is an online portal for green and ethical living in Bristol. The website aims to connect green activity in the city, get more people involved, and promote the work of local green businesses, organisations and initiatives. The site allows people to keep up-to-date with the latest local environmental and community news, discover and give away unwanted household items, and find job and volunteer opportunities. A visitor can also search the directory for businesses selling more sustainable products and services, and for organisations and community groups based in Bristol.

Ecojam was officially launched in November 2008 by Matt Fortnam, a researcher at the University of Bristol. He and his colleagues had run 'Sustainability Cafés' throughout 2006 and 2007 that provided a forum for academics, entrepreneurs, educators, community and voluntary organisa-tions and local government to discuss how to create a sustainable Bristol. Over 300 people took part in the Cafés, which led to the formation of the Bristol Sustainability Network. As mentioned during the discussion of the Green Capital Partnership, these cafés contributed to the development of the vision of Bristol as a 'green capital'. The Bristol Sustainability Network also enabled different people working on different issues in Bristol to come together and find opportunities for collaboration.

Matt realised that there was a real need to join up what was already happening in the city and get more people involved. With this in mind, Ecojam was designed to be inclusive. Matt suggests: "You don't have to be a 'diehard green' to use Ecojam. Some want to discuss how to make Bristol sustainable, but others want to volunteer for a charity, avoid sending their unwanted items to landfill, or go to a food festival." [196]

With 5,000 members, Ecojam could be the largest green community in Bristol. These members add all the content on Ecojam; 340 events were posted in the last year, in addition to over 200 jobs. As Ecojam's con-cept has worked well, the team behind it have ambitious plans for the future. They want to redevelop the site to improve the user experience and fully integrate online green communications in Bristol. The site will integrate fea-tures from popular social network and online sites such as Facebook, Twitter, Flickr and YouTube to enable Ecojam's members to continue to interact through discussion as well as imagery and film.

The original features of the site – events posting, jobs adverts and news – remain, and the team aim to promote these further afield through social networking sites like Twitter and Facebook to ensure that they are reaching as many people as possible. Ecojam is also looking for people who would like to replicate Ecojam Bristol's success in their towns and cities to form a UK-wide network of local green portals.

Bristol also has a whole host of annual events which engage with envi-ronmental issues. We have already mentioned the Festival of Nature and The Organic Food Festival, but the city has many street fairs in local areas across the city every year. One of these is the Best of Bedminster Show which began in 2006. Climate Action Bedminster developed out of the Sustainable Southville Project and was founded as a separate group. This group felt that the many things happening across the Greater Bedminster area needed to be signposted to demonstrate the different low-carbon activities in which local people could take part.

Jim O'Shaughnessy and Emily Stokes (then Nicholson) discussed the idea of a 'Best of Bedminster' show. They felt that this kind of event could enable local businesses, community groups and organisations to display the amazing variety of things already going on in the area rather than 'telling people what to do'. It was hoped that this would then encourage people to take part in more low-carbon activities as well as encourage and help the local economy.

The fair took place on North Street in the heart of Southville and Bedminster and incorporates traditional 'Best of' shows, but also has stalls for organisations like City Car Club and Sustrans. In 2010, they had a Local Traders Tent for businesses and community groups to publicise themselves.

Sustainable Westbury-on-Trym (SusWot) have also discovered the benefits of local events. During the Eco-Fiesta that they organised in Westbury-on-Trym in 2009 they closed down the local main road to create a space for this community fair.

The Fiesta was based on four themes; energy, waste and recycling, transport and green spaces. The mix of stalls and children's entertainment aimed to encourage both having fun and sustainable living. A bike-powered smoothie maker showed an innovative way to use less energy, and the Fiesta's 'pledge-tree' invited people to make pledges such as 'switch to a green electricity supplier' and 'grow some veg'. Another Ecofiesta was held in 2010, and the popularity of closing the road to cars means that SusWot are working with a local councillor to look into part-pedestrianising the space.

By bringing together the local community to celebrate all that is good in an area, fairs, street parties and events provide a perfect way of encouraging people to share skills, talk and help one another. These events lend themselves well to Transition and sustainability groups which are trying to develop local resilience and community spirit.

Sustainable thinking also has a place in learning and education. Bristol's organisations and initiatives have often run training courses and advice centres, such as UCAT's demonstration house on Philip Street. Shift Bristol, launched in 2010, offers people in Bristol specific training courses in preparation for a low-carbon, post-oil, creative, dynamic and community-centred future, including permaculture, alternative energy, green building and group dynamics to aid decision-making.[197] Sarah Pugh, a director of Shift Bristol, was involved with the beginnings of Transition Bristol and notes that people have a huge desire to get involved with sustainability issues but often lack the skills to do so.[198] Shift Bristol offers training to enable people to be able to do the things they want as well as work better with others.

Open Platform (OP) is another programme that helps people discover new skills and new ideas. OP is a community enterprise and was originally developed through The Schumacher Institute. It is now a separate entity.

Tim Barker, a member of the OP committee, says that the initiative "exists to help people build the ethical career they seek and to support them in their efforts to turn great ideas into reality. The group holds discussions, practical activities and presentations from outside speakers. It provides a network of like-minded individuals for support, idea sharing and collaboration." [199] This popular programme has become its own community of people who share ideas, advice and food. It has proved especially useful at a time when many young people are coming out of universities and colleges and are faced with high levels of unemployment.

Knowle West Media Centre (KWMC) is a registered charity and arts organisation based in South Bristol. It helps people engage with and benefit from digital technologies and the arts, and aims to develop and support cultural, social and economic regeneration. KWMC runs a variety of groups, projects and activities for young people, giving them the opportunity to learn valuable technical and creative skills and use digital media, including photography, filmmaking and music to express themselves.

The origins of the organisation date back to an arts and health photography project run by Carolyn Hassan (now the KWMC Director) at the Knowle West Health Association in 1996. The success of the first project inspired another one for over 200 young people and linked media arts to community development. Further projects followed, and the decision was taken to unite them as the Knowle West Media Project.

KWMC was formally constituted as an independent charity and registered organisation in June 2002. Since then KWMC's work has developed and expanded to include design, filmmaking, music production, journalism, photography, website design and related media activities.

In 2008 local residents and young people were involved in designing a new building for the organisation. Young people, members of the Archimedia Project, were heavily involved in the discussions about design and were keen for the new building to be environmentally friendly and sustainable. The building is now one of the largest straw-bale buildings in the south-west, and has solar panels, rainwater to flush the toilets and a vegetable patch.

KWMC is based in Knowle West, an estate in South Bristol which has great community spirit but ranks highly in statistics for poverty, unemployment, mental and physical health problems and educational underachievement. KWMC takes a grassroots approach and supports residents to improve their quality of life, publicise local successes and give young people access to new and exciting opportunities.

During the course of the Bristol's Green Roots project we ran three workshops with the young people of Digital Fish (film-making group) and discussed Bristol's history of environmental achievements and action. They then made their own short filmed piece about what they wanted Bristol to look like in 50 years' time. These are some of the perspectives from the workshops and their filmed piece:

I think it is important to know about your city's history because you can learn a lot about the past and then improve on any mistakes that have been made and make sure you don't do it again.

Michael Summers

It is important that Bristol is sustainable because we need a future for everyone. . . We would like everyone to live life to the full and get what we have now because you might not think it but we are actually very privileged in what we have. We need to keep that going and maybe make it even better for the future generation.

Emily Butler

I believe that it is very important to know about the past of my city because it's a reference to go back to and learn from. . . it's very important to know about your history so you can prepare yourself for the future.

James Wall

In the future I'd like to see Bristol a lot more sustainable with local produce, for it to be greener, for there to be more recycling because a lot of the stuff you have to take to the supermarket to recycle and not everybody can take it there, people using more public transport so there are less CO_2 emissions. From this project I have learnt that other people feel the same sort of way, they care about Bristol's future.

Chloe Shiner, Digital Fish

2011 and onwards: the future of Bristol

What does it hold and where can it go?

You never change things by fighting the existing reality. To change something, build a new model that makes the existing model obsolete.
Buckminster Fuller

To talk about the future is useful only if it leads to action now.
E. F. Schumacher

The most successful campaigns, organisations and initiatives in Bristol have been the ones that have demonstrated the positives of change by making the changes themselves.

Sustrans wanted new cycle paths. They made them, and people used them. Avon Friends of the Earth wanted Bristol to recycle, so they collected Bristol's recyclable waste. AVAG did not want a big new development within their community, and so determined the use of the space themselves.

We cannot guess what will happen 10, 20 or 50 years from now. We know that people in Bristol will work hard to make the city a better place for themselves, their children and the people they love and, a lot of the time, for people they do not even know. We also know that there are people working quietly and tirelessly in Bristol who do not get the recognition they deserve.

We know that things will change as energy, especially oil, becomes less available and more expensive. Whether we see this now as an opportunity to change our economy, our models of living and ways of thinking or wait until it is a catastrophe, is down to us. We know that there are a lot of people already trying to seize this inevitability as an opportunity and shift towards a low-carbon, community-orientated, well-being-focused model of living.

What we do not know is whether this dedication, passion and hard work will make changes that will make the city 'sustainable'. It certainly will not be due to a lack of trying.

Something which became clear during this project is that people felt that perhaps Bristol's environmental movement was a 'whole that was less than the sum of the parts'.* There is no denying that Bristol has a vast wealth of people, communities, organisations, initiatives and businesses working towards making their work, lives and local areas more sustainable. This passion and dedication, however, has not always made as much change as could have been hoped for.

Whether this is because of lack of authority support, lack of public uptake, lack of funding or lack of joined-up thinking is not easy to determine. All seem to play a part and, generally, those interviewed throughout the project have been both pleased with the advances that Bristol has made but frustrated by the fact that Bristol can be a 'graveyard for ambition'.

There is still a long way to go. We are not as far along the path as many European cities, and according to Forum for the Future's Index, other UK cities are overtaking us. We need to make sure that different projects across the city are not too disparate and we are not constantly 'reinventing the wheel'.

Those at the Bristol's Green Roots community workshop also noted that rivalry and competition need to be kept in check. While competition helps progress and improve work, it can also prevent collaboration.

Blame is also a dangerous game. It is easy to get stuck in dichotomies of blame and praise, and easy conclusions like: community led = good and corporate = bad. These judgements can lead to divisions, tensions and mistrust, which actually holds back change.

The participants at our community workshop also discussed the great potential that business involvement in sustainability can have, in terms of funding, support, publicity and the development of markets for sustainable goods. Having said this, sustainability needs to be taken as integral part of business and our economy. and not just an add-on.

Partnership is a word that gets used a lot as a proposed tool for decision-making and encouraging sustainable development across the city. It is clear that partnerships do provide space for organisations, community groups and the council alike to develop initiatives which can tackle big concerns like transport, energy and food.

---

* Jeff Bishop, community engagement consultant, used this term specifically, and many other people alluded to this.

We need the decision-makers in the city to make some difficult decisions, and people in the city need to have more say in these decisions. Schemes like the Freebus and the examples of community energy projects show how people can take back the organisation of public services for the benefit of the community.

The rethinking of our priorities is going to be an important aspect of this. Darren Hall, manager of Green Capital, spoke of his concern that "we were still veering towards a growth model rather than a well-being mode". While economic security is important, it is clear that unregulated economic growth and obsession with money is not good for the planet or for us. If you put the well-being, health and equality of people first, the protection of the environment follows closely.

These conclusions are all easy to say and perhaps overly simplistic, especially with the differing priorities, boundaries and targets that exist across the city. Ultimately, as is clear from the organisations, initiatives, community groups and the people we have quoted and spoken to, all that can be done is to try to make the changes wanted by showing their viability and the benefits that will accrue from them.

We want to leave the rest of this section for the perspectives and thoughts of a few of the people we have spoken to. We realise that there are many more perspectives in the city, and that these are just a few of them. We hope that other projects will continue to document the voices and opinions of the people of Bristol and further contribute to the rich dialogue that, with the help of so many Bristolians, we have been able to present in this book.

Is Bristol on its way to becoming a sustainable city?

I'm not sure if any city is on its way to becoming a sustainable city at the moment. It's really hard to know what that looks like. I don't know anybody who's really got a convincing answer. It's definitely going to be a co-creation of a lot of different people. I think the first step is recognizing the real challenges of surviving and thriving with a lot less energy – and if we can do that in a celebratory way, all the better. But at the moment I think the idea of 'what a city is' is going have to change a lot before we really start to understand what a sustainable way to live in cities is going to look like.

Ciaran Mundy, Director of Transition Bristol and member of Transition Montpelier

I think Bristol's got a long way to go to become a sustainable city. I think it is too easy to think that because we talk about Bristol being a 'green city' [and] our ambitions to be a 'green capital' that therefore we are somewhere near it. I think we are a million miles away from being a sustainable city. I believe that Bristol has great natural advantages and we should build on those natural advantages, but to be a 'green city' we need to have more independent local business, we need to fight back against the big chains, multiples and internationals that have taken over an awful lot of the trade and business in this city. It is a radical movement that needs to make those changes.

George Ferguson, Architect and Social Entrepreneur

It has some real hurdles to get over but I can't imagine that all this effort ultimately will be wasted. I think eventually it will bear fruit rather than just being disparate projects all over the city . . . but [Bristol] clearly dodges, keeps dodging, some big issues. It keeps backing off from making good green decisions . . . it's probably too complacent for its own good but it is quite a commercial city, there's quite a lot of private money here. I think if – if – people see the green vision as the way to make money, Bristol will get into gear quite clearly, as it seems to be doing in the renewable energy field.

Richard St George, Renewable Energy Consultant and former Director of Schumacher Society

I wish I could say yes. I suspect it's going the other way . . . one of the reasons that kicked Sustainable Southville off was a concern about the traffic, the deluge of cars – not just locally, but also coming in as commuters and so on. The situation is worse now than it was. So until we start to crack that particular one, the best we can claim is that we've slowed the development down, but I'm not even sure if that's true. . . . I guess that there is a lot more talk about doing the right thing, not yet enough walking of the right thing, but having a strong voluntary sector is good. Having people at least saying the right thing is a start. It's not easy because often short-term advantages are grasped rather than long-term implications because that's just so much easier.

Ben Barker, Southville Community Development Association and Sustainable Southville Project

The future is very unpredictable. I think that the only thing that we can be sure of is that the next 20-30 years are going to be quite different from the last 10-30 years. Quite often what happens in those situations is, some people have been saying 'look at these pressures we need to change in this way and that way' and everybody else has said 'we don't even like thinking about that'. It takes some kind of a shock, it could be an economic shock, it could be an extreme climate event, and then everybody will go 'where were all those plans you were drawing up?' So I don't know quite how we will get there, but at the moment we are not sustainable at all.

Angela Raffle, Director of Transition Bristol and member of Sustainable Redland

I think that Bristol has got a long way to go before it can claim to be a truly sustainable city, let alone one of the greenest cities in Europe. The transportation system is really so poor – in green terms – this is just one example of the lack of serious green credentials. We [also] need to make progress on a plan to give Bristol food security and resilience against future shocks. Food could be one of the litmus tests of how we could justify such a claim. This could find expression in many different ways, including much more food growing in the green spaces of inner Bristol such as the parks and gardens.

Patrick Holden, former Director of the Soil Association

Bristol is on its way to becoming an environmental city, but it has got a long way to go. There is a huge amount of motivation and fantastic abilities, skills and knowledge here, but getting everybody to understand why it is really important to get behind it is going be key to making it happen here.

Amy Robinson, Network Director of Low Carbon South West

In truth it's still got a long way to go, but then any city in the developed world has got this problem. There are some particular challenges around transport and transport links, and I think some of the problems related to transport are difficult for Bristol to deal with on its own, so it needs to work and indeed is working with the neighbouring authorities. I think it is going to be very challenging in the light of the public expenditure cuts at the moment, and I am very anxious about the impact that those cuts will have on the voluntary and community sector which I think are the seed bed for many new ideas. Bristol is fortunate that it has a number of local entrepreneurs who are very sustainably minded and have over a number of years supported initiatives in the city, but there is still a long way to go in really galvanising the whole of the private sector to look at business being more sustainable. Having said that, there are lots of green shoots, if you look at what's happening south of the river at the Tobacco Factory and in Stokes Croft. There are a number of things that are moving in the right direction, but it will require substantial leadership and imagination as to how to co-ordinate all the various initiatives and activities to make sure that effort is focussed and doesn't become very fragmented with initiatives working against each other. That's always going to be a challenge when you've got lots of different people doing lots of different things.

Jane Stephenson, involved with Avon FoE, Resourcesaver and The Recycling Consortium, and Chief Executive of Resource Futures

I don't think that Bristol is particularly on its way to becoming a sustainable city, I think there are a lot of very interesting small initiatives going on in the cracks and crevices and the fringes and the edges, but my overall feeling would be that they're not even stemming the tide, let alone reversing it. As exciting as the food projects are, it's a tiny percentage of the population that is involved and a tiny percentage of the land area. If there was to be a significant shift just in desire or the will to do stuff, people would soon come up against the amount of land that is available and the amount of people who are skilled and experienced enough to coordinate or facilitate it. A lot of the good agricultural land that remains is under threat from property development, which is often council-backed. There are a whole bunch of smallholdings in the city that could be used in a much more socially and environmentally positive way, but seem to be pretty much off the radar. There would probably need to be quite a big economic depression to get any real change.

Tim Lawrence, Community Vegetable Grower

That's a fascinating question because there are so many signs that it is. We've got vast ambition to be a Green Capital City, there are huge numbers of good green organisations in the city and for the first time ever I think, we now have a city administration that's deeply sympathetic. We will become a sustainable city if we're intelligent about what we know and apply what we know. We won't if people insist on following the current, the old economic model. So, will it? If I would put money on it I will say that it will become green-er, but unless something major happens in the next couple of years it will probably never be green enough.

**Alastair Sawday, Founder of Avon FoE
and Chair of Sawdays Publishing**

Right now, no! It's got all kinds of good intentions and there are plenty of people working towards it and aspiring towards it. There are individual projects which are very good but if you look at it strategically, if you look at the whole of Bristol, Bristol as a city-region, Yate is in a sense part of Bristol, Thornbury is part of Bristol, the little villages out there, in the north and the south down to the Mendips are a part of Bristol in the social and systemic sense, so you've got to look at the whole thing and is the whole thing going in the right direction, right now? No. Over so many generations Bristol has been going, effectively, in the wrong direction. So we've got to look at it in a different way and take it much more seriously than we have been able to so far. Words are almost a waste of time, it's action that counts and we haven't had the real strong action.

**Hugh Barton, Founder member of UCAT, Professor of Planning,
Health and Sustainability at UWE**

That's a good question. Is Bristol on its way. . . yes, I think it is on its way. But I'm starting to hear lots of stuff about growing our way out of the problems we've got at the moment. And that's not the answer. I honestly believe that if Bristol adopts a strategy that says we're going to grow our way back to success, then Bristol has got it wrong. And we're at a moment of choice right now, in learning from the banking crisis and saying let's not go back to that, let's look forward to a proposition which is workable, that's not oil-based, that's not consumer-based. We need to be talking about a well-being model. So I think Bristol is right at the point in time when it can choose and there's a real danger we're going with the growth model. We need to go the other way. So ask me again in a year's time.

Darren Hall, Manager of Green Capital Partnership

Bristol's doing a lot of work to become a sustainable city across the board. On sustainable food issues we have strengths and weaknesses, strengths and vulnerabilities. And we've got some great building blocks to really make use of – and value – but we've got some big challenges. So if you look at how we might make Bristol a sustainable food city we would need to look at production, processing, distribution, retail, catering, food waste . . . so it's a big question. But I do think we have a lot of very aware people here in this city. We've had some great reports, and what we now need is a clear plan and really good leadership which enables the people with ideas, and who are already doing stuff, to get as much support as they can. And for the city planners and decision-makers to understand what a fantastic opportunity putting food at the heart of the sustainability plans actually is – because it impacts on health, environment and the economy. It's right there at the heart of making Bristol a really green city.

**Joy Carey, Freelance Consultant
and primary author of 'Who Feeds Bristol?' report**

Do you know I think that's a really difficult question, I think that Bristol's got a lot of really interesting initiatives in it, but if we talk about a sustainable city as one that, shall we say, you can draw a line around it and you're not buying in gas and you're not buying in oil, of course it's not. It's a city that uses and consumes a vast amount, and in the field of transport it hasn't really made any strides at all. The streets are clogged, they're clogged with stationary cars and moving cars – it would be quite correct that if somebody came down from Mars and looked at Bristol they would see it as a city that is run and managed and built for cars and people are just some sort of little robots servicing them. . . . I fear it's going to take gigantic shocks and huge fuel shortages or something of that sort to really bring about change. I mean there are places in the city where the council have done wonderful things: Queen's Square where the old A42 Wales road has been removed and from outside the Cathedral too, but these are tiny compared with the scale of the problem. All of us have seen far too many plans for traffic and public transport just come and go, and we don't seem to have either the public will or the style of management of a city state to make radical changes.

**John Grimshaw, Civil Engineer, Founder Member of Cyclebag,
and former CEO of Sustrans**

I feel very hopeful most of the time. There are times when I feel much less optimistic about the city, and Friday afternoon at 3.30 is probably a low point. If you ever try to get into the city centre then it just feels like a great big car park. My own personal feeling about what Bristol needs is a mayor. Having lived in London for most of my life and having seen the benefits of having a mayor, I think Bristol needs that. Bristol needs a dedicated, strong, rather belligerent leader to effect change. Because what happens in Bristol is, you get all these lovely grassroots ideas and then they stop somewhere. There is this invisible barrier to make real change in the city.

Lucy Pedler, Director of The Green Register

It's a difficult journey, and there are still many obstacles to be overcome and I think that although we're blessed with a large number of people who have this vision of Bristol being a sustainable city and largely understand the direction in which we need to move – we have supportive politicians, we have supportive businesses, and we have a good mass of community organisations that are all working towards that end – we still have problems and we still have by and large a business community that sees sustainability as an add-on if you like. . . it's still only a minority that are taking a broader view of what the sustainable future of the city must look like.

Mike Birkin, South West campaigner with Friends of the Earth

There are indeed a lot of challenges in Bristol . . . we've got a lot more to do with transport, we've got a lot more to do with some of the inequalities in the city. Bristol is known as a city committed to environmental activism and social action and grass roots projects . . . we have immense grass roots local activism around local food, waste and resource reuse, cutting waste and recycling. There are so many community energy projects, it's amazing. There are lots of positive signs of hope, but at the same time we've got this immense battle of stuff that needs sorting out, all this old housing stock that is still not refurbished and renovated and saving enough energy. We've still got far too much traffic and congestion; it's probably only the recession that's reduced levels of traffic and pollution. I don't think the amount of traffic can keep going up forever, so let's hope some of those things will actually be dealt with, and there are some very positive signs of sustainable energy initiatives at the local level in neighbourhoods, not just on individual houses but collaborative solutions, which are going to bring more sustainable energy to the city and that's pretty fundamental to tackling the carbon footprint and dealing with peak oil, which is so urgently needed.

Martin Fodor, Bristol environmentalist and campaigner

What are your hopes for the future of Bristol?

I would love to see market gardens again in and around Bristol . . . there is some fantastic, high quality agricultural land very close to the city as you go up the M32. I think in the future the UK has to take very seriously increasing domestic production of fruits and vegetables. And that is something that the government are saying. So just that particular angle is one part of making Bristol a more sustainable food city. But I would love to see more people growing food . . . market gardens, community orchards, commercial orchards and horticultural units. And [that] the city actually supports those businesses to make them viable. And I'd love to see more diversity of retail outlets. So more local food shops, more markets, more people, more festivals. We've already got great stuff going on. More people engaged and a more down-to-earth Bristol food culture . . . I think that would work really well for Bristol.

Joy Carey

I hope Bristol's going to become a very green city. I hope that the current administration grasps the nettle, bites all the bullets and makes itself politically unpopular in the short term to do what Bristol needs. We need decentralised energy systems, we need a radically overhauled public transport system, we need to totally abandon Bristol's domination by the motor car, we need to focus much more on well-being, not at the expense possibly of economic well-being but we need to focus on it more. We need to jump off the economic-growth-for-its-own-sake bandwagon which means finding an alternative economic model, which is a big ask but I think there are a lot of models all over the world where there are other cities that are doing a lot better than we are, I mean all over northern Europe for example and southern Europe, there are cities who are way ahead of us so we've got a lot of people showing us the way. I hope that Bristol will learn from its European partners and from its own green citizens. I hope Bristol will be a green city – it's a faint hope, but it's glowing brightly enough for me to follow it.

Alastair Sawday

I would hope that it would continue developing its waste and recycling initiatives. I would like to see it moving much more to looking at waste prevention and to giving good sound advice to local business . . . getting the right sort of energy supply for the city is going to be challenging, and we keep coming back to transport. I would hope that transport will rise up the list of priorities. I would hope that the city would continue to have a thriving voluntary and community sector that will continue to have an influence on policy and direction at a local government level . . . I would like to think that Bristol will continue to be at the forefront, but we're obviously faced with a lot of cuts at the moment and it is going to be very challenging to balance the sustainability initiatives against social services and education and other council services which clearly also need to have a priority.

Jane Stephenson

I hope that it will become more sustainable . . . as simple as that. [Bristol] needs to have a transport system which is public rather that private, which is low on consumption of fuels and low production of toxic gases and so on . . . our dependence on oil seems to me to be one of the key questions for us in the future, and we'll either crack it and we'll become a prosperous and sustainable city or we won't and we'll gradually degenerate into a big traffic jam which won't be pleasant to live in.

Ben Barker

My hopes for the future of Bristol are that it's a much more connected up city, that it's much more aware of its resources, both its natural and its cultural resources – and bringing those to bear on creating a sustainable, good life for the people who live here. [Bristol] has an amazing range of physical attributes and the surrounding land as well and the city's hinterland, which could enable this city to really be a shining example for many other parts of the developed world.

Ciaran Mundy

I would hope that we can create the future that we would like to step into. That we could redesign food systems, so that they can not only provide us with sustainable supplies of food but we can increase our personal involvement with growing the food and [creating] relationships with the farmers and growers who produce it. This would be transformative to the city's health. I think the potential for enhancing the quality of life in a time of recession and austerity is enormous.

Patrick Holden

I hope that the future of Bristol is a place where my grandchildren can really look back and say that this generation made a difference and made it one of the best places in the world to live. That needs really strong, determined leadership. . . there is a realisation that we have to move in that direction, but I have a terrible feeling that party politics and big business will get in the way of it. I think if Bristol could have the ambition like Freiberg in Germany, of being 'the green city', it could build its own green industries, it could become the place that everybody comes to see what to do to make a special place, then I think [Bristol] will be a very prosperous city as well as a green and delightful place to live in.

George Ferguson

I would like [Bristol] to step up to the mark and for it to be a lot braver than it is. I hope that Bristol will take on bigger aspirations. Bristol was innovating like mad a couple of hundred years ago – we had the first suspension bridge, the first intercity rail road, the first screw-driven ship, the first iron ship – all this was going on in Bristol. I don't where those genes have got to, but we need to rediscover those genes that were able to innovate and could take risks and have a vision for the future.

Richard St George

I'm an optimist so I hope things will get better and I hope people will collaborate more . . . there are a lot of interesting ethically-minded business people and social enterprises, especially in the city, that are helping to take us in the right direction. And my hope is that all of that strengthens and grows and connects better. And I hope people also learn lessons from the past, because if you've seen things going round a few times decade by decade, you realise that we can't be too optimistic or naïve, we've got to be well informed enough to say 'that has been tried, we need to know why it didn't work last time, what were the barriers that we might be able to move this time'. I'm hoping Bristol will be a more sustainable city and we'll learn all those lessons and thrive and share some of its lessons [but] I don't want it to keep trumpeting the fact that it is the most sustainable city or the greenest capital . . . There's a lot of hard work that's needed all around that and year after year after year to make it keep happening, keep it moving in the right direction. I want it to keep moving in the right direction and be a wonderful city to live in, which it is.

Martin Fodor

What are my hopes for the future of Bristol? That we do have strong action. I suppose absolutely key to that is public transport. Currently we've got one of the worst public transport systems and most expensive transport systems for a city of this size in the country . . . currently the vast majority of trips are by car so we've got to look at an integrated transport system and develop our land use, where we put the shopping, how we develop commerce and business, where people live and what options we give them when they live there. We've got to think absolutely holistically and integrate it through, otherwise it simply won't work and it's a long slow haul. It's a generation job. It's 25-30 years to turn a city like this around to something going really in the right direction so it's going to be very tricky and you've got to have political leadership of the first order . . . it's an opportunity, when there is change there is an opportunity for rethinking, for making new alliances, for building a different kind of world.

Hugh Barton

Just to keep on going in the right direction. Shake out some of the dead wood, try to get some impetus, try and get some of the blocks that are currently there. I had a very depressing conversation with the taxi driver when we first moved here. He said 'Bristol is the city where good ideas fail.' Well, I want Bristol to be the place where good ideas succeed.

Lucy Pedler

I hope it will go on becoming a more and more attractive place to be. I always sort of have this hope that one day we'll be able to walk and live in a city where you really don't feel overpowered by traffic and public transport and by cars and you don't have the endless noise. So if you ask me to be quite radical I'd quite like to see car-free Sundays, for example, which is what Italy had at the peak of the oil crisis. I would like to see whole roads where priorities are given to walkers and cyclists certain days. For example the Portway could be closed every Sunday all day, not just on the occasional event, and that would become a wonderful playground for Bristolians. I would like to genuinely see the whole city brought down to a gentler speed. I suppose the last thing I'd like to see is that every single one-way street in the city made into two-way for cycling, as is the law in Brussels.

John Grimshaw

My hope for the future of Bristol is for it to be more just, more fair, or less damaging to the environment [and] to try and find ways in which to do it without going head to head with the sort of consumer capitalist way of doing things, find ways to undermine it and create alternatives to it that kind of help it fall in on itself. Another strand of my hope for Bristol . . . is to try and develop pathways where people can learn new skills and make new relationships and learn new ways of being and being more productive from what's around us and using natural resources in terms of what comes through nature and the environment [but] also in terms of people. So with the community allotment, a key part of it is the therapeutic aspect and to make friends and share cross-culturally.

Tim Lawrence

Bristol is an incredibly diverse place and there are people from every back-ground, people doing an incredibly versatile amount of things . . . dynamic, exciting things [including] 9-5 jobs, music, arts, crafts, and underneath all of that I think people want the same thing. I think it's the responsibility of the council to allow people to understand that they can make change and it's about individuals coming together and understanding and believing that they can make change themselves and joining en masse to do it together.

Sam Valentine, Musician in Bristol

My hope for Bristol is that it will continue to commit as much time and energy as it has been in the last few years to pushing the environmental and low-carbon agenda. It's made so much progress and it's really shouting about what it's doing – my hope is that this will continue, the enthusiasm will continue and our successes will only grow.

Amy Robinson

In the future I'd like the outdoor spaces in Bristol to be used more and for more people to be involved with green issues such as fringe people who have different perspectives on things and for more people to feel like they are involved [in the environmental movement]. And for the Floating Harbour to become a swimming pool!

Chris Richards, Cycling Advisor

We've just asked the [Green Capital] partnership that question. We called it our 'What if' Event. What if Bristol was a true sustainable city in ten years time? And it was interesting, because people didn't talk about process or physical stuff. They talked about how it felt. So they talked about it being calmer. The noise we would hear might be less traffic and more birds and more water. So I think we've got to turn that kind of sense of what we want Bristol to be into something practical. And so my hope is that if you are walking round the city Bristol in ten years time you'd feel and hear some of those things. And we would have been able to change some of the way Bristol develops so it becomes more about those kinds of feelings.

Darren Hall

I would like for Bristol's environmental movement to grow and encompass everybody. There are incredible resources in Bristol, and we need to make the most of these. It is growing, but not quickly enough. There need to be more joined-up activities and work. We need to work smarter and look at new ways of working which make us more productive and less stressed.

Sarah Pugh, Founding Member of Transition Bristol and Director of Shift Bristol

My hopes for the future of Bristol are that these initiatives, the community organisations, the political support, the businesses and the campaigning organisations generate enough of a change that it actually becomes the whole city changing with us and that . . . social enterprises would take on matters such as energy, regeneration and transport, but do so from a genuine sustainability perspective. And my hope is that that kind of approach grows such that it becomes the mainstream economy of the city and my hope might be that . . . in 25 years' time it will be the people of Bristol that own and run a sustainable transport system, own and run sustainable energy companies.

Mike Birkin

My hope for the future of Bristol is that it will continue to be a happy city to live in for the next thousand years.

Angela Raffle

Conclusion

These case studies, stories, perspectives, thoughts and hopes that we have gathered here have shown some of the achievements that Bristol has seen over the last 40 years. They are evidence of the tireless work of people within the city, and what can be achieved with a group of fiercely dedicated individuals.

They are examples of just a few of the many initiatives, people and organisations that have dedicated themselves to making Bristol a better city for people and the environment, but are an indication of how far-reaching and comprehensive this work has been.

Bristol's environmental movement has been a strong voice in the city even when it is not being listened to. Moreover, sustainable thinking is being implemented city-wide in all different sectors and is beginning to be seen as 'common sense' or practical.

We have examples of pioneering, innovative and creative thinking with people working with a single-minded determination to make Bristol, and elsewhere, a better place to live. These organisations and initiatives have dealt with environmental concerns as well as making Bristol more community-minded, more about fun rather than 'things', safer and less polluted, and have encouraged equality.

It is hard to say what Bristol's 'best achievements' are, as each organisation, initiative and community group have achieved such different things. The big organisations such as Sustrans, the Soil Association, CSE, Forum for the Future and Resource Futures have contributed to substantial city-wide and national changes making everyday life more sustainable in terms of transport, energy, food, resource use and local and national policy making. Smaller projects, like the Bristol Bike Project, Hartcliffe Health and Environment Action Group and the Asylum Seekers Allotment Project, seek to tackle concerns within the community and work steadfastly to put sustainability at the heart of projects which tackle local social and environmental concerns.

All the initiatives, organisations and community groups have shown that people of every age and from all backgrounds are keen to make Bristol a more sustainable, healthier, cleaner and more equal place to live than it is already.

Perhaps the biggest achievement is that people have not given up. One question that we could have asked people is 'why do you do this? Why do you work so hard for something so difficult to achieve?' The 'why' is clear, however; people just want to make Bristol, the UK and even the world a better place to live.

These observations are also true for many other cities across the UK. Bristol does have the enviable accolade of being the only UK city nominated for the EU Green Capital Award but, as we have seen, there have been many instances when calls for sustainable thinking have often fallen on deaf ears – protests and direct action have not been able to achieve their aims.

The radical, innovative ideas have not always come to fruition in th context of local politics, financial difficulty or lack of support from decision-makers. This is never through lack of trying by those involved, but is because our social, cultural, economic and political systems have not moved quickly enough and do not accommodate truly sustainable behaviour.

The story of Bristol is a 'tale of two cities': the city which is founded on the wealth of social injustice contrasted with the modern historical dedication to protect the planet and better the lives of many; the city that wants to grow and expand side-by-side with calls for sustainable development; the city with some of the most economically affluent areas in the UK and some of the most economically deprived.

These tensions show the crossroads that we are at. In the midst of an economic crisis, we have an opportunity to shift towards a planet and people-friendly way of living. While environmental protection can be at odds with social justice at times, and the costs of 'environmental' goods or practices such as organic produce, renewable energy retrofitting, taxation on energy use and ethical fashion can be prohibitive, there are many ways in which sustainable living can have a positive impact upon quality of life.

The retrofitting of houses, local food, recycling and creative reuse of resources, the improvement of the local environment, preservation of green space, the development of sustainable transport and urban planning can minimise environmental damage, protect us from future environmental threats while benefiting people socially and economically.

The need to involve a more varied representation of the population in the sustainability movement was highlighted as essential to its success and validity. Everything that is done, and the way it is communicated, must be accessible, applicable and relevant for everyone.

If there was one thing we had to take away from this project it would be that you cannot overemphasise the importance of cross-sectoral collaboration, partnership and diversity of action. The individual sectors of the city, the campaigners, the businesses, the council and the community groups all have a part to play, and together can make visible change.

The different kinds of environmental involvement, from recycling to direct action to judicial reviews to community consultation, are all necessary parts of making change happen and having a variety of perspectives and voices heard.

Community work, social enterprises and local businesses also need to be able to rely on the city's organisations, businesses and the council for support. The help that these larger organisations can provide, whether this be in the form of a building, a start-up fund or advice, has proved to be invaluable.

Ultimately, no one knows what a sustainable city will really look like. Those interviewed think it will minimise its impact on the planet by not using fossil fuels and by recycling materials, reducing pollution, respecting nature and developing local facilities, housing and amenities in creative ways which maximise social benefit while minimising environmental damage. It will source locally as far as possible, develop fair and just provision of services, eliminate discrimination, engage all people and have high levels of happiness. Most importantly, a sustainable city will only exist if all other communities across the world are sustainable.

While we can be proud of the achievements that Bristol's people have made, and be thankful to those pioneers in the 1960s, 70s, 80s and 90s who have paved the way for a better Bristol, there is still a long way to go.

There is hope though when we see that Bristol, and other communities, will continue to have dedicated individuals who realise the importance of safeguarding the future and leaving the planet a better place than they found it.

References

A PDF of these references with clickable web links can be downloaded from http://www.schumacherinstitute.org.uk/bristols_green_roots

1. http://www.oed.com/view/Entry/195210 Date Accessed: 28.02.11

2. http://www.sustainablemeasures.com/Training/Indicators/Def-Br1.html Date Accessed 09.01.11

3. The Natural Step's Fourth Condition cited in Cook, D., *The Natural Step: Towards a Sustainable Society*, Schumacher Briefings, Green Books 2004, p.14

4. Pontin, J. and Roderick, I., *The Converging World: Connecting Communities in Global Change*, Schumacher Briefings, Green Books 2007, p.17

5. Pontin, J. and Roderick, I., *The Converging World*, p.18

6. http://www.sweethistory.org/timeline Date Accessed: 11.11.10

7. Mike Birkin, Filmed Interview, Bush House, 27.01.11

8. George Ferguson, Filmed Interview, The Tobacco Factory, 6.12.10.

9. http://www.bbc.co.uk/bristol/content/articles/2007/02/28/abolitionists_feature.shtml Date Accessed: 26.05.11

10. Coules, V., *Lost Bristol*, Birlinn Limited: Edinburgh, 2008, p.177

11. http://www.sweethistory.org/
http://www.bbc.co.uk/insideout/west/series11/week9_slavery.shtml
http://www.voscur.org/system/files/Consortium+of+Black+Groups+statement.pdf Date Accessed: 08.01.11

12. http://www.bbc.co.uk/bristol/content/articles/2007/02/28/abolitionists_feature.shtml Date Accessed: 11/11/10

13. Simms, A. Schumacher Lectures, Bristol 2008

14. Muir, J., *My First Summer in the Sierra*, Canongate, 2007, p.xxii

15. Schumacher, E.F., *Small is Beautiful: A Study of Economics as if People Mattered*, Blond and Briggs, 1978, p.11

16. McNeill, J., *Something New under the Sun: An Environmental History*, Norton, New York, 2000, p.325

17. Carson, R., *Silent Spring*, Mariner Books, New York, 2002, p.277

18. History of Greenpeace,
http://www.greenpeace.org/international/en/about/history/founders/ Date Accessed: 5.04.11

19. History of Greenpeace, http://www.greenpeace.org/international/en/about/history/founders/ Date Accessed: 5.04.11

20. Hunter, B., 'The Greenpeace to Amchitka', on Greenpeace Website http://www.greenpeace.org/international/en/about/history/amchitka-hunter/ Date Accessed: 2.08.11

21. History of Friends of the Earth, http://www.foe.co.uk/resource/press_releases/1107obit.html Date Accessed: 22.02.11

22. http://www.earthisland.org/index.php/aboutUs/legacy Date Accessed: 22.02.11

23. http://www.foei.org/en/who-we-are Date Accessed: 22.02.11

24. http://www.foe.co.uk/resource/press_releases/1107obit.html Date Accessed: 22.02.11

25. http://www.clubofrome.org/eng/about/4/ Date Accessed: 13.02.11

26. http://www.clubofrome.org/eng/about/4/ Date Accessed: 13.01.11

27. http://recession.org/history/1970s-oil-crisis Date Accessed: 16.02.11

28. Hulme. M., *Why we disagree about climate change*, Cambridge University Press, 2009, p.58

29. Ibid., p.58

30. Clayton, Anthony M. H., Radcliffe, N. J., *Sustainability: A Systems Approach*, Earthscan, 1996. p.7

31. Schumacher, E. F., *Small is Beautiful*, p.44

32. Schumacher, E. F., *Small is Beautiful*, pp.23-4

33. Economic and Social Research Council, Friends of the Earth, London School for Hygiene and Tropical Medicine, *Environmental Justice: Rights and Means to a healthy environment for all*, 2001, p.3 http://www.foe.co.uk/resource/reports/environmental_justice.pdf Date accessed: 15.03.11

34. Smith, J.B. et al, 2001. *Vulnerability to climate change and reasons for concern: a synthesis, Climate Change 2001: Impacts, Adaptation, and Vulnerability.* Contribution of Working Group II to the Third Assessment Report of the Intergovernmental Panel on Climate Change, J.J. McCarthy, O.F. Canziani, N.A. Leary, D.J. Dokken and K.S. White, Eds., Cambridge University Press, 913–967 referenced in *Climate change 2007: Impacts, Adaptation and Vulnerability*, IPCC, ch. 19, p.18. Date Accessed: 27.04.11

35. Devall, Bill and Sessions George, 'Deep Ecology', *Resurgence* Magazine, Issue 113, November-December 1985, p.21

36. Ibid., pp.18-19

37. http://www.un.org/apps/news/story.asp?NewsID=37731&Cr=unep&Cr1 Date Accessed: 3.3.11

38. http://www.worldometers.info/population/ statistics derived from UN data. Date Accessed: 3.3.11

39. Eames, M., http://www.jrf.org.uk/sites/files/jrf/ 1934-reconciling-environmental-social.pdf p.11

40. Priest, G. and Cobb, P., *The fight for Bristol: Planning and the Growth of Public Protest*, Bristol Civic Society and Redcliffe Press, 1980, p.18

41. Brian Price, Filmed Interview at Horizon House, 4.3.11

42. Avon FoE, Western Environmental Bulletin, 1981

43. Brian Price, Western Environmental Bulletin, 1981

44. 'Street by Street, the poor die younger', New Scientist, Issue 1524, 4th September 1986, pp.24-25

45. Simon Hooton, Interview (not filmed), 27.01.11

46. John Grimshaw, Interview at Wool House, 10.02.11

47. Hugh Barton, Filmed Interview at UWE Frenchay Campus, 2.02.11

48. Urban Centre for Alternative Technology Draft Prospectus, March 1980

49. Irene Galant, Phone Interview, 5.04.11

50. Andy King, Filmed Interview at Bush House, 18.01.11

51. www.soilassociation.org

52. Patrick Holden, filmed interview, 30.03.11

53. John Purkiss, interview, 10.05.11

54. Roberts, E., Roberts, M. and O'Shea, S., 'We live there, we should know . . .' A report of local health needs in Hartcliffe, August 1980.

55. Sue Walker, requested quotation, 05.08.11

56. Martin Fodor, Filmed Interview, 15.02.11

57. Boyle G., 'Ecotechnics: The Quarry Effect', *Resurgence*, July-August 1985 Issue 111, p.9

58. Bristol Health Profile 2010 compiled by Association of Public Health Observatories, www.healthprofiles.info. Date Accessed 20.04.11

59. Ingleheart, R., 'Post-Material Value Thesis' (1990) cited in Burningham, K. and Thrush, D., *The environmental concerns of disadvantaged groups*, p.1. http://www.jrf.org.uk/sites/files/jrf/1842631462.pdf Date Accessed: 5.4.11

60. Ben Barker, Filmed Interview at Southville Centre, 5.01.11

61. Osborn, S. 'Building a Positive Future for Bristol after Peak Oil', Bristol Local Strategic Partnership, 2009, p.4. http://www.bristol.gov.uk/ccm/cms-service/stream/asset/?asset_id=32277111. Date Accessed: 3.11.10

62. Schumacher, E.F., *Small is Beautiful*, p.12

63. UCAT's 'What is Appropriate Technology Flyer', CSE's Archive

64. The Centre for Sustainable Energy, 'Switched on since 1979'

65. http://www.nei.org Date Accessed 26.04.11

66. *The Ecologist*, Vol 8, No. 6, November – December 1978, p.202-3, http://exacteditions.theecologist.org/exact/browse/307/308/6378/2/24

67. Boardman, B and Houghton, T, 1991, 'Poverty and Power', Bristol Energy Centre

68. http://www.bristolfoe.org.uk/?Content=Campaign=Biofuels http://www.bbc.co.uk/news/uk-england-bristol-11627025 Date Accessed: 9.06.11

69. http://www.acseb.co.uk/ Date Accessed: 9.06.11

70. http://www.cse.org.uk/pdf/pub1055.pdf Date Accessed: 9.06.11

71. http://www.bristol.gov.uk/ccm/content/Environment-Planning/Planning/planning-policy-documents/bristol-development-frame-work/bristol-citywide-sustainable-energy-study.en Date Accessed: 22.04.11

72. Osborn, S. 'Building a Positive Future for Bristol after Peak Oil', p.14

73. Simone Osborn, Interview (not filmed), 10.01.11

74. Osborn, S., Bristol Peak Oil Report, p. 71

75. http://www.bristol.gov.uk/ccm/cms-service/stream/asset/?asset_id=34399204&

76. Dan Narayanan, Phone Interview, 9.03.11.

77. Kate Watson, Interview (not filmed), 22.2.11

78. www.decc.gov.uk Date Accessed 11.07.11

79. Reverend Burnett, Phone Interview, 5.5.11

80. Stephen Moore, requested quotation, 14.06.11

81. Monbiot, George, 'Let's face it: none of our environmental fixes break the planet-wrecking project', *The Guardian*, 2 May 2011, http://www.guardian.co.uk/commentisfree/2011/may/02/environmental-fixes-all-greens-lost Date Accessed: 20.04.11

82. Patrick Holden, Filmed Interview, 30.03.11

83. Term from work done by Richard Spalding http://www.bne.uwe.ac.uk/staff/staffDetails.asp?staffid=12-spalding Date Accessed: 14.04.11

84. http://www.bristol.gov.uk/ccm/content/press-releases/2010/nov/land-boost-for-community-food-growing-projects-.en Date Accessed: 9.04.11

85. Sims Hill Shared Harvest website: http://simshillsharedharvest.wordpress.com Date Accessed: 12.12.10

86. Tim Lawrence, Filmed Interview, 06.05.11

87. Tim Lawrence, 06.05.11

88. http://www.independent.co.uk/news/uk/green-revolt-of-the-ordinary-citizens-new-supermarkets-are-opening-in-britain-at-a-rate-of-more-than-one-a-week-often-despite-bitter-opposition-by-local-residents-louise-downes-examines-one-dispute-1531331.html Date Accessed: 3.6.11

89. http://www.independent.co.uk/news/uk/protesters-lose-fight-with-tesco-to-save-lime-trees-1540402.html

90. http://www.prsc.org.uk/index.htm

91. Tesco Corporate Responsibility Report 2009, p.24 http://cr2010.tescoplc.com/~/media/Files/T/Tesco-Corporate-Responsibility-Report-2009/Tesco_CSR_2010.pdf Date Accessed: 5.05.11

92. The Grocery Market: Office of Fair Trading's Reasons for making a reference to the Competition Commission May 2006, p.2 http://www.oft.gov.uk/shared_oft/reports/comp_policy/oft845.pdf Date Accessed: 05.03.11

93. UK supermarkets set for shake-up, BBC News, February 2008, http://news.bbc.co.uk/1/hi/business/7245944.stm Date Accessed: 05.03.11

94. http://notesco.wordpress.com Date Accessed: 7.03.11

95. Patrick Kingsley, Stokes Croft: The Art of Protest, Thursday 26 May 2011. http://www.guardian.co.uk/uk/2011/may/26/stokes-croft-protest-tesco-rioting Date Accessed: 6.6.11.

96. http://www.bristollocalfood.co.uk/wp-content/uploads/bristols-local-food-update-july-aug1.pdf 2009

97, Osborn, S., 'Bristol Peak Oil Report'. p. 17

98, Joy Carey, Filmed Interview, 11.05.11

99. http://www.sustainablebristol.com/2010/08/dig-bristol-submits-city-food-plans Date Accessed: 29.03.11

c=100. The Ecologist, Blueprint for Survival, http://www.theecologist.info/page34.html.Date Accessed: 21.03.11

101. http://www.john-adams.co.uk Date accessed 9.05.11

102. Adam, J., 'The Social Consequences of Hypermobility', RSA Lecture, 21 November 2001, pp.1-6

103. Sustrans Website: http://www.sustrans.org.uk Date Accessed: 22.3.11

104. Karen Bell, requested quotation, 23.06.11

105. Mike Ginger, Interview (not filmed), 10.12.10

106. http://www.thisisbristol.co.uk/Bristol-wasting-cycling-millions/story-11315194-detail/story.html

107. Cars only. Compared to Unitary Authorities, 2009

108. http://www.forumforthefuture.org/project/sustainable-cities-

index/overview Date Accessed: 20.01.11

109. http://www.westofengland.org/transport

110. Transport for Greater Bristol Alliance: http://www.tfgb.org.uk/campaigns.htm Date Accessed: 06.06.11

111. Sustraco Bristol Tram Proposal, November 2010

112. http://www.freebus.org.uk Date Accessed: 23.05.11

113. Gus Hoyt, Requested quotation, 13.06.11

114. Ben Barker, Filmed Interview, 5.01.01

115. James Lucas, Interview (not filmed), 15.12.11

116. Adams, J., *The Social Consequences of Hypermobility*, p.4.

117. The Bristol Bike Project, http://vimeo.com/9469007

118. The Ecologist, Introduction: The Need for Change, in *Blueprint for Survival*. http://www.theecologist.info/page33.html

119. Schumacher, E. F., *Small is Beautiful*, p.55

120. Richard Walker, Interview (not filmed), 3.11.10

121. Nick Francis, Filmed Interview, 15.02.11

122. Robert Lambourne, Filmed Interview, 15.02.11

123. 'Introducing the Create Centre', Bristol Record Office, ref no. 35510/Com/20/2/2.

1234. http://www.ethicalfashionforum.com/the-issues/energy-and-waste Date Accessed: 16.05.11

125. http://www.bishopstontrading.co.uk/shop/index.php Date Accessed: 18.05.11

126. http://www.fairtrade.org.uk/what_is_fairtrade/history.aspx Date Accessed: 17.05.11

127. http://www.bristolfairtrade.org.uk/News-archive.html Date Accessed: 17.05.11

128. Jim O'Shaughnessy, requested quotation 14.06.11.

129. Muir, John, *Our National Parks*, Cosimo, New York, 2006 (1901), p.56

130. http://www.bristolnats.org.uk/about

131. Susan Carter, Interview (not filmed), 16.06.11

132. Mark Durk, requested quotation, 03.08.11

133. http://www.avongorge.org.uk/index.php Date Accessed: 12.03.11

134. *The Fight for Bristol*, p.62

135. http://www.rspb.org.uk/ourwork/casework/details.aspx?id=tcm:9-228221 Date Accessed: 12.04.11

136. Mike Birkin, Filmed Interview, 27.01.11

137. http://www.sd-commission.org.uk/publications.php?id=607 Date Accessed: 25.05.11

138. http://www.avonwildlifetrust.org.uk/wildlife/78-severn_estuary.htm http://www.rspb.org.uk/ourwork/casework/details.aspx?id=tcm:9-228221 Date Accessed: 25.05.11

139. http://www.bbc.co.uk/news/uk-wales-11565056 Date Accessed: 24.06.11

140. http://egc.gecoloco.com/winning-cities/previous-finalists/bristol Date Accessed: 02.05.11

141. D. A. Lambert, 'Bristol's Own Twyford Down?', Summer InFoE 1994, p.2

142. Anderson, Jon, 'Spatial Politics in Practice: The Style and Substance of Environmental Direct Action', p.3 http://www.cardiff.ac.uk/cplan/resources/JA_SpatialPoliticsPractice.pdf Date Accessed: 04.04.11

143. Anderson, Jon, 'Spatial Politics', p. 3

144. Wilding, Jo, 'Ashton Caught', InFoE Winter 1998, p.4

145. Wilding, Jo, 'The Right to (Say) No', InFoe Summer 1999, p.8

146. Bristol City Council, 'Bristol Quality of Life Indicators 2009', p.43

147. Steve Micklewright, Interview (not filmed), 12.01.11

148. http://www.bristol.gov.uk/ccm/content/Environment-Planning/Parks-and-open-spaces/wildlife-folder/wild-city.en;jsessionid=4FA0558B09300F110CAD38F7B756E925.tcwwwaplaws1 Date Accessed: 19.06.11

149. http://franc.org.uk Date Accessed: 22.05.11

150. Bland, R., The Wildlife of the New Cut, p.1 http://www.franc.org.uk/wildlife Date Accessed: 07.05.11

151. Bristol Civic Society Website: http://www.bristolcivicsociety.org.uk/en/about-us/history/76?start=1 Date Accessed: 25.04.11

152. Priest, G. and Cobb, P., *The Fight for Bristol*

153. *The Fight for Bristol*, p.9

154. *The Fight for Bristol*, p.51

155. *The Fight for Bristol*, p.59

156. George Ferguson, Filmed Interview, 6.12.10

157. Adburgham, R., *A View to the Future: JT Group a radical approach to building and development*, Redliffe Press, 2006, p.68

158. John Pontin, Filmed Interview, 13.04.11

159. Adburgham, R., A View to the Future, p.152.

160. Pontin, J., quoted in Adburgham's *A View to the Future*, p.147

161. Ferguson, G., 'The Good the Bad and the Ugly', http://www.georgeferguson.co.uk/bristol%E2%80%99s-recent-planning-and-architecture-%E2%80%93-the-good-the-bad-and-the-ugly Date Accessed: 12.07.11

162. Bruges, J., 'Sustainability and the Bristol Urban Initiative for Bristol Urban Village Initiative', A forum of The Western Partnership for Sustainable Development, April 1999, pp.22 – 23

163. Bruges, J., BUVI, p.24

164. Keith Hallett, requested quotation, 19.05.11

165. Ethical Property Website: http://www.ethicalproperty.co.uk/site/en/_OurMission.php Date Accessed: 13.04.11

166. Bristol Sustainable Development Guide for Construction, p. II http://www.bristol.gov.uk/ccm/cms-service/stream/asset/?asset_id=36292251 Date Accessed: 18.07.11

167. Lucy Pedler, Filmed Interview, 24.3.11

168. http://bristolgreenhouse.co.uk Date Accessed: 19.07.11

169. Rik Lander, requested quotation, 21.07.11

170. Grant Shapps, Twitter, 5th Jan 2011

171. Jackson Moulding, Interview (not filmed), 1.12.10

172. http://www.communitylandtrusts.org.uk/upload/public/Publications/2011%20CLTs%20in%20a%20Nutshell.pdf p.2 Date Accessed: 04.04.11

173. http://coexist.hamiltonhouse.org/p/about.html

174. Sennen Timcke, Interview (not filmed), 1.02.11

175. Jane Stevenson, Interview (not filmed), 15.12.10

176. http://transitionculture.org/2007/11/22/transition-bristols-big-event-latest-news/

177. http://www.bbc.co.uk/birmingham/content/articles/2008/05/22/transition_city_birmingham_feature.shtml http://transitionculture.org/2007/03/21/transition-city-bristol-kicks-off-tonight-with-a-talk-by-dr-chris-johnstone Date Accessed: 24.06.11

178. Ciaran Mundy, Filmed Interview, 10.05.11

179. Angela Raffle, Filmed Interview, 10.05.11

180. http://www.forumforthefuture.org/project/sustainable-bristol-city-region/overview

181. Paul Rainger, requested quotation, 4.08.11

182. Amy Robinson, Filmed Interview, 27.04.11

183. http://www.bitc.org.uk Date Accessed: 30.06.11

184. http://www.guardian.co.uk/environment/2002/jul/10/society.ethicalshopping

185. Bristol Partnership, Community Strategy 2003, p.30, http://www.bristol.ac.uk/esu/groups/comm_strategy.pdf Date Accessed: 12.04.11

186. http://www.bristolgreencapital.org Date Accessed 08.04.11

187. Mark Leach, Interview (not filmed), 9.12.10

188. Darren Hall, Filmed Interview, 8.04.11

189. http://www.lets-linkup.com/4114-UK-South%20West.htm Date Accessed 08.04.11

190. Ciaran Mundy, Filmed interview 10.05.11

191. Bristol Pound Website: http://www.bristolpound.org/about Date Accessed: 2.05.11

192. Ciaran Mundy, Filmed interview 10.05.11

193. http://www.bristolpound.org/about/

194. http://www.neweconomics.org/blog/2009/09/15/brixton-pound-launches-this-week Date Accessed: 07.05.11

195. http://www.happycity.org.uk/

196. Matt Fortnam, requested quotation 04.08.11.

197. http://www.shiftbristol.org.uk/# Date Accessed 08.04.11

198. Sarah Pugh, Phone Interview, 17.06.11

199. Tim Barker requested quotation 12.05.11

Bibliography

Books

Adburgham, R., *A View to the Future: JT Group a radical approach to building and development* (Redliffe Press: Bristol 2006)

Carson, R., *Silent Spring* (Mariner Books: New York 2002)

Clayton, Anthony M. H., Radcliffe, N. J., *Sustainability: A Systems Approach* (Earthscan: London 1996)

Connelly, J. and Smith, G., *Politics and the Environment: From Theory to Practice* (Routledge: London 1999)

Cook, D., *The Natural Step: Towards a Sustainable Society* (Schumacher Briefings, Green Books: Dartington 2004)

Coules, V., *Lost Bristol* (Birlinn Limited: Edinburgh 2008)

Doppelt, B., *The Power of Sustainable Thinking* (Earthscan: London, 2008)

The Ecologist, *Blueprint for Survival* (New American Library: New York 1974)

Hulme. M., *Why we disagree about climate change* (Cambridge University Press: Cambridge 2009)

McNeill, J., *Something New under the Sun: An Environmental History* (Norton: New York 2000)

Muir, J., *My First Summer in the Sierra* (Canongate: Great Britain 2007)

Pontin, J. and Roderick, I., *The Converging World: Connecting Communities in Global Change* (Schumacher Briefings, Green Books: Dartington 2007)

Priest, G. and Cobb, P., *The fight for Bristol: Planning and the Growth of Public Protest* (Bristol Civic Society and Redcliffe Press: Bristol 1980)

Schumacher, E.F., *Small is Beautiful: A Study of Economics as if People Mattered* (Blond and Briggs: Great Britain 1978)

Wickers, D., *Millennium Miles: The Story of the National Cycle Network* (Good Books: Whitley 2000)

Wilkinson, R. and Pickett, K., *The Spirit Level: Why Equality is Better for Everyone* (Penguin Books: London 2010)

Articles, Magazines and Publications

Adams, J., 'The Social Consequences of Hypermobility' (http://john-adams.co.uk/wp-content/uploads/2006/hypermobilityforRSA.pdf 2001)

Anderson, Jon, 'Spatial Politics in Practice: The Style and Substance of Environmental Direct Action' (http://www.cf.ac.uk/cplan/resources/JA_SpatialPoliticsPractice.pdf 2004)

Bland, R., 'The Wildlife of the New Cut' (http://www.franc.org.uk/wildlife.)

Boyle G., 'Ecotechnics: The Quarry Effect', *Resurgence* 111 (July – August 1985)

Bruges, J., *Sustainability and the Bristol Urban Initiative,* for Bristol Urban Village Initiative A forum of The Western Partnership for Sustainable Development, April 1999

Carey, J., 'Who Feeds Bristol? Towards a Resilient Food Plan', (Bristol Partnership, March 2011)

Centre for Sustainable Energy, Barton, H. speaking at 30th Anniversary of CSE, Founding Faith: The Origins of CSE, 30 Years Ago. (http://www.cse.org.uk/downloads/file/Founding_Faith_Hugh_Barton%283%29.pdf)

Devall, Bill and Sessions, George, 'Deep Ecology', *Resurgence Magazine* (Issue 113, November – December 1985)

Eames, M., 'Reconciling Environmental Concerns' (http://www.jrf.org.uk/sites/files/jrf/1934-reconciling-environmental-social.pdf Joseph Rowntree Foundation, 2006)

The Ecologist, Volume 8, Number 6 http://exacteditions.theecologist.org/exact/browse/307/308/6378/2/24 November – December 1978)

Wildlife, 20 in 2000: Celebrating 20 years of achievement (Winter 1999, Number 58)

Economic and Social Research Council, Friends of the Earth, London School for Hygiene and Tropical Medicine, 'Environmental Justice: Rights and Means to a healthy environment for all'. (http://www.foe.co.uk/resource/reports/environmental_justice.pdf 2001)

Ingleheart, R., 'Post-Material Value Thesis' (1990) cited in Burningham, K. and Thrush, D., 'Rainforests are a long way from here' (http://www.jrf.org.uk/sites/files/jrf/1842631462.pdf Joseph Rowntree Foundation, 2001)

IPCC, Climate change 2007: Impacts, Adaptation and Vulnerability. (http://www.ipcc-wg2.gov/AR4/website/fi.pdf 2007)

Lambert, A., Bristol's Own Twyford Down? (Summer InFoE 1994)

'Street by Street, the poor die younger', New Scientist, Issue 1524,

Osborn, S. 'Building a Positive Future for Bristol after Peak Oil' (Bristol Local Strategic Partnership, 2009)

Roberts, E., Roberts, M. and O'Shea, S., 'We live there, we should know . . .' (A report of local health needs in Hartcliffe, August 1980)

Wilding, Jo, Ashton Caught, Bristol Friends of the Earth Magazine (Winter 1998)

Wilding, Jo, The Right to (Say) No, *Bristol Friends of the Earth Magazine* (Summer 1999)

Website References

Action for Sustainable Energy for Bristol: www.acseb.co.uk

The Avon Gorge & Downs Wildlife Project: www.avongorge.org.uk

Avon Wildlife Trust: www.avonwildlifetrust.org.uk

BBC News: www.bbc.co.uk

Bishopston Trading Company: www.bishopstontrading.co.uk

Bristol Civic Society: www.bristolcivicsociety.org.uk

Bristol Evening Post: www.thisisbristol.co.uk

Bristol Friends of the Earth: www.bristolfoe.org.uk

Bristol Green House – Rik Lander's blog: www.bristolgreenhouse.co.uk

Bristol Health Profile: www.healthprofiles.info.

Bristol Local Food Newsletter: www.bristollocalfood.co.uk

Bristol Pound: www.bristolpound.org

Bristol Quality of Life survey 2010: www.bristol.gov.uk/ccm/cms-service/stream/asset/?asset_id=36565057

Business in the Community: www.bitc.org.uk

Centre for Sustainable Energy: www.cse.org.uk

Club of Rome: www.clubofrome.org

Community Land Trusts: www.communitylandtrusts.org.uk

Earth Island Institute: www.earthisland.org/index.php/aboutUs/legacy/

Ecojam: www.ecojam.org

Ethical Fashion: www.ethicalfashionforum.com

Ethical Property Company: www.ethicalproperty.co.uk

EU Green Capital Award: www.egc.gecoloco.com

Fairtrade Foundation: www.fairtrade.org.uk

Forum for the Future: www.forumforthefuture.org

Forum for the Future's Sustainable Bristol Project: www.sustainablebristol.com

FreeBus: www.freebus.org.uk

Friends of the Earth International: www.foei.org

Friends of the Earth UK: www.foe.co.uk

Friends of the New Avon Cut: www.franc.org.uk

George Ferguson's blog: www.georgeferguson.co.uk
Greenpeace International: www.greenpeace.org
The Guardian: www.guardian.co.uk
Happy City Initiative: www.happycity.org.uk
The Independent: www.independent.co.uk
New Economics Foundation:www.neweconomics.org
No to Tesco: Stokes Croft: www.notesco.wordpress.com
Royal Society for the Protection of Birds: www.rspb.org.uk
Sims Hill Shared Harvest: www.simshillsharedharvest.wordpress.com
Sustainable Development Commission: www.sd-commission.org.uk
Transition Network: www.transitionculture.org
United Nations: www.un.org
Voscur: www.voscur.org

About the author

Emmelie has a research and critical thinking background and a degree in English Literature and Cultural Criticism from Cardiff University. She is interested in the way that cultural frameworks shape our way of thinking and behaving and thinks that an understanding of this is pivotal in order to develop sustainable lifestyles.

This research has also made her aware of the important role that well-being plays in the sustainability movement.